Dishonest Dollars

Dishonest Dollars

The Dynamics of White-Collar Crime

Terry L. Leap

ILR Press
AN IMPRINT OF
Cornell University Press
Ithaca and London

First published 2007 by Cornell University Press

Printed in the United States of America

Library of Congress Cataloging-in-Publication Data

Leap, Terry L., 1948–
    Dishonest dollars : the dynamics of white-collar crime / Terry
L. Leap.
        p. cm.
    Includes bibliographical references and index.
    ISBN-13: 978-0-8014-4520-0 (cloth : alk. paper)
    1. White collar crimes—United States.   2. Criminal
behavior—United States.   I. Title.

HV6769.L43 2007
364.16'8—dc22

                                                    2006026569

Cornell University Press strives to use environmentally
responsible suppliers and materials to the fullest extent
possible in the publishing of its books. Such materials include
vegetable-based, low-VOC inks and acid-free papers that are
recycled, totally chlorine-free, or partly composed of nonwood
fibers. For further information, visit our website at
www.cornellpress.cornell.edu.

Cloth printing   10 9 8 7 6 5 4 3 2 1

To my parents, Henry W. Leap and Barbara L. Leap,
and my father-in-law, Harold P. Coston

Contents

Preface

Work on this book began several years ago when I decided to make an oblique shift from the study of mainstream management topics to the study of white-collar criminology—a topic that has been of interest to me for many years. After receiving my doctorate in business administration, I have spent most of my academic career in the field of human resource management. Over the years, I read numerous books and articles about crime and watched the ever-expanding array of television crime documentaries on channels such as A&E, Discovery, and TLC. I was especially intrigued with the works of the criminologists Stanton Samenow, Marcus Felson, and John Douglas.

Then it occurred to me. Why not develop a course in white-collar crime for business students? By the late 1990s and early years of the twenty-first century, dozens of major corporate scandals were in the news. AACSB International, the major accrediting body for business schools, began emphasizing ethics training for undergraduate business majors and MBA students. In response, I developed a senior seminar for undergraduates and referred to it as an "applied ethics" course on white-collar crime. After offering the class for several semesters to senior management majors at Clemson University, I developed an advanced version of the course for MBAs. Both courses were well received by my students. And, for me, teaching had never been so much fun!

Books on white-collar crime usually fall into one of four categories. First, some books provide a detailed account of a major white-collar crime (or set of related crimes) such as the Enron or WorldCom debacles. Second, other books focus primarily on the sociological aspects of white-collar crime. Since academics who teach criminology often have doctorates in sociology and work in university sociology departments, it comes as no surprise that academic books on crime are often written by sociologists. Third, crime has also caught the attention of economists. Although books have been written about the economics of crime in general, I am not aware of a book devoted exclusively to the economics of white-collar crime. Fourth, several legal case books on white-collar crime have been written for attorneys and law students.

My book might fit a fifth category. Unlike other books on white-collar crime with which I am familiar, this book provides an integrative model that incorporates the events and influences surrounding white-collar crime, the decision-making processes of white-collar criminals, and the impact and aftermath of these crimes. It integrates the perspectives from sociology, psychology, public policy, and business. The book also borrows heavily from the journalistic accounts of white-collar crime. Although the book discusses major categories of white-collar crime, it recognizes that different crimes still have common elements. Criminals in the suites and criminals in the streets have more similarities than differences.

Acknowledgments

I would like to thank my colleagues and students in the College of Business and Behavioral Science at Clemson University. My discussions with them have sharpened my thinking on white-collar crime. I would also like to thank Frances Benson of Cornell University Press. It has been my pleasure to have worked on several projects with Fran for the past twenty-five years. Also at Cornell, I thank Nancy Ferguson, Ange Romeo-Hall, Scott Levine, and Mahinder Kingra for their work on the project, and I extend appreciation to the two reviewers of the manuscript, D. Quinn Mills and Stanton Samenow. Thanks also to Kathy Kegley of Clemson University for her technical assistance. I owe a debt of gratitude to my wife Carolyn, my daughter Cathy, and my son Christopher who listened patiently to my thoughts and ramblings about the book. Finally, I would like to acknowledge Bo, a faithful friend of fourteen years, who was often curled up asleep at my feet as I typed away on my laptop.

Dishonest Dollars

Introduction: The Big Picture

Some Typical White-Collar Crimes

Robert Ligon, a former weight-loss franchisee, purchased regular dough-nuts from a Chicago bakery and sold them as low-fat doughnuts to un-suspecting consumers. The doughnuts were labeled as having 130 calo-ries and 3 grams of fat when they actually contained over 500 calories and 18 grams of fat. Customers loved the taste of the "diet" doughnuts but became suspicious and contacted the U.S. Food and Drug Adminis-tration (FDA) when they started gaining weight and discovered that the doughnuts left grease spots on napkins. The FDA investigated, confis-cated the pastries, and Ligon was convicted of fraud and sentenced to fif-teen months in federal prison (where doughnuts are not on the menu).[1]

The CEO of a South Carolina regional transportation authority was accused of "willfully and maliciously" using taxpayer money for lavish meals, personal expenses, and trips to Africa, Honduras, and New York City. He was indicted on four felony counts of public corruption and two misdemeanor charges. After being fired, he requested $115,000 in sev-erance pay. The transit authority responded by filing a civil suit against him seeking reimbursement for $145,000 in unauthorized expenses and an additional $485,973 to compensate the agency for lost government grants and private contracts.[2]

A Missouri woman admitted to embezzling $24,000 from a small tourist business. At the time of the theft, she was already on probation for stealing over $57,000 from a former employer in Illinois. During her subsequent job interview in Missouri, she told her prospective employer that she had experienced a "little problem" at her previous job over a "discrepancy" that was the result of a "misunderstanding." She was hired after a cursory background check failed to reveal her felony conviction in Illinois.[3]

All of these acts fall under the rubric of white-collar or organizational crime, yet none is especially egregious. They are typical of the hundreds of white-collar crimes that are committed by individuals who receive little or no prison time and experience only brief notoriety. There are many similarities, however, between these crimes and the marquee media crimes at major corporations. One purpose of this book is to explore those similarities as well as the similarities between white-collar criminals and street criminals.

Looking Back

Organizational corruption has been a social problem since ancient times. Plato's critique of democracy expressed his disillusionment with corrupt ancient Athenian leaders. Over two thousand years later, the writings of Marx, Rousseau, and Freud made reference to corruptive influences in organizations and in society at large. Prominent examples of such corruption can be found in a variety of contexts from John Quincy Adams's controversial ascent to the presidency in 1825 to Napoleon III and his concern with avoiding graft and corruption during his ambitious revitalization of Paris during the 1850s to the U.S. industrial robber barons of the late nineteenth century.[4] The twentieth century was marked by major scandals such as Watergate, Iran-Contra, and the savings and loan industry collapse. During this time, corporate criminals such as Billy Sol Estes, Ivan Boesky, and Michael Milken became household names.

By the early years of the twenty-first century, investigative journalists, talk show hosts, and business news commentators were chronicling the events at WorldCom, Enron, Adelphia, Tyco, Global Crossing, Waste Management, and Martha Stewart Living Omnimedia. Congressional subcommittees investigated acts of corporate malfeasance, and Congress passed legislation such as the Sarbanes-Oxley Act in 2002 to curb irresponsible corporate leaders. Business schools intensified their interest in ethics education, and corporations developed stricter codes of conduct.

Media accounts of major corporate scandals describe falsified financial statements, securities fraud, misappropriation of corporate assets, and insider trading. These crimes damaged financial markets, shook the confidence of investors, and created a public distrust of corporate leaders. Pundits and cartoonists had a field day lampooning the major scandals that engulfed the business world.[5] Less spectacular, but more insidious, white-collar crimes such as petty theft by employees and minor acts of fraud, however, were largely overlooked by the media.

Criminologists, psychologists, sociologists, business analysts, and legal scholars continue to explore the causes and consequences of white-collar crime and corruption. Opinions range from greed by top management to lax oversight by corporate boards and regulatory agencies to a long-standing indifference toward white-collar crime by the public. Egocentric executives intoxicated by power, corrupt organizational cultures, stock options gone awry, and conflicts of interest in investment banks and accounting firms have also been cited as root causes.

White-collar crime and corruption carries a huge price tag. Multi-billion-dollar damage estimates are commonly affixed to fraud, embezzlement, environmental pollution, the sale of counterfeit products, and cyber crimes. But the widespread economic impact is only part of the destruction. White-collar crime imposes a degree of physical and emotional trauma on its victims that far exceeds the trauma inflicted by street criminals.

Plan for the Book

This book integrates the work of academicians and investigative journalists into a dynamic model of white-collar crime. Emphasis is placed on the process that occurs when executives, managers, and employees engage in illegal or corrupt behaviors that damage their organization and its stakeholders. The model starts with the conditions underlying white-collar crime and discusses the range of crimes, risk assessment strategies and psychological ploys of the perpetrators along with the aftermath of and societal responses to white-collar crime. Rather than treating each major category of white-collar crime as a distinct social problem, I explain them by using an integrative model. Furthermore, criminals in the "suites" and criminals in the "streets" commit distinct crimes. But as Stanton E. Samenow, a psychologist with nearly four decades of experience working with criminals observes:

> Despite a multitude of differences in their backgrounds and crime patterns, criminals are alike in one way: *how they think*. A gun-toting, uneducated criminal off the streets of southeast Washington, D.C., and a crooked Georgetown business executive are extremely similar in their view of themselves and the world. This is not to deny individual differences among criminals in their aesthetic tastes, sexual practices, religious observances, or favorite sports team. But all regard the world as a chessboard over which they have total control, and they perceive people as pawns to be pushed around at will. Trust, love, loyalty, and teamwork are incompatible with their way of life. They scorn and exploit most people who are kind, trusting, hardworking, and honest. Toward a few they are sentimental but rarely considerate. Some of their most altruistic acts have sinister motives.[6]

What Is White-Collar Crime?

In this book I use the terms *white-collar crime* and *organizational crime* interchangeably since both are part of organizational life. The term *white-collar crime* was coined in 1939 by the Indiana University professor and criminologist Edwin Sutherland. Sutherland defined white-collar crime as "crime in the upper, white-collar class, which is composed of respectable, or at least respected, business and professional men."[7] Criminologists and others have since debated the precise meaning of white-collar crime (as well as who qualifies as a white-collar criminal).[8] Sutherland's definition was developed at a time when there was a sharp distinction between the managerial and blue-collar segments of the labor force. By the second half of the twentieth century, this distinction had become less clear as the majority of employees in advanced industrialized economies were doing white-collar work. Sutherland also did not account for the possibility that managers and professionals may commit the same crimes as street criminals.[9]

Marcus Felson's modern-day definition of white-collar crime is *crimes of specialized access* that are committed by managers and professionals in the course of their work activities.[10] Felson makes two critical points. First, he regards the term *white-collar crime* as an "unfortunate expression" that encourages us to define crime primarily by the people who commit it. Classifying crimes as "white-collar" provides little insight into how and why these crimes occur. Second, access to power, money, and resources provides executives with the opportunity to misbehave. A clerical worker does not have the power to commit an antitrust violation, whereas a CEO does. Similarly, crimes such as embezzlement require that the perpetrator have access to money or other valuable resources; otherwise the crime cannot take place.[11]

Felson's definition of white-collar crime ties in nicely with the term *corruption*. Corrupt behaviors are those in which managers and professionals use their formal power for personal gain. Acts of corruption may or may not violate a criminal statute, but they almost always violate a professional code of ethics, an organizational policy, or a societal norm. Nepotism, cronyism, throwing lavish parties at shareholders' expense, or taking indecent liberties with a vulnerable client are forms of corruption. With the passage of time, additional laws have been passed that prohibit a wide range of dissolute behaviors. Sexual harassment, for example, has long been viewed as a corrupt workplace behavior, but it was not until the late 1970s that the courts also began to view it as a form of illegal sex discrimination.

The FBI defines white-collar crime as illegal acts that are: (1) characterized by deceit, concealment, or violations of trust, (2) not dependent on the application or threat of physical force or violence, and (3) committed by individuals or organizations to obtain money, property, or services or to secure personal or business advantage.[12] The nonviolent nature of white-collar crime in the FBI's definition, however, is misleading. Executives who condone environmental pollution, ignore serious workplace safety hazards, and design and manufacture unsafe products are, in reality, committing violent crimes. The primary difference between violent street crimes and violent white-collar crimes is a matter of timing. Street crimes are "in your face" events where the threat of bodily harm is immediate, whereas white-collar criminals inflict illness, injury, and death on their victims over a period of years or even decades.

An Overview of the Dynamic Model

An illustration of the dynamic model of organizational crime and corruption can be found in the appendixes at the end of this book. The model recognizes three contributing sources to criminal behavior: individual, organizational, and societal. These sources affect: (1) whether a person will commit a white-collar crime, (2) the profile of the perpetrator, (3) the type of white-collar crime the perpetrator will commit, (4) the psychological defense mechanisms used by the perpetrator before, during, and after the crime, (5) the aftermath of the crime, and (6) organizational and societal responses to white-collar crime and corruption. The components of the model are summarized here and explored in detail in later chapters.

The model starts with the premise that persons who engage in criminal or corrupt acts are not psychotic but are instead rational and sane beings with a firm grasp of reality.[13] Personality traits (and sometimes personality disorders), relationships with supervisors and co-workers, and perceptions of justice and fairness in the organization all determine whether an individual might engage in white-collar crime.

Many white-collar crimes involve conspiracies in which two or more persons plan a crime. The courts usually punish accomplices to a crime with the same severity as they punish the the ones who actually commit the crime. Criminals are usually aware at the outset that they are committing fraud, theft, or dangerous acts. There are situations, however, in which a manager may be pulled unwittingly into a crime and not recognize his culpability until it is too late. Given the harsh view of the judiciary toward those who participate in criminal conspiracies, a manager could face serious penalties even when he or she played a minor role in a white-collar crime.

The organization offers both opportunities to engage in crime as well as threats for those who do. Cohesive and corrupt work groups, weak accounting controls, and poor security all represent opportunities for white-collar criminals, whereas rotating work groups, strong ethical policies, and sophisticated security technology all create threats for professionals and managers with a criminal bent.

Similarly, society both encourages and discourages criminal and corrupt behavior. A society's emphasis on materialism, personal competitiveness, and a belief that many white-collar offenses are not serious crimes all encourage executive malfeasance. At the same time, society imposes sanctions (incarceration, fines, disbarment, restitution, probation, and ostracism) on those who engage in criminal and corrupt acts.

Some industries and organizations are more prone to criminal activity than others. The term *criminogenic* has been coined to describe organization and industry environments that are conducive to crime.[14] A notorious example of a criminogenic industry is automobile sales and service. Automobile dealers and brokers have long been known for their price gouging, financing scams, odometer rollbacks, and repair fraud. Labor unions also have a tarnished reputation for being criminogenic and attractive to elements of organized crime. Union officials collect money for membership dues, insurance premiums, and pension contributions, and money is easy to steal. Unions also control the supply of skilled labor in many urban areas, allowing union officials to extract bribes from employers in exchange for labor peace. Likewise, the health care industry has become increasingly criminogenic because of the money-making potential of fraudulent medical treatments and insurance scams.

Three types of white-collar criminals are discussed in subsequent chapters: crisis responders, opportunity takers, and opportunity seekers. Crisis responders commit crimes out of financial desperation. Opportunity takers are responding to a situation that is too good to resist. Opportunity seekers are habitual criminals who commit multiple offenses.[15]

White-collar crimes contain any of the following characteristics: illicit transfer of money or other resources (e.g., theft or embezzlement); misinforming others (e.g., accounting or financial fraud); manipulating others (e.g., sexually harassing a subordinate); and endangering the health and safety of others (e.g., placing counterfeit UL certification labels on electrical products not meeting Underwriters Laboratory standards).[16]

Contrary to popular belief, criminals neither act impulsively nor do they fail to learn from experience. Nearly all crimes—both white-collar and street crimes—occur only after the perpetrator has weighed the risks associated with the crime. Furthermore, law-abiding citizens look at the lives of repeat offenders and conclude that some criminals are not capable of learning from their mistakes. This view, too, is erroneous. First, habitual criminals regard "making a mistake" as being synonymous with "getting caught." Committing a crime was not the mistake in their mind; becoming entangled in the chain of events that led to their apprehension was their real mistake. Second, criminals often learn valuable lessons from their arrest and prosecution. After a few hard knocks, a criminal may decide to go straight. More than likely, however, their illegal acts and brushes with the law provide insights that are helpful in planning future crimes.[17]

After planning a crime and assessing the risks, the white-collar criminal makes a conscious decision either to abstain from the crime because it is too difficult or too risky or commit the crime, perhaps by making adjustments to the original crime plan.[18]

If the criminal believes that the economic, social, and psychological benefits of the crime exceed the risks of getting caught, he or she will implement the crime plan. Some crimes represent once-in-a-lifetime opportunities after which no additional crimes are committed (crisis responders and opportunity takers). Career white-collar criminals (opportunity seekers), on the contrary, view crime as an integral part of their lifestyle. Some make crime their full-time job, whereas others confine their criminal activities to off-duty hours. Still other opportunity seekers work at legitimate jobs that serve as a cover for their illegal activities.

Most criminals—especially white-collar criminals—do not see themselves in a negative light. If they commit a crime but are not apprehended or punished, they may believe that their crimes are not serious or they may believe they are somehow immune from prosecution. Even when faced with felony charges and potentially severe penalties, white-collar criminals do not regard themselves as criminals. They instead view themselves as scapegoats or victims of a gross misunderstanding. If incarcerated, white-collar criminals regard themselves as superior to other inmates who are the real criminals.

White-collar criminals use a variety of psychological ploys or defense mechanisms to minimize the severity of their transgressions or to justify their corrupt actions. A convenience-chain store owner may claim that his price gouging of low-income customers at his inner-city stores is necessary to offset losses from shoplifting. When confronted with evidence that the inventory shrinkage from shoplifting at his inner-city stores is not significantly different from that of his suburban stores, he may justify his actions on the grounds that inner-city customers are of no account and deserve to be cheated.

White-collar criminals use psychological coping processes before, during, and after they commit a crime or an act of corruption. An employee who embezzles money may rationalize that she will pay the money back before the crime is discovered. After the employee realizes that restitution is impossible, she may justify her theft by claiming she has been underpaid for years and the company owes her the additional money.

In a subsequent chapter, I discuss several psychological tactics that executives and managers use to minimize their bad deeds or to escape culpability for their crimes. These excuses have been gleaned from dozens of accounts of white-collar crime, and they also have a foundation in the psychological literature.[19]

Law enforcement agencies and criminologists are interested in measuring the impact of different categories of crime. Most assessments of crime are limited to how often such crimes occur and their economic impact. Since many white-collar crimes go undetected or unreported, we do not have a good idea as to their prevalence or whether they are increasing or decreasing. There are numerous studies that place a price tag on major white-collar crimes (e.g., theft, embezzlement, fraud, environmental crimes, and cyber crime). Most white-collar crimes come with multi-billion-dollar price tags, but estimates of their impact vary widely. Whether employee theft amounts to $20 billion or $40 billion in losses a year, for example, depends on which expert opinion you solicit and the methodology they use to make their estimates.

In addition to the economic assessments of white-collar crime, I explain the concept of *moral intensity*. Moral intensity takes into account the severity of a crime, the time lapse between the criminal act and the damage wrought by the act, how the impact of the crime is concentrated (few versus many victims), and the proximity of the crime to those who judge its impact.

Like all crimes, white-collar crimes have both direct victims and indirect victims. The direct victims of financial fraud, for example, are the company shareholders whose holdings diminish in value once the scheme becomes public knowledge. The indirect victims are the law-abiding firms that must absorb higher regulatory costs as the government enacts legislation to curb financial fraud. Similarly, white-collar crimes also benefit certain groups. The most obvious beneficiaries are the primary criminals and accomplices who reap the financial rewards of their crimes while avoiding prosecution. Other beneficiaries of crime include fraud investigators, auditors, law enforcement personnel, and security firms that profit from criminal activity.

Once a corporate board or management becomes aware of a crime or act of corruption, they may respond by instituting tighter financial controls, beefing up security, or rethinking the way executives are compensated. Society may respond to a significant wave of crime or organizational corruption by passing new laws or increasing the strictness with which current laws are enforced. The news media may play up the devastating effects of white-collar crime on the public and call for a strong stand against it by government and corporate officials.

As organizations and society respond to crime, criminals too make adjustments in the way they behave. The passage of a new criminal law may deter some individuals from committing additional white-collar crimes. Some identity thieves, for example, may decide to abandon their life of crime because of threats posed by the beefed-up federal identity theft legislation. Others may either ignore the law or frustrate the purpose of the act by using new tactics to steal personal identities. Still other identity thieves may switch to a different type of white-collar crime such as securities fraud. Criminals adapt either by getting out of the crime business or by taking new approaches to the way they commit crimes.

Not a Predictive Model

The model illustrates the dynamics of white-collar crime, but it must be emphasized that many individual crimes are difficult to predict. It is likely that a person with a lengthy criminal history will commit additional crimes in the future. Some white-collar criminals, however, do not have criminal records because they were able to break the law but avoided detection. Others do not commit crimes until later in life. A shrewd psychologist would have been hard-pressed to foresee the misdeeds of Enron's Kenneth Lay, Jeffrey Skilling, or Andy Fastow. Similarly, Bernard Ebbers or Scott Sullivan of WorldCom infamy exhibited no criminal behaviors during their early careers. The same could be said for members of the Rigas family (Adelphia), Martha Stewart (Martha Stewart Living Omnimedia), or David Duncan (Arthur Andersen and Enron). On the contrary, these individuals were noted for their community service and philanthropy. It was only after these high-profile executives were accused or charged with a crime that journalists and others began to dig into their pasts in hope of finding danger signals that would have suggested the potential for trouble.

The difficulties encountered in predicting white-collar crime are similar to the difficulties found in predicting workplace violence. During the 1990s, criminologists and law enforcement officials developed a profile of the typical violent perpetrator in the workplace. Violent individuals were usually white males, thirty-five to fifty years of age with a history of workplace problems, single or divorced with no social support group, fascinated with weapons and violence, and openly unhappy with their current employment situation.[20] What the literature tends to ignore is the low base rate of workplace violence. That is, only a very small number of individuals who fit this profile ever became violent at work.[21] White-collar crime also has a low base rate that makes it difficult to identify potentially unscrupulous professionals and managers.

Profiling versus Predicting Criminal Behavior

The FBI's Behavioral Science Unit has developed a system of criminal profiling that has proven useful for identifying suspects in violent crimes such as murder, rape, or arson. Profilers gather information about the victim and the crime scene to make inferences about the unknown perpetrator's sex, age, race, ethnicity, physical characteristics, personality, occupation, and motives. This technique has been especially useful in solving serial or spree crimes, but it has not been used widely for solving white-collar crimes.[22] John Douglas, a legendary FBI profiler, has written several books on crimes that have been solved with the help of criminal profiling techniques.

Profiling techniques are used after a crime has occurred, whereas predictive models attempt to identify the likely perpetrator of a crime before it happens. FBI agents and forensic scientists have spent many years interviewing criminals and compiling data from crime scenes, autopsy reports, and court records. This database, along with the decision-process models and crime-assessment techniques, provides a rigorous methodology for criminal investigations. Profiling requires painstaking investigative work, and it usually does not lead to the easy resolution of a criminal case.[23]

Gathering Insights from Criminals

Criminologists strive to understand the causes and consequences of criminal behavior. But they encounter major obstacles when interviewing and gathering information from criminals. Persons accused of a crime almost always have self-serving motives. They not only want to profess their innocence and be viewed positively by others but also may have legal reasons for not disclosing information about their activities. As a result, criminals have long frustrated researchers with distorted accounts of their backgrounds and behaviors. Criminals with antisocial personality disorder are especially manipulative and skillful at misleading interviewers and putting them on the defensive. Others are adroit at eliciting sympathy from naive interviewers.[24]

A Classification of Organizational Crime and Corruption

White-collar crimes fall into five classifications: (1) organized crime, (2) collective embezzlement, (3) corporate crime, (4) occupational crime, and (5) individual crime. Note that a white-collar crime may fall into more than one category. A corporate crime such as financial fraud, for example, is committed primarily for the benefit of the company. Yet, executives at the center of this crime may benefit personally, which also makes the act an occupational crime.

Organized Crime

Organized crime has not historically been linked to white-collar crime. Prostitution, gambling, racketeering, money laundering, and drug trafficking have long been the staples of organized criminals. Since the early

1980s, however, they have begun to make inroads into white-collar crimes such as securities fraud.[25] It appears that members of organized crime are expanding their networks into other white-collar crimes such as illegal immigration, credit card and social services fraud, and cyber crimes.[26] Organized crime has existed both to provide goods and services that are not obtainable through legal sources and to infiltrate and control legitimate businesses as a means of promoting the goals of organized criminals (known as *racketeering*).[27]

A robust market exists for these illegal goods and services. Criminals who provide them charge a premium for the risks they assume and the infrastructure they maintain. Illicit goods and services are often sold under monopolistic arrangements in which each organized crime syndicate has a prescribed territory that is off-limits to competitors. Thus, the highly profitable nature of organized crime can be attributed to the higher level of risk that is associated with selling something that is illegal and the sale of these goods and services under restrictive or monopolistic conditions.

Organized crime may consist of both legal and illegal operations. A legitimate business such as a restaurant, warehouse, insurance company, or labor union may be used as a front by organized criminals to conceal their unlawful businesses and to launder money obtained from criminal enterprises. One of the most infamous fronts for organized criminals was the "Pizza Connection" case. Heroin was smuggled from Asia through Sicily and into the United States where it was distributed by a criminal syndicate and sold through pizza restaurants in the Northeast and Midwestern states.[28]

The core group of organized criminals depends heavily on the support of protectors such as corrupt police officers, judges, lawyers, bankers, and other business people. Protectors, who are on the payroll of organized criminals and who are often sympathetic to their cause, enable the core group of criminals to operate their illegal businesses without outside interference or fear of prosecution. Organized crime also solicits the services of others who provide specialized and social support. These specialized persons include pilots for drug smuggling, accountants for advice on taxes, and law-abiding business people for entrees into the legitimate business world. Individuals who provide services and social support do not necessarily share the values of organized criminals. Finally, and most important, organized criminals must have a user support group such as drug users, gamblers, prostitution patrons, and buyers of stolen goods.[29]

Most members of organized crime work within an organizational structure that determines their rank, defines their duties, and requires a strict code of silence when dealing with law enforcement and other outsiders. Organized criminals, other than terrorists, have no political or religious ideology that drives their criminal activity; their primary goal is to make money and expand their territories.

Less traditional forms of organized crime are also emerging. Identity thieves have begun to form rings to steal, sell, and trade financial data on individuals using underground Internet sites. One network, Shadowcrew, had approximately 4,000 members before being shut down by federal agents. Shadowcrew, according to an indictment handed down to nineteen ringleaders by a Newark, New Jersey, federal grand jury, traded at least 1.5 million stolen credit card numbers and inflicted losses of over $4 million. The U.S. Department of Justice called Shadowcrew one of the largest online centers for trafficking stolen identity information.[30]

The Italian-based Mafia and La Cosa Nostra are household terms that are synonymous with organized crime. Membership in organized crime, however, has become global in scope. Ethnic groups from Asia, Latin America, Eastern Europe, and the Caribbean have established organized crime rings. Some organized crime groups are formed along lines other than national origin. Organized groups of convicts (both in and out of prison), motorcycle gangs, and street gangs all share attributes of organized crime.[31]

Collective Embezzlement

Collective embezzlement might best be summarized by the adage "The best way to rob a bank is to own one." In essence, collective embezzlement occurs when white-collar criminals assume control or ownership of an organization for the purpose of stealing from it. Thus, collective embezzlement is a crime by the organization against itself.[32]

The best example of collective embezzlement occurred during the savings and loan scandals of the late 1970s and early 1980s. A combination of poor economic conditions (the stagflation of the 1970s), deregulation of the savings and loan industry by the Reagan administration, and the highly competitive nature of the banking industry created a criminogenic environment that made savings and loan institutions attractive targets for white-collar criminals who used them as personal piggy banks. In addition, outside business people collaborated with criminal-minded savings and loan officers in a series of get-rich-quick schemes such as land flips (buying and selling land repeatedly to inflate its value) and collusive loan practices.

Collective embezzlement creates a situation in which a legitimate business becomes both the perpetrator of a crime and its victim. Some Enron executives allegedly used a complex corporate structure of special-purpose entities and other arrangements to commit both major financial fraud and to misappropriate millions of dollars disguised thinly as loans, bonuses, and commissions.

Corporate Crime

Corporate crimes are committed by executives and managers for the benefit of their organization. Price fixing (an antitrust violation), stealing proprietary information from competitors, entering into sweetheart arrangements with union officials to the detriment of union members, illegally dumping hazardous waste to avoid the cost of proper disposal, false advertising, cheating employees out of overtime pay, and the sale of unsafe products are all examples of corporate crime.

Most corporate crimes involve an element of fraud. The key ingredients of a fraudulent act are deception and misrepresentation.[33] Making false claims about a product, convincing the elderly to donate money to a phony religious charity in exchange for eternal salvation, and misleading investors about the financial health of a company are examples of fraud. The athletic director at a Midwestern community college along with former basketball and track coaches were indicted by federal jurors on fraud charges. They were accused of helping student-athletes obtain federal money by submitting falsified time cards for work that was never performed. Wire fraud charges were also filed in conjunction with the forwarding of fraudulent school transcripts.[34]

In line with Felson's crimes of specialized access, both the perpetrators of collective embezzlement and the perpetrators of corporate crime occupy positions of power. A crucial difference, however, is that those who engage in collective embezzlement are acting in their personal interest, and those engaged in corporate crimes are acting primarily for the benefit of their organization.

Occupational Crime

Occupational crimes are the classic crimes of specialized access and probably account for most white-collar crime. Nearly all occupations present some opportunity for crime or corruption. Bank employees can embezzle money, warehouse supervisors have access to supplies, purchasing agents can extract kickbacks from vendors, health care providers have the opportunity to commit insurance fraud, and police officers are in a position to take advantage of vulnerable citizens. Positions of power and trust present opportunities for these crimes.

Unlike collective embezzlement and corporate crime, occupational crimes can be committed at every level of the organization. Occupational crimes are committed primarily for the benefit of the perpetrator, usually to the detriment of the organization. Examples of occupational crime vary from the general manager of a building supply firm who accepts an under-the-table payment from a contractor in exchange for providing the contractor with lumber at below cost, to the janitor at a computer software company who rummages through trash cans in search of proprietary information that can be sold to the firm's major competitor.

Occupational crimes, like corporate crimes, usually involve fraud. Both the *New York Times* reporter Jayson Blair and the *Washington Post* reporter Janet Cooke fabricated stories that embarrassed their newspapers and tarnished the credibility of journalists. Blair committed frequent acts of journalistic fraud by inventing comments, concocting scenes, lifting material from other newspapers and wire services, and claiming to cover the news from Maryland and Texas when he was actually in New York. *New York Times* journalists discovered problems in at least thirty-six of the seventy-three articles written by Blair.[35] Cooke won a Pulitzer Prize for her heart-wrenching tale of Jimmy, an eight-year-old heroin user.[36] After Cooke described Jimmy's horrible plight, the authorities sought to locate him. She refused to provide information on Jimmy's whereabouts, however, or to name her sources for fear they would suffer retaliation at the hands of drug traffickers. The intensive search eventually revealed that Jimmy did not exist. It was also discovered that Cooke had falsified credentials on her resume when she had applied for the job at the newspaper. The *Washington Post* returned the Pulitzer Prize.[37]

Many occupational crimes are the result of a conspiracy by two or more employees. As organizations strengthen their security and refine their accounting controls, the likelihood of one person being able to commit an act of embezzlement or fraud is reduced. Two or more employees acting in concert, however, can frequently circumvent security devices or accounting procedures and perpetuate criminal activity over a long period of time. One classic example of an occupational crime conspiracy that also had links to organized crime was the Lufthansa heist of 1978 that netted $5 million in cash and $850,000 in jewelry. With the assistance of an insider who worked at the Kennedy International Airport, eight men known as the "Robert's Lounge Crew" disabled the alarm systems, overpowered security guards, and escaped in a waiting van with the stolen money and jewelry.[38] The crime was later the subject of a movie *The Big Heist*, and it also composed a prominent segment of the film *Goodfellas*. The two major elements of the Lufthansa heist are the indispensable role of the inside employee who stood to profit from this occupational crime and the fact that it involved a well-orchestrated conspiracy. Both of these elements appear repeatedly in other occupational crimes.

Most occupational crimes pale in comparison to Lufthansa. Instead, they are usually the work of employees who repeatedly embezzle small amounts of cash, set up fictitious business and vendor accounts to siphon off money, steal checks from a mailroom, file false or inflated travel expense claims, or misappropriate company resources. Although the majority of occupational crimes are small and often go undetected or unreported, the cumulative economic impact of such crimes can be significant.

Individual Crime

The final category of white-collar crime is individual crime. As the name implies, these crimes are committed by individuals operating alone or in a small, transient group. Scam artists, identity thieves, or tax evaders are examples of individuals who commit crimes on a freelance basis. In some cases, individual crimes involve several people who operate fly-by-night businesses. Some boiler room operations, for example, use tele-marketers to sell worthless securities or counterfeit goods, solicit for phony charities, or commit vacation scams. These operations often use temporary employees who are paid in cash and work out of cheap office space.

Putting White-Collar Crime in Perspective

Crime has two important dimensions: the public's perception of the se-riousness of a crime, and the complexity of the crime itself.

The Public's Perception of a Crime

The public is likely to perceive a crime as serious if it is violent, if the victim is not at fault and is relatively powerless, or if the crime causes se-rious economic damage. Terrorism, murder, rape, violent assault during a robbery, a burglary that financially devastates a business, injuries or deaths caused by inebriated drivers, violence toward children, and arson that results in millions of dollars in damage are usually regarded by the public as serious crimes.[39] Such crimes receive extensive media cover-age, and there is likely to be a great deal of pressure on law enforcement and on the judicial system to apprehend and punish the offenders. The public is less concerned about simple assaults (especially in cases where both sides played a part in initiating the dispute and the combatants were evenly matched), public drunkenness, recreational drug use by adults, or prostitution. These crimes are regarded by many as being less deviant, having no unwilling victim, or affecting only a small and more fringe segment of the population.

Similarly, white-collar crimes have traditionally been regarded as being of low severity by the public. As noted earlier, white-collar crimes do not involve violence or at least not the immediate application of vio-lence. The victims of white-collar crime often elicit little public sympa-thy because they may have contributed to the crime through their poor judgment, inattention, or greed. Furthermore, white-collar criminals do not have a sinister physical appearance. They are often personable and well dressed, in stark contrast with the menacing presence of many street criminals.

The Complexity of a Crime

Simple crimes can be detected and resolved with a modest expenditure of money and effort. Bringing the perpetrator of a complex crime to justice, however, may require millions of dollars and thousands of hours of work by investigators and prosecutors. The first aspect of the complexity of a crime is ease of detection. Crimes such as murder, rape, and assault have a detection rate of almost 100 percent. That is, either the victim or someone other than the perpetrator is aware that the crime has occurred. White-collar crimes, on the other hand, are insidious and are detected with less frequency. Some white-collar crimes such as embezzlement, medical fraud, and environmental crimes may go unnoticed for months or years.

Even if a crime is detected, it may not be reported to the authorities. Companies and individuals who are victimized by white-collar criminals may refuse to report the incident for fear of adverse publicity or a loss of investor confidence. They may elect, instead, to fire the offending party without pressing criminal charges.

Crimes that are reported may not result in charges being filed. Street crimes such as burglary, robbery, or assaults are often committed by anonymous individuals who have no connection with the victim. Even when the perpetrator is known to the victim, there may be insufficient evidence to prosecute the case. White-collar crimes are especially perplexing because once detected, it is fairly easy to identify the suspects.[40] Federal and state courts, however, have strict legal rules of evidence and demand a high burden of proof (guilt beyond a reasonable doubt) in criminal cases. The evidence in street crimes includes weapons, fingerprints, DNA analyses, eye-witness testimony, and video surveillance footage. Evidence in white-collar crimes is often in either paper or electronic form. Legal rules may prevent such evidence from being introduced into court proceedings and, when admitted, it may be difficult to link the evidence to the accused. This problem is exacerbated because documents and information associated with white-collar crimes are increasingly being stored on computers. As John Douglas and Steven Singualar explain:

> When doing an "autopsy" on a computer, after someone has been arrested and that individual's property has been seized, the authorities have to follow meticulously the Constitution's Fourth Amendment rules regarding reasonable "search and seizure" or the evidence will never stand up in court. This creates enormously time-consuming tasks and complexities. Most law enforcement people are used to getting a search warrant and going out and looking for a particular item. What happens if you obtain a warrant for someone's hard drive but then you find things on the disk that you were not specifically hunting for? What if you are investigating one kind of crime but find evidence of several others?
>
> The moment you turn a computer on, you change the configuration of everything that's in it, which is to say that you can alter the evidence of a crime. The windows and the files "start cookin" and when that happens, you've likely ruined some of the raw data that you most wanted to preserve. Instead of getting the computer and immediately turning it on, which seems to be the natural thing to do, specialists have learned to copy everything off the hard drive first, making exact duplicates of the evidence and then working off the copy and keeping the original data in tact.[41]

So while the identification of suspects in white-collar crimes is often easy, the successful prosecution of complex cases is time consuming, expensive, and highly uncertain. For these reasons, federal and state prosecutors are selective in deciding which white-collar crime cases to pursue. "In white-collar crimes, top brass are tough to prosecute. They rarely participate personally in fraudulent transactions, legal experts say, and aren't likely to come right out and say cook the books. If they instead say ambiguous things about hitting targets or 'making numbers,' others who take this as a code for 'cheat' are at risk because 'their fingerprints are all over the documents,'" says Howard Schiffman, a former Securities and Exchange Commission enforcement lawyer.[42]

When a conviction is obtained, white-collar criminals have usually received light sentences in minimum-security prisons. Street criminals are subjected to more severe penalties for crimes of low economic impact.

It should be emphasized, however, that street criminals often commit dozens of crimes before they are caught; the one for which they are arrested and convicted is often the tip of the iceberg.

Why White-Collar Crimes Have Fallen below the Radar

There are two crucial points about white-collar crime that explain why these crimes fall below the radar. First, violent street crimes are taken more seriously than white-collar crimes. Second, white-collar crimes are more complex and difficult to prosecute than street crimes. Because of public pressures and limited resources, federal and state prosecutors are reluctant to pursue white-collar criminals with so many violent criminal cases vying for their attention.[43]

In the wake of Enron, WorldCom, and other high profile cases, it appears that the public, along with prosecutors, juries, and judges, are taking a less sympathetic view of white-collar criminals. It should also be noted that when federal government prosecutors decide to move forward with a case, the odds of a conviction are high. The federal government has the resources to outgun even the wealthiest defendant although, as the Martha Stewart case illustrates, the sentence received is often lenient in light of the resources expended to obtain a conviction.

Conclusion

There is growing concern about the complex social problem of white-collar crime and corruption. The model discussed in this book describes the dynamics of this form of criminal behavior, its aftermath, and the organizational and societal responses to it. Although the model does not provide a means of predicting individual criminal behavior, it does do the following: (1) examines the thought processes used by white-collar criminals before, during, and after their crimes, (2) places the impact of white-collar crime into a realistic perspective, and (3) identifies points of attack that can be used to combat white-collar crime and corruption.

Chapter one discusses the individual, organizational, and societal factors that contribute to organizational crime and corruption. Chapter two focuses on the types of white-collar crime, and chapter three deals with the major categories of white-collar criminals, the risk assessment process of criminals, and the psychological mechanisms that they use to justify their deeds. Chapter four analyzes the economic, psychological, and social consequences of organizational crime and corruption. Chapter five discusses possible societal and organizational responses to white-collar crime, and the Conclusion provides a summary and closing remarks.

1

What Influences Organizational Crime and Corruption?

The causes of crime defy simple explanation. Over the past century, dozens of theories on crime and criminal behavior have been set forth. These theories include genetic explanations (the XYY chromosome theory, phrenology), biological causes (brain dysfunctions, exposure to toxic substances that impair neurological functioning), early childhood traumas (parental abuse and neglect, traumatic head injuries, exposure to violence), psychological problems (attention deficit disorders, impulsive behaviors, low IQ, personality disorders), environmental influences (criminal role models, drug abuse, pornography, overindulgent parents), and societal factors (materialism and the accumulation of surplus wealth, the acceptability of bending rules, a win-at-all-costs mentality, economic downturns and unemployment). The appendix at the end of the book provides a thumbnail sketch of some major theories of crime.

Whenever a complex phenomenon such as crime becomes the subject of numerous explanations, three conclusions can be drawn. First, each of these explanations probably contains an element of truth. Second, numerous explanations likely means knowledge is incomplete; the vast differences among crime theories indicate that we do not fully understand criminal behavior, and we often find it difficult to explain the differences between criminals and law-abiding citizens. Third, it is easier to explain than to predict; criminologists and other social scientists are more adept at analyzing crime than knowing when it will happen. Crime levels would actually be much higher if the standard explanations for crime were always true, but most persons who are exposed to criminal role models, physical or psychological trauma, or economic adversity do not resort to crime.[1] Conversely, persons who have benefited from a stable family life, a quality education, and a fulfilling career are not immune from crime.

Predicting the behavior of criminals has long been a practical concern to judges and parole boards. Judges set bail and decide between prison time and probation for convicted felons. Parole boards are asked to determine whether a prisoner can be released without posing an undue danger to society. Employers have begun to use background checks and integrity testing to avoid hiring persons with criminal records or dishonest attitudes. Judges and parole boards, however, have an advantage over employers in predicting criminal behaviors. The former are dealing with individuals who have been arrested or convicted of a crime, whereas the latter are dealing with job applicants who usually have no criminal record.

A discussion of the multiple factors that help explain criminal behavior follows. Since crime starts with the individual, individual influences on crime are discussed first followed by organizational effects on criminal behavior and, finally, society's impact on crime.

Sorting out these multiple factors or conditions, however, is not easy. For example, we know in retrospect that the demise of WorldCom involved several key persons, events, and conditions: (1) a wealth-driven management team and a board that failed to challenge top management's decisions, (2) research analysts who exaggerated the financial health of the company and the growth potential of the telecommunications industry, (3) investors who trusted the analyst's reports and projections, and (4) a fragmented industry structure that enabled WorldCom to acquire and integrate small firms into their empire.[2]

At the individual level, we can ask: What made the top WorldCom managers so ambitious, yet so careless? Why did accountants and security analysts knowingly inflate their assessments of WorldCom's financial health? At the organizational level, we can ask: How did the culture at WorldCom contribute to its corruption? What flaws existed in its accounting system that allowed WorldCom to hide hundreds of millions of dollars in expenses and falsely inflate the company's profit picture? At the societal level, we can ask: What industry characteristics contributed to the WorldCom debacle? Why did auditors and government regulators fail to detect problems at WorldCom until it was too late?

As another example, the woman described in the introduction who embezzled money from a Missouri tourist business: (1) probably had a high degree of impulsivity and optimism that her embezzlement would go undetected (individual influences), (2) worked unsupervised for an owner who lived over 100 miles from the business (organizational influences), and (3) received leniency for her previous crime in Illinois (societal influences). The questions relevant to this case are: Why did the owner hire and place trust in someone he did not know? Why did a background check fail to reveal the woman's criminal history? Why was she left unsupervised by the criminal justice system after embezzling a large sum of money from her former employer?

Individual Characteristics

Professionals and managers have their individual personality traits, knowledge, experience, level of integrity, and personal needs. These characteristics play an integral but inexact role in determining whether they will engage in white-collar crime.

Personality Traits and Disorders

Personality is undoubtedly linked to crime. The problem is that we do not know precisely how personality and crime are related. An individual's personality is composed of dozens of individual traits. There are approximately 18,000 words in the English language that describe some type of personality trait or characteristic.[3] Psychologists, however, use a much smaller number of traits in their work on personality and personality disorders. One popular grouping of personality traits is the Big Five: (1) conscientiousness, (2) agreeableness, (3) emotional stability, (4) openness to new ideas, and (5) extraversion. Of these, conscientiousness, and to a slightly lesser extent, agreeableness appear to have the most influence on job performance and deviant behaviors.[4] That is, the higher executives and managers score on psychological measures of conscientiousness and agreeableness, the less likely they will be to commit deviant acts such as white-collar crime. A note of caution: These relationships, while statistically significant, still fail to explain a great deal of deviant managerial behavior.

Traits such as impulsiveness and recklessness have also been attributed to criminals, and it appears that both white-collar and street criminals may exhibit these behaviors to a greater extent than the population at large. The terms "impulsive" and "reckless" are subjective, however, and they might just as easily be used to describe noncriminal behaviors such as sexual promiscuity, rock climbing, skydiving, or accumulating excessive debt. Furthermore, we should not assume that quick actions are impulsive actions. Criminals are often poised to move quickly once an opportunity for crime presents itself. They may have already decided when, where, and under what conditions they will commit a crime. Impulsive acts, in contrast, occur when someone does little planning before the commission of a crime. As with persons with low levels of conscientiousness and agreeableness, most impulsive and reckless persons are not criminals.

A personality disorder is any mental condition that adversely affects an individual's quality of life or ability to function. Psychologists have defined and catalogued a large number of personality disorders.[5] Examples include mood disorders, anxiety disorders, and paranoid personality disorder. These enduring patterns of inner experience or behavior deviate markedly from cultural expectations across a range of personal and social situations. The pattern of personality disorders are stable and long-lasting and can be traced back to adolescence or early adulthood.[6] Many criminals who have been incarcerated for violent crimes have personality disorders, although the majority of persons with such disorders are not criminals.

Few white-collar criminals are diagnosed with personality disorders. There are two disorders, however, that may explain the behavior of some white-collar criminals: antisocial personality disorder and narcissistic personality disorder.

By definition, a person diagnosed with antisocial personality disorder has already committed multiple criminal, corrupt, or highly irresponsible acts.[7] Persons with antisocial personality disorder (formerly known as sociopaths or psychopaths) exhibit harmful behaviors, ranging from the rare cases of serial murder to the more prevalent cases of chronic physical and mental abuse of family members or co-workers, neglect, unreliability, substance abuse, lying, fraud, and theft. About 3 to 4 percent of the population has this personality disorder, with males having a higher prevalence than females. Persons with antisocial personality disorder often end up in prisons, mental institutions, or drug rehabilitation centers. There are those, however, whose family ties, appearance of respectability, intelligence, craftiness, and access to legal protection allow them to avoid detection or prosecution.

The psychologist Robert Hare, who has spent his career studying individuals having antisocial personality disorder, comments: "I always said that if I wasn't studying psychopaths in prison, I'd do it at the stock exchange. There are certainly more people in the business world who would score high in the psychopathic dimension than in the general population. You'll find them in any organization where, by the nature of one's position, you have power and control over other people and the opportunity to get something."[8] These individuals are known as subcriminal or high-functioning psychopaths.[9] An intelligent person with antisocial personality disorder hides behind a "mask of sanity."[10] They are usually articulate, glib, and superficial in their dealings with others.

Persons with antisocial personality disorder will engage in almost any act of treachery. They tend to view people as objects to be manipulated, not as human beings with feelings and needs. Persons with antisocial personality disorder have one chilling common characteristic: a complete lack of remorse for the harm they cause. White-collar criminals with this personality disorder are oblivious to the careers they damage, the jobs they destroy, the financial losses they cause, or the bodily harm they inflict. When confronted with their misdeeds, they will either attempt to talk their way out of trouble, intellectualize or rationalize their actions, or claim they are the victim of a misunderstanding.[11]

Narcissistic personality disorder may also be a factor in white-collar crime. Narcissistic people are extremely egocentric (self-centered) and egotistical (an inflated self-perception).[12] They possess a grandiose view of themselves and their importance, and they fantasize about their power, brilliance, and lofty accomplishments. At the same time, they devalue the accomplishments of others. They expect to be idolized and placed on a pedestal, and they feel entitled to hold the best jobs, attend the most prestigious schools, and enter the most elite social circles. Not surprising, persons afflicted with this personality disorder are even more galling, but less dangerous, than those with antisocial personality disorder. They are power-seeking, ruthless self promoters with insatiable ambition. Persons with narcissistic personality disorder are adept at ingratiating themselves to persons of high status and power. They like to socialize with and drop names of prominent persons and celebrities.

At the same time, the narcissist has no regard for persons of lower status who have nothing to offer him or her. Like the person with antisocial personality disorder, the narcissist has no concern or empathy for others. Despite their self-important bravado, they have a fragile self esteem, and they react negatively when others either fail to appreciate their importance or criticize them.

Persons who aspire to positions of power may, at times, exhibit egocentric and egotistical behaviors although they do not meet the diagnostic criteria for narcissistic personality disorder. Although narcissistic individuals are less likely than antisocial personalities to become embroiled in crime, they believe they are above everything, including the law. A narcissistic and ruthlessly ambitious scientist might falsify experimental data or fail to recognize the contributions of colleagues as he blindly pursues professional fame. A corporate chief financial officer might engage in fraudulent accounting practices to boost her company's profits because her narcissism will not allow her to be part of an organization that is not an industry leader. Similarly, the narcissistic and corrupt televangelist who claims to have a direct conduit to the supernatural may feel no guilt about spending lavishly and living regally on the donations of his faithful, but naïve, followers.

Antisocial personalities and narcissists are arch manipulators. They can be ingenious at using others to achieve their goals and, at the same time, they resist manipulation by others. Compliant individuals represent the other extreme. Such individuals may be drawn into white-collar crime because of a strong desire to please their superiors or clients. The Arthur Andersen accountant David Duncan represents an example of a solid citizen who was probably intimidated by the relentless pressure and presence of Enron executives bent on engaging in accounting fraud and, later, shredding documents to cover their tracks.[13]

Compliant individuals may also be pulled unwittingly into crime because they are trusting and naïve; if their boss tells them to do something, they will do it without question. Some extreme cases of compliant behaviors may be the result of dependent personality disorder. Individuals with this personality disorder are highly submissive and go to excessive lengths to please others. They will submit to what others want even when the demands are unreasonable.[14]

It is easy to imagine an antisocial or narcissistic boss running roughshod over a compliant subordinate who will commit theft or fraud on command. It is also easy to imagine that the antisocial or narcissistic individual will try to escape culpability by shifting blame for the crime to the gullible subordinate.

Intelligence, Knowledge, and Skills

Being a criminal requires knowledge and skill. Street criminals such as robbers and pickpockets learn how to select and approach victims, commit the crime, and make a getaway. Car thieves may spend a great deal of time examining repair manuals of the latest models so that they will be able to disable or sidestep antitheft technology. Thieves who prey on wealthy victims have learned the complex business of entering highly secure residences, disarming alarm systems, and stealing valuable items while leaving few clues for law enforcement.[15] Identity thieves have learned how to steal or manufacture "breeder" documents such as birth certificates or social security cards, as the following case describes.

> At 19 years old, Douglas Cade Havard was honing counterfeiting skills he learned in online chat rooms, making fake IDs in Texas for underage college students who wanted to drink alcohol. . . . By the age of 21, Mr. Havard had moved to England and parlayed those skills to a lucrative position at Carderplanet.com, one of the biggest multinational online networks trafficking in stolen personal data. . . . Having reached a senior rank in the largely Russian and Eastern European organization, he was driving a $57,000 Mercedes and spending hundreds of dollars at clubs and casinos. . . . Now 22, Mr. Havard is in a Leeds prison cell, having pleaded guilty to charges of fraud and money laundering. The Carderplanet network has been shut down. . . . The officers discovered $28,000 worth of forged traveler's checks and a portfolio of identities bearing his photo, including phony drivers' licenses and fake or doctored passports from Spain, Ireland, and the U.S. . . . The policemen also found high-resolution images of bank and credit-card logos stored on a computer along with fake holograms, blank plastic cards and a heat press for embossing numbers.[16]

White-collar criminals have more education than other criminals and, as a result, they usually score higher on intelligence tests.[17] Whether white-collar criminals are more intelligent than street criminals is debatable, especially when one looks at the ingenuity displayed by some burglars and drug traffickers. Specific knowledge and skills can provide excellent tools for certain white-collar crimes. Accounting fraud requires knowledge of generally accepted accounting principles and the ability to detect weaknesses in an accounting system. Medical fraud requires an understanding of health care providers and health insurance claim mechanisms. Criminals who engage in computer fraud must have a current knowledge of programming, software design, the Internet, and the location of protected information. White-collar criminals who commit securities, real estate, or consumer fraud must have insights into human behavior that enable them to manipulate and gain the trust of their victims. Counterfeiters and forgers have specialized expertise in the banking system as well as the latest graphics and color copying technology.[18] In essence, knowledge and skills provide the specialized access needed to commit crimes.

Propensity for Risk

Criminals appear to have a higher tolerance for risk than noncriminals.[19] The degree of risk taking and intelligence exhibited by criminals varies widely, ranging from crimes that only someone with high intelligence and extreme daring could commit to episodes featured on *America's Dumbest Criminals*. A seasoned criminal may decline a risk that a novice one might take. Experienced and intelligent criminals may also take precautions to reduce risk prior to committing a crime. A savvy computer expert may develop meticulous plans for hacking into the computer system of a large bank, whereas a less-knowledgeable hacker may attempt to enter the system with little forethought or planning.

Street criminals often appear to be impulsive and ignorant of the risks they face while white-collar criminals appear to be more conservative and calculating. White-collar crimes, however, are more complex and probably require more planning than most street crimes. Experienced street criminals may have formulated a set of rules that enable them to capitalize quickly on a crime opportunity. As noted earlier, behaviors that appear to be more risky and impulsive may, in fact, be less risky because of the criminal's knowledge and experience. Risk assessment is discussed in more detail in chapter three. Suffice it to say that criminals have varying propensities for risk, but few are careless, reckless, or impulsive. They plan their crimes, reject those that are too risky, and are able to bide their time until a safer opportunity comes along.

Both white-collar and the street criminals may be motivated by the emotional thrill they receive from committing a crime. In fact, a thief may get more gratification from the act of stealing and avoiding apprehension than from the monetary value of the stolen items. Getting high on danger and risk taking is thought to be the result of a neurotic need for power and flirtation with death that provides what Frank Bruno calls "the *excitement* that comes with a close look at the abyss of oblivion."[20]

Honesty and Integrity

Criminals are regarded as being less honest than law-abiding citizens, but most dishonest people are not criminals. Most people exhibit some form of dishonesty at some point in their lives. If dishonesty is defined broadly, many of us are dishonest on an almost daily basis. We may greet someone by saying, "It's nice to see you," even when we barely know that person and are indifferent to their presence. When asked for an opinion on a garish piece of art, most "honest" people—not wanting to offend the owner—will reply that they like the bright style of the work, while thinking that nothing could be further from the truth. We often say or do dishonest things for the sake of tact or diplomacy.

Criminals behave in ways that go well beyond the polite distortions or falsehoods of others. The dishonest behaviors of criminals inflict financial loss, physical damage, or pain and suffering on others. Dishonest behaviors may be usefully divided into three categories: stealing, cheating, and lying. Stealing obviously involves taking something of value that belongs to another with the intent of permanently depriving that person (or organization) of the use of that item. Cheating entails breaking rules to secure an unfair advantage. The college football coach who buys an automobile for a blue-chip recruit is violating NCAA rules and obtaining a competitive advantage over coaches who refuse such accommodations to star high school athletes. Lying, of course, is making a statement that one knows to be false.[21] Most white-collar crimes such as fraud involve combinations of these basic offenses.

White-collar criminals are especially adept at telling lies because lies form the foundation for fraud, and fraud is the backbone of white-collar crime. There are two types of lies: lies of commission and lies of omission. Lies of commission are those in which someone says something that they know is not true. A manager who intentionally falsifies sales data and then denies doing so has committed a lie of commission. Lies of omission occur when pertinent information is withheld. A job applicant for a nursing supervisor position who fails to mention that his nursing license has been revoked is committing a lie of omission.

Philosophers from Socrates to the present day have asked the question: "How should we behave?" This question has evolved into a mainstream philosophical issue, and it forms the foundation for the study of ethics.[22] Discussions about when it is acceptable to break the law can be traced to Greek mythology and plays such as *Antigone*, the tale of a woman who insisted on the proper burial of her brother even though it violated the decree of a despotic ruler. Thoreau, Gandhi, and Martin Luther King Jr. encouraged civil disobedience under certain circumstances, and philosophers have long debated the definitions of ethics, honesty, integrity, and goodness.

When criminals wax philosophical, they are usually trying to tailor the concepts of honesty and integrity to fit their special circumstances. Although most criminals do not spend time thinking deeply about the texts of great philosophers, they often attempt to place their crimes in perspective by engaging in ethical arguments. One way of doing this is to distinguish between crimes of necessity and crimes that are senseless, always emphasizing that their crimes fall into the former category. Another way is to argue that crime is defined subjectively and capriciously by legislators and judges who are themselves corrupt. Yet another way of placing crime into the criminal's perspective is to contend that definitions of honesty and integrity are culturally biased. Actions such as bribery when committed in the United States are illegal. But white-collar criminals are quick to point out that bribes are an acceptable business practice in many other countries.

Perceptions of Fairness and Equity

Occupational crimes such as theft are thought to be caused primarily by an employee's reaction to unfair treatment. J. Stacy Adams's famous equity theory explains motivation in terms of employee outcome-input ratios.[23] Employees receive outcomes from their work such as pay, benefits, and social amenities, and they bring inputs to their work such as effort, time spent on the job, knowledge, skills, and abilities. At the same time, employees select referent others (persons performing similar work in the same or similar organizations) and compare their outcome-input ratio with the ratio of the referent employee. If the outcome-input ratios are approximately the same, then a condition of equity exists. If the employee's ratio is less than that of the referent other, then a condition of under reward exists. The process of computing outcomes and inputs and selecting referent others for comparison is a personal and subjective process, but it has real consequences for the employee.

To eliminate or reduce an under-reward situation, the employee must either increase outcomes (e.g., receive a pay raise) or decrease inputs (e.g., decrease effort at work). Few employees can simply ask for and receive a pay raise and, in controlled work environments, few employees have the opportunity to make a significant reduction in their effort. One way to increase outcomes is to steal. Theft of money, equipment, merchandise, or supplies can increase the employee's outcome-input ratio and restore a sense of equity. Similarly, the falsification of time cards, recording phony sales to increase commissions, padding expense accounts, and setting up false vendor accounts to channel money to an employee's personal business are all ways of increasing outcomes and achieving equity by eliminating the condition of under reward.

An extraordinary compensation package does not always prevent feelings of inequity. White-collar and professional employees may believe they are under rewarded because their compensation, while well into six figures, is still less than that of similarly situated executives (referent others). The same phenomenon occurs when a professional athlete rejects a multi-million-dollar contract offer because he believes that another athlete received a better deal. It is the relative amount of compensation that an executive receives (not the absolute amount of compensation) that is critical.

Outcome-input ratios may also be affected by more than the economic aspects of work. Employees who feel unappreciated by their superiors may have less compunction about stealing from their organizations than do employees who feel they are treated with dignity and respect. Furthermore, a phenomenon known as hostile attribution bias may affect the way employees view their treatment in the workplace. Mentally ill persons suffering from paranoia might attribute hostility to even the most innocuous or well-intended actions of others. To a lesser degree, employees who perceive that they are treated disrespectfully by their supervisors, customers, co-workers, or others may retaliate by committing crimes against their organizations.

An Individual's Utility for Money

Money is almost universally valued. Most people have a positive utility for money (i.e., more is better), but a decreasing marginal utility for money (i.e., a $10,000 pay raise brings more pleasure to us if we make $50,000 a year than if we make $1 million a year). The desire for more money, either for lifestyle improvement or crisis needs, probably explains acts of theft and embezzlement by some lower- and mid-level employees.

One puzzling aspect of some white-collar crimes is: Why do executives who already make millions of dollars per year feel compelled to commit fraudulent acts such as those that occurred at Enron, World-Com, Tyco, and Adelphia? What economic needs could these executives possibly have when they already live in palatial homes, own expensive automobiles, yachts, and airplanes, wear the most elegant and stylish clothing, dine on the finest food, and travel first class to wherever they desire? Why would they risk losing such an opulent lifestyle, facing criminal charges, and suffering irreparable damage to their reputations when they already have more money than they can spend? A standard journalistic explanation for white-collar crimes committed by extremely wealthy executives is "greed." This explanation, however, begs the question as to what causes greed.

Beyond a certain income level, most people prefer additional leisure time to additional money. For some highly paid individuals, however, money becomes a scorecard of success. Even though their economic needs have been met in every conceivable way, they still have an obsession with wealth. Former Enron CEO Kenneth Lay said that he not only wanted to become rich but also to become "world class rich."[24] The psychology behind such greed is difficult to comprehend. An obsession with wealth may be attributable to relative egotistical needs, narcissism, obsessive-compulsive behavior, a high need for power, or a quest for perfectionism. Psychological issues such as these distort a person's utility for money. Wealthy but corrupt executives may underestimate the risks associated with white-collar crime. In retrospect, Martha Stewart took a great deal of risk to protect a fraction of one percent of her wealth. At the time she sold 3,928 shares of ImClone stock based on inside information from her broker, she may have thought her risk of being detected was minimal to nonexistent. Yet her connection to then ImClone CEO Sam Waksal and her misstatements to FBI agents led to her indictment on charges of securities fraud and obstruction of justice. Stewart's timely stock sale enabled her to avoid losses of $45,673, a scant sum when one considers the costs associated with her conviction and incarceration.

A Comparison of White-Collar and Street Criminals

A central thesis of this book is that white-collar criminals and street criminals exhibit comparable thought patterns and possess similar views of people and the world around them. There are, however, notable socioeconomic differences between white-collar and street criminals.

Table 1.1 summarizes the differences between white-collar criminals and their counterparts on the street, and it reinforces Felson's previously mentioned notion of white-collar crime as crimes of specialized access.

Table 1.1. White-Collar versus Street Criminals

White-Collar Criminals	*Street Criminals*
Older	Younger
Males and a significant number of females	Mostly males
Commit primarily property crimes (theft, embezzlement, fraud)	Commit both property crimes and violent crimes (murder, rape, assault)
Stable lifestyle (homeowner, employed, no drugs)	Unstable lifestyle
Educated (usually some college or college degree)	Less educated (often lacking a high school diploma or GED)
Commit few crimes	Commit numerous crimes
Suspect easy to identify once the crime is detected	Suspect difficult to identify once the crime is detected
Individual crimes have high economic impact	Individual crimes have low economic impact
Crimes committed within an organizational context	Crimes committed alone without organizational sanction or support
Crimes committed with others	Crimes committed alone
Indictment causes humiliation and damages reputation	Indictment causes little humiliation or damage to reputation

White-Collar Criminals	Street Criminals
Primarily federal or state prosecution	Primarily state or local prosecution
Private criminal attorney is likely to be used	Public criminal attorney is likely to be used
Attorney often involved before charges are filed	Attorney likely to be involved only after charges are filed
Probation or short prison term	Prison term of significant length
Sentenced to a minimum-security prison	Sentenced to a medium- or maximum-security prison
Prosecutors retain advantage during retrial	Prosecutors lose advantage during retrial (element of surprise is lost)

Street criminals, being younger and less educated, lack the opportunity to hold white-collar jobs, have less money and stability in their lives, and they do not enjoy prominence in their communities. If a career street criminal were hired for a white-collar job, however, he would commit white-collar crimes. As noted earlier, some white-collar workers and professionals also commit street crimes such robbery, burglary, shoplifting, sexual assaults, and murder.

The Organization's Impact on White-Collar Crime

I once toured the Missouri State Penitentiary. A corrections officer escorted me through the cell blocks, past guard stations, and around the recreational areas of the old and decaying maximum-security prison (which has since closed). He said that the inmates, all of whom were convicted felons serving lengthy sentences, committed every type of crime within the prison walls that could be committed in society, with one exception—auto theft. While the high-population density, close confines of the prison, and prevalence of violent inmates provided the ideal environment for murders, rapes, thefts, vandalism, acts of intimidation, and scams, the inmates had no way of stealing a motor vehicle. Had inmates gotten access to motor vehicles, the corrections officer opined, they would have stolen them, if only to go for a short joyride within the prison walls. This situation illustrates, in an extreme way, how an organizational environment provides both opportunities and barriers to crime.

Criminogenic Organizational Environments

Criminogenic environments are those that encourage criminal behaviors. Some organizations provide numerous opportunities for crime, whereas others provide few opportunities. Criminogenic organizations have been depicted as crime-coercive and crime facilitative.[25]

Crime-coercive organizations expect their members to engage in criminal behavior. The best example of crime coerciveness is an organized crime group that employs or does business with people who understand they are expected to commit criminal acts. The crooked banker, for example, who helps drug traffickers launder money does so with the full knowledge that he is violating federal law.

Crime-coercive organizations may hire unsuspecting individuals who are then pulled into criminal activity. Once they discover that crime is part of their job, they may either resist or participate willingly. Other individuals may be deceived into committing a crime and then become trapped in a situation from which they cannot escape. Usually the employee is enticed into committing a minor crime such as accepting a small but illegal gratuity. The employer, vendor, or contractor who provided the small gratuity then uses this illegal act to blackmail the employee into committing more serious crimes.

All organizations, to varying degrees, are crime facilitative. Every organization has security-system flaws, accounting rules that can be bent and manipulated, and dishonest employees who will steal merchandise or embezzle funds if conditions are right. The remainder of this chapter deals primarily with conditions found in crime-facilitative environments.

Physical Security

Organizations use a variety of physical security devices, ranging from simple key-operated door locks to highly sophisticated electronic surveillance systems.[26] Security systems are designed to regulate physical access to specific areas, detect an intrusion, and slow down an intruder. The technology of physical security systems has improved tremendously over the past twenty years as witnessed by the advent of motion-and-heat detection devices and satellite (global positioning system) technology.

Physical security systems, however, have several common vulnerable elements. First, all security systems depend on human intervention, and humans make mistakes. Security guards are occasionally inattentive or distracted; they fail to make rounds as scheduled (or they adhere to a regular schedule that is known to the criminal), or they do not use electronic surveillance devices properly. Second, physical security devices, while designed to protect the organization from both outsiders and insiders, can be disabled. Employees may learn how to unplug a security device, or they may discover areas in a warehouse that are not monitored by surveillance cameras. Third, physical security systems do little to combat common white-collar crimes. An army of security guards using state-of-the-art surveillance would have little impact on the commission of crimes such as accounting and financial fraud, the manufacture of unsafe products, securities fraud, or scams against consumers.

Accounting and Financial Controls

Organizations use accounting procedures to record and measure assets, liabilities, revenues, expenditures, and cash flows. An accounting system that is designed properly also provides a system of checks and balances that helps to prevent acts of theft, embezzlement, and fraud. Independent auditors periodically examine a corporation's accounting system to ensure that the company's procedures are being followed properly and that they comply with generally accepted accounting principles. Accounting systems that are designed poorly or that are used improperly can provide opportunities for white-collar crime. Auditors who do not perform their duties diligently or who have conflicts of interest with the client firm also contribute to white-collar crime.

Accounting fraud involves the creation of fraudulent paperwork or entries in ledgers either to conceal acts of theft or embezzlement or to misrepresent a company's financial condition. Executives commit financial fraud by overstating assets and revenues or by understating liabilities and expenses (or some combination of these things) on corporate financial statements. By exaggerating the financial strength of the company, executives can boost stock prices, mislead investors, and increase their wealth through their stock option grants that are tied to inflated short-term stock values.

Job Characteristics, Organizational Structure, and Accountability

There is evidence that job characteristics and organizational structures have an impact on organizational crime and corruption.[27] Jobs that provide employees with autonomy and lax supervision create more opportunity for crime than do jobs in which the supervision is more intense. Executives, sales personnel, attorneys, and other professionals have more freedom to conceal illegal activities than do many blue-collar workers.

Large organizations may have a higher incidence of crime and corruption than small organizations because they conduct business with a wide variety of people (employees, customers, vendors, and investors). Sheer size increases the odds of criminal and corrupt activity. Large organizations are also more likely to be decentralized and subject to less-rigid controls than smaller organizations. Decentralized structures are usually geographically dispersed. A manager at an Asian subsidiary cannot be closely supervised from U.S. corporate headquarters. Far-flung units may also be pressured to meet unrealistic sales or profit goals. A combination of unrealistic sales, production, or financial goals and management's sense of isolation from the rest of the organization, for example, may encourage accounting, financial, or other forms of fraud.

Diffusion of responsibility is another influence on organizational crime. Individuals who are monitored closely and held strictly accountable for their work have few opportunities for illicit behavior. A classic example is allowing only one employee to have access to a cash register and holding that employee responsible for any cash shortages. Managers and employees who work in poorly defined jobs with minimal supervision, lax accounting controls, flexible working hours, and freedom of movement within and outside of their work site are in a better position to hide their criminal activities and avoid individual responsibility.

Work Groups and Crime Enablers

Professionals and managers who commit white-collar crimes or who engage in acts of corruption rarely do so without the participation or knowledge of others.[28] Many white-collar crimes involve conspiracies in which two or more individuals work together to plan and commit a crime. Persons who actually commit the crime are the primary criminals, and those who aid and abet in the planning, execution, or cover-up are regarded as either accomplices or accessories after the fact. In the case of embezzlement, the primary criminal steals the money, a co-worker accomplice alters accounting records to conceal the theft, and an accessory after the fact might protect these parties by feigning ignorance or by providing misleading information to bank examiners or federal authorities.

Work groups that become involved in organizational or occupational crimes are cohesive and have a high degree of trust among members. By working together, they can alter documents, destroy evidence, and bypass security procedures. Illicit work groups usually steal and embezzle cash, merchandise, supplies, or equipment. They may also extort kickbacks from suppliers, run illegal drug or gambling rings in the workplace, and sell trade secrets to competitors. At higher organizational levels, groups of executives may engage in price fixing, cultivate relationships with corrupt politicians, or misappropriate corporate funds or assets.

Inadequate Oversight by Corporate Boards

Corporate boards shouldered a significant amount of blame for the flurry of corporate scandals that occurred during the late 1990s and early years of the twenty-first century. Boards of directors are supposed to provide guidance to the CEO and members of top management on the strategic direction of the company. They are also expected to oversee how the company is managed.

The criticisms leveled at corporate boards are twofold. First, boards have failed to control corporate crime and corruption because they have been kept in the dark and mislead by top management.[29] Corporate boards are made up of prominent individuals who are not full-time employees of the companies they serve. The information that board members receive regarding their firm's financial picture and operations is provided by the CEO and top-management team. CEOs and others who are involved in corporate or occupational crime will obviously not reveal information of their misdeeds to board members. The problem is compounded by the fact that board members meet only periodically throughout the year. Board members are inundated with information during these meetings, making it difficult for them to detect if something is amiss.[30] Second, corporate boards may be compromised by generous salaries and lavish perquisites. Once seduced, board members lose their objectivity in controlling CEOs and may themselves become coconspirators in a civil or criminal case.[31]

Compensation Practices That Encourage Crime and Corruption

One of the most controversial aspects of corporate life is the exorbitant compensation and benefit packages of CEOs and other top executives. Multi-million-dollar annual salaries have become commonplace among the corporate elite, with the most significant component of executive pay being stock options.

In theory, stock options are designed to align the interests of top managers with the interests of corporate shareholders. Executives are appointed by the board of directors who, in turn, were elected by the company's shareholders. As agents of the owners, executives are expected to manage the company in ways that are in the best interests of those who have invested in the firm. In practice, stock options have tempted top managers to act in personally selfish ways that are contrary to the interests of shareholders. Executives who are issued stock options as part of their compensation package have the right (or option) to purchase company stock at a specified price (usually the current market price). If the stock price of their company's stock rises, executives can sell their shares for a profit. In some cases, the corporation loans the executive the money needed to purchase the stock at a low interest rate with attractive repayment terms.

Executives are expected to formulate innovative strategies, build core competencies within their firms, manage financial and other assets wisely, and make decisions that will generate long-term profits and financial stability for shareholders. Instead of building a business the legitimate way, some executives use short-term strategies, including financial fraud, to deceive the market and to raise the price of their company stock. During the short time that their stock values are artificially inflated, these executives sell their stock and reap huge profits.

Still another form of stock option fraud is the practice of backdating. According to a *Wall Street Journal* investigation, some companies awarded option grants to executives just before a sharp rise occurred in their share prices. Although the fortunate timing of these grants could be attributable to luck, it is possible that they were awarded at a later date and then backdated to a more favorable time, giving the executive an instant profit. Between 1994 and 2001, the CEO of a semiconductor firm received ten grants that were all followed by a jump in the firm's share price. The statistical probability of such an event occurring by chance, according to the *Journal*, was approximately one in twenty million. Questions about the timing of stock options at more than a dozen companies led to a federal probe during the spring of 2006. Former SEC chairman Arthur Levitt stated that backdating options "represents the ultimate in greed. It is stealing, in effect. It is ripping off shareholders in an unconscionable way."[32]

Organizational Cultures That Foster White-Collar Crime

Corrupt organizational cultures have been cited as a root cause for major corporate scandals. Among the most significant causes of this corruption are executives and managers who fail to serve as ethical role models and set a bad example for others. When the CEO and other top executives engage in fraud or the misappropriation of assets, some lower-level managers and employees will take notice and follow suit.

Another aspect of organizational culture that can enhance corruption is the concept of groupthink. Groupthink occurs within highly cohesive work groups. These groups could be an inner sanctum of top managers as well as key members of a department, project team, or cross-functional team. Bolstered by their successes, these tightly knit groups develop feelings of self-importance and invincibility. Members of the group usually disregard the opinions and criticism of persons outside the group and view them as evil or inept. Groupthink also stifles the thoughts and actions of group members. Self-appointed "mind police" protect the group from threatening information and push for conformity in thought. Since groupthink promotes a shared illusion of unanimity, members who think and speak independently of the group are ostracized.[33]

The groupthink mentality has been blamed for poor group decision making. But it also appears that this phenomenon can foster white-collar crime. The Watergate episode of the early 1970s, perhaps the most notorious of all white-collar crimes, might have been attributable to groupthink. Other well-publicized corporate scandals may also have been caused by this organizational problem.

Another aspect of the organizational culture that has often been linked to white-collar crime is the constant pressure by the board of directors or top management to achieve strong financial results. The super-ambitious expectation of increasing revenues and profits with each subsequent quarter soon becomes unrealistic, even under the most favorable economic conditions. Once chief financial officers and other executives realize that lofty financial goals are no longer attainable, the temptation to commit accounting and financial fraud increases.

Society's Impact on White-Collar Crime

Society creates conditions that are widespread and that neither the organization nor the individual can control. These conditions play an indirect but influential role in organizational crime and corruption.

Accumulation of Surplus Wealth

Unlike many third-world and tribal societies, prosperous industrial economies have a surplus of wealth that enables individuals to accumulate goods and purchase services that go well beyond meeting their basic economic needs. In Western cultures, status is linked directly to economic wealth. This wealth is displayed by the acquisition of luxury homes and automobiles, fine jewelry, rare art, and membership in exclusive clubs. Less-tangible achievements such as mastering an academic discipline, performing volunteer work, or displaying civility are admired less than the accumulation of vast wealth. The *nouveau riche* executive with a penthouse adorned with expensive art and overlooking New York's Central Park enjoys a higher status than a middle-income curator who has spent many years becoming an expert on the work of Italian Renaissance artists.

Corporations originally displayed their power through the construction of large and impressive office buildings that dominated city skylines. Individuals do the same by engaging in conspicuous consumption. People who commit white-collar crimes are often driven by the "impatient wealth" phenomenon that emphasizes the rapid and sometimes dishonest accumulation of tangible assets as a mark of status and as a source of personal power. Tyco's Dennis Koslowski owned a yacht worth

$17 million and houses in Boca Raton, Florida, and Nantucket worth a total of over $37 million. His number-two man, Mark Swartz, who allegedly looted Tyco for more than $150 million, owned real estate in Florida and Virginia worth over $28 million.[34]

The Culture of Competition

Western societies encourage free markets, competition, and survival of the fittest. People who attain powerful leadership positions are thought to have done so because they worked harder and were smarter than those who did not reach the pinnacle of organizational life. One theory that has been used to explain the exorbitant levels of compensation received by executives is tournament theory. This theory views the CEO as the winner of a long and competitive tournament through the corporate world. Not only is the tournament championship accompanied by a huge compensation package but also it serves as a visible incentive for aspiring CEOs.[35]

People who rise to the level of CEO through hard work, intelligence, and ethical behavior are deeply admired. Few would begrudge the financial rewards that these individuals receive. People who rise to the top and profit financially through treacherous, exploitative, and unethical behavior, however, are becoming more commonplace. What is even more disturbing is that these cutthroat individuals are often admired for their aggressive behavior. The win-at-all-cost mentality is regarded as part of rugged American individualism that is at the core of a free-market society.

Business ethicists should carefully consider these questions: Are there situations in which self-interests or corporate interests should trump societal interests? How do we know when we have crossed the line between these two sets of interests? At what point do executives make decisions that benefit their corporations (or themselves) but take unfair advantage of customers, employees, vendors, and the public? The hatchet-man mentality of Al "Chainsaw" Dunlap garnered accolades by the business press as he closed plants, slashed costs, and evicted people from their jobs. It was not until it was discovered that his managerial philosophy also included a liberal dose of accounting and financial fraud that the business press revised their lofty opinion of Dunlap.[36]

Criminogenic Industries

Like criminogenic organizational cultures, industries also vary in their tendencies to coerce or facilitate crime and corruption. Two examples of criminogenic industries are the automobile and liquor industries.[37]

There are a range of criminogenic industry characteristics:[38] (1) A high degree of competition and performance pressures among firms within an industry might encourage corrupt behavior such as antitrust violations or the wrongful interference with contracts.[39] (2) Avoidance of detection is another key element in criminogenic industries. Police officers are often able to commit opportunistic theft, extract kickbacks, and shake down criminals because they work with little direct supervision, and they are protected by the time-honored "blue code of silence." (3) Complex rules with gray areas can also help to create a criminogenic industry environment as witnessed by the numerous corporate scandals in which accountants and auditors have bent accounting rules to facilitate crime. (4) Industries that are characterized by jobs with inadequate control mechanisms also facilitate criminogenisis. Health insurance fraud occurs, in part, because insurance companies want to settle claims quickly. By attempting to be responsive to their customers, insurance companies have relaxed fraud detection procedures. (5) Some industries have built-in conflicts of interest. One conflict of interest in the investment banking industry is the diverse interests among security analysts, investment banks, and potential investors. Security analysts are supposed to provide objective assessments of the financial health and investment potential of client companies. But they have been known to bias their analyses to favor the investment bank rather than the prospective shareholder. (6) Another criminogenic industry factor is asymmetric information or knowledge between organizations and their customers. Fraud and various forms of consumer scams are often predicated on the fact that the perpetrator possesses knowledge that is not available to the victim. (7) Finally, some industries are criminogenic because of the susceptibility of theft of their merchandise. Jewelry, computer chips, designer clothing, software, compact disks, and automotive parts are attractive to thieves. These items are simple to conceal, difficult to trace once stolen, and are sold easily for cash.[40]

The Regulatory Environment

White-collar crime can be prosecuted under a plethora of federal and state laws and associated regulations.[41] These laws cover conspiracies, mail fraud, wire fraud, securities fraud, computer crime, environmental crime, bribery and gratuities, extortion, false statements, perjury, obstruction of justice, tax crimes, currency transactions and money laundering, and racketeering.[42]

Federal white-collar crime laws are enforced through independent and nonindependent regulatory agencies. Independent agencies, such as the Securities and Exchange Commission, Environmental Protection Agency, and the Consumer Product Safety Commission, are headed by president-appointed commissioners. These agencies have executive, legislative, and prosecutorial powers, and they have three prosecution alternatives: administrative action, criminal referral to the Department of Justice, and civil prosecution by agency attorneys. Nonindependent agencies, such as the IRS and the Customs Service, rely on the U.S. Department of Justice for criminal and civil prosecution.[43]

Despite the abundance of laws and ways to prosecute, enterprising white-collar criminals and their legal representatives know that these laws contain ambiguities and loopholes that can be exploited. Many agencies lack the resources and expertise to prosecute complex organizational crimes, relying instead on voluntary compliance. There is also concern that these agencies adopt a collegial rather than an enforcement relationship with the organizations they are supposed to regulate.

Technological Advances

Technology, especially computer technology, has opened new avenues to white-collar criminals. Table 1.2 summarizes the types of crime that fall under the rubric of computer crime.

Table 1.2. Types of Computer Crimes

Crimes and civil wrongs facilitated or expanded by computers:
embezzlement
credit card fraud
tax fraud
securities fraud
theft

espionage
sabotage
telecommunications fraud
child pornography
copyright violations and theft of intellectual property
denial of service
jeopardizing national security
harassment and stalking
criminal inducement and enhancement
violations of personal privacy
identity theft
consumer fraud (failure to provide products, sale of defective products, shill bidding,
    false advertising)
counterfeiting money and securities

Crimes and civil wrongs directed at computers:
hacking
software piracy
website defacement
computer equipment

Table 1.2 reveals an important point: Technology has created few totally new crimes, but it has facilitated the commission of many white-collar crimes that existed before the emergence of computer technology. Embezzlement, sabotage, and various forms of fraud, with computers are now easier to commit and more difficult to prosecute because of complex evidentiary rules and jurisdictional issues. A white-collar criminal in Russia, for example, can commit credit card fraud against a victim in California. Identifying and prosecuting the perpetrator, however, is nearly impossible.

Crimes that were once containable have now flourished because of computers and the Internet. In the past, child pornography was restricted to underground sources, but the Internet has now spawned a vast international distribution network.[44] The use of computers and the Internet in the developing and trafficking of child porn have created a legal quagmire in the U.S. as Congress has attempted to pass legislation that will protect children and at the same time withstand Constitutional challenges under the First Amendment.

Technology such as scanners and color printers make it easy for white-collar criminals to reproduce or manufacture a variety documents such as fake birth certificates, Social Security cards, driver's licenses, immigration documents, tickets to premiere athletic and cultural events, retail gift certificates, and securities. Color copiers have proven to be a boon to counterfeiters. Money launderers use technology to move large sums of money from one country to another. Technology that we now take for granted, such as ATMs (automatic teller machines), creates numerous opportunities for theft.[45]

Technology, especially e-mail messages, can also be used against white-collar criminals in legal proceedings. E-mail provided incriminating evidence against the Credit Suisse First Boston banker Frank Quattrone (whose 2004 conviction for obstruction of justice was thrown out in 2006 by a U.S. Court of Appeals), Merrill Lynch & Company's Henry Blodgett, and senior Enron executives.[46] Now that e-mail use is routine, law enforcement is becoming skilled at using the messages of accused white-collar criminals as crucial evidence against them in legal proceedings.

The Presence of Victims

Victims of white-collar crime may be people or institutions. Felson views victims in terms of their relationship to the criminal. Some victims share overlapping activity spaces with the criminal. A home-repair scam artist, for example, may con elderly people who live near his or her apartment complex. Other victims have personal ties to the criminal. A perpetrator may learn, through a mutual friend, that a potential victim recently inherited a large sum of money. This information could entice the perpetrator to concoct a securities fraud scheme. As technology makes white-collar crime more impersonal, however, overlapping activity spaces and personal ties may become less important to criminals as they target their victims.

Finally, as noted earlier, Felson describes the criminal-victim relationship as one of specialized access. White-collar criminals commit their crimes because they have access to victims (or the victim's property). Police officers can shake down criminals and accept bribes from small businesses requiring protection. Family members and acquaintances of an elderly person suffering from dementia can take advantage of his confused mental state to pilfer money from his bank account.

At the same time, victims aid criminals through their ignorance, gullibility, and greed. Some consumers know little about the products and services they purchase, and they depend on the integrity of sales personnel or professionals not to mislead them. In the automotive, health care, and insurance industries, consumer ignorance is especially prevalent. Criminals also know that victims can be gullible. Children and the elderly are especially trusting, which makes them vulnerable to a variety of crimes.

Greedy victims can also be duped by criminals. Criminals who commit real estate or securities fraud are looking for victims who want to make an easy windfall profit. These criminals convince their target that they have an inside track on a lucrative investment opportunity, but they also emphasize that the deal must be completed immediately, as the following example illustrates.

Real estate is fast becoming a favorite of the confidence man. The attraction of real estate lies in the fact that the stakes are high. Measured by numbers of six or seven digits, real estate can offer quite a large potential haul for a trickster. One con works this way: The con-artist stands in an upscale residential area, on a busy thoroughfare, and stops people on the street, saying, "Excuse me, but are you the Mr. Green who is to meet Mr. Black here? Most will say No, but occasionally one will answer "Why?"

The con-artist will zero in on his or her prey, giving the victim a business card, which bears the name of a well-respected real estate firm. (Actually, the con artist stole the cards from one of those plastic bins that salespeople sometimes have on their desks.) The confidence man explains to the mark that he or she was to meet Mr. Green, who was to sign a contract to purchase "that particular house" on the corner. It must be sold on that day, by order of probate court, so that the estate can be dissolved. If the intended victim expresses any interest, the con-artist will say that the property could be bought at a most attractive price, because with the estate closing that afternoon, there wasn't sufficient time to contact others who had shown an interest in the property.

The conversation continues, and the prospective purchaser is inveigled into giving the con-artist a certified check as earnest money. The victim receives the crook's promise that the closing attorney will meet with him or her at the victim's office 2 days later. Only then does the bargain seeker realize that greed has cost him or her a great deal of money.[47]

Despite the multitude of warnings by consumer protection advocates about scams such as this, overly anxious victims make poor decisions and sacrifice large sums of money in financial deals that should look too good to be true. Furthermore, a shady online merchandiser may offer unbeatable deals as a way of obtaining credit card or personal information from customers. This information is then sold to others or used to commit credit card fraud or identity theft.

Conclusion

This chapter outlines the major influences on white-collar crime, yet it is key to remember that crime resides with the individual, not with the organizational or industry structure, not with emerging technology, and not with the lack of corporate or university ethics training. Organizations and society can encourage or discourage criminal activities, but it is the individual who decides whether to commit a crime.

Some influences on white-collar crime are direct, such as a criminal's strong desire for money that leads to the theft of substantial sums from bank accounts. The criminal must also have knowledge of and access to the technology that is necessary to hack into the bank's computer system. Without this technology, the crime is nearly impossible to commit. Other influences are less direct, such as society's lack of sympathy for incompetent bank managers who allow themselves to be outsmarted by computer-savvy criminals. Indirect influences add fuel to the fire, but they do not provide a necessary condition for white-collar crime.[48]

2

The Many Facets of White-Collar Crime

Criminologists, law enforcement professionals, and policymakers have debated the best way to classify the vast range of property and violent crimes. Existing classifications are based on the premise that some crimes are sufficiently distinct from others. Measuring and tracking white-collar crime, however, which ranges from petty theft to major frauds and from minor violations of safety and health regulations to the deaths of workers and consumers, is difficult because of the many ways such crimes can be categorized and because white-collar crimes often overlap across classifications.

White-collar crimes can be categorized by:

1. the traditional descriptions of crime: fraud, theft, embezzlement, and bribery;
2. perpetrator profiles: crisis responders, opportunity takers, opportunity seekers, as well as by the age, race, sex, and occupation of the perpetrator;
3. victim profiles: age, race, sex, socioeconomic status, purchasing habits;
4. methods used to commit crime: mail or wire transmittals, manipulation of accounting records or financial documents, illicit use of color copy machines, acts of deception or misrepresentation;
5. location of the crime, perpetrator, or victim: crimes committed in commercial establishments, on government property, in a public space, in a private residence;

6. organizational bases for crime: organized crime, collective embezzlement, corporate crime, occupational crime, individual crimes committed outside of the formal organization;
7. industry bases for crime: automobile, insurance, banking; and
8. objectives of the criminal or criminal enterprise: financial gain, revenge for wrongdoings, thrill of committing an illegal act.

The Uniform Crime Reports (UCR) and the National Crime Victimization Survey (NCVS) provide statistics on crimes that are well-known to law enforcement.[1] Both the UCR and NCVS compile data on seven index crimes, four of which are violent crimes and three of which are property crimes. The violent crimes are murder, forcible rape, robbery, and aggravated assault; and the property crimes are burglary, larceny-theft, and motor vehicle theft. Arson is treated separately by the UCR, and homicides are not included in NCVS data. Both UCR and NCVS crime data enable criminologists and policymakers to measure the incidence of crime, analyze crime trends, and develop programs to reduce crime.

In 1985, the U.S. Department of Justice began developing measures of white-collar crime by revising and expanding the Uniform Crime Reporting (UCR) data system. This program, known as the National Incident-Based Reporting System (NIBRS), categorizes white-collar crime based on fraud, bribery, counterfeiting and forgery, embezzlement, and bad checks.[2] The NIBRS also provides information on the location of white-collar crimes and the age, race, sex, ethnicity, and resident status of white-collar offenders and victims. In addition, the NIBRS includes property type, property stolen and recovered, and computer usage in its database.[3]

The NIBRS has several limitations that affect its reliability. First, many white-collar crimes are not recorded because they are neither detected nor reported. Second, some acts of white-collar corruption are adjudicated through administrative or civil proceedings rather than through criminal proceedings. Civil and administrative cases are excluded from criminal databases unless these cases also include criminal charges. Third, most index crimes are prosecuted at the state or local level. White-collar crimes, however, typically originate at the state or local level but may be prosecuted at the federal level. The gap between where a crime originates and where it is prosecuted may cause important data to fall between the cracks and not appear in criminal databases. Fourth, many criminal activities resist neat, well-defined categories. Criminal and civil cases overlap as do crimes involving a mixture of fraud, embezzlement, and bribery. Crimes that fit into more than one category make the collection and analysis of data difficult. Fifth, different criminal activities are interrelated, and a decrease in one crime may result in an increase in another crime. Burglaries have now begun to decrease because criminals have found that drug trafficking, fraud, and theft from motor vehicles are more lucrative and less risky than breaking into residences and commercial establishments.[4] Drug trafficking, in turn, may have increased the incidence of robberies because drug users are often desperate for quick cash.[5] Sixth, the incidence of crime may change artificially because of changes in the law or because of changes in how certain crimes are perceived. Assault cases appear to be on the rise, not because people are more violent but because society and law enforcement officials have become less tolerant toward those who engage in any assault, however slight.[6]

Law enforcement authorities and criminologists typically classify crimes based on the criminal behaviors involved in the commission of a crime. Table 2.1 summarizes white-collar crimes by their behavioral features.

Table 2.1. Classifications of White-Collar Offenses

National Incident-Based Reporting System (NIBRS) Crimes
academic crime
adulterated food, drugs, or cosmetics
antitrust violations
ATM fraud
bad checks
bribery
check kiting
combinations in restraint of trade
computer crime
confidence game
contract fraud
corrupt conduct by juror
counterfeiting
defense-contract fraud
ecology-law violations
election-law violations
embezzlement
employment agency and education-related scams

environmental-law violations
false advertising and misrepresentation of products
false or fraudulent actions on loans, debts, and credits
false pretenses
false report or statement
forgery
fraudulent checks
health and safety laws
health care–provider fraud
home-improvement frauds
impersonation
influence peddling
insider trading
insufficient-fund checks
insurance fraud
investment scams
jury tampering
kickbacks
land-sale frauds
mail fraud
managerial fraud
misappropriation
Ponzi schemes
procurement fraud
religious fraud
restraint in trade
RICO violations
sports bribery
strategic bankruptcy
subornation of perjury
swindle
tax-law violations
telemarketing scams
telephone fraud
travel scams
unlawful use of vehicle
uttering
uttering bad checks
welfare fraud
wire fraud

White-collar crimes that overlap with the NIBRS
bankruptcy fraud
breach of public trust
collusion
credit card fraud
economic espionage (theft of proprietary information)
false or double billing
falsification of credentials, licensure, educational achievements
falsification of quality of merchandise or parts
falsification of test results (medical, pharmaceutical, product tests)

identity theft
loan fraud (residential, commercial, consumer educational)
money laundering
securities fraud
unsafe products or services

How organizations and individuals operating within organizations may commit an overlapping set of crimes can be understood by examining how categories of crime are related. Primary crimes (or object crimes) represent the main focus of the criminal. They consist of crimes such as fraud, consumer scams, counterfeit products, identity theft, bribery and kickbacks, and crimes that endanger people and the environment. Facilitating crimes are committed to support primary crimes. Mail and wire fraud, money laundering, tax evasion to avoid the detection of illegal activities, and conspiracy are the major facilitating crimes. These crimes are not only used to aid in the commission of a primary crime but also to conceal evidence. A corrupt physician who engages in Medicare fraud might also be subject to prosecution for mail or wire fraud (because the postal service or the Internet was used to submit false claims to Medicare), money laundering (if the physician attempts to hide the illicit income or make the income appear to be from legitimate sources), income tax evasion (if the illegal income is not reported to the IRS), and conspiracy (if two or more individuals are involved in the medical fraud).

The facilitating crimes described here may also be committed in conjunction with some street crimes. Drug traffickers, for example, are frequently charged with money laundering and tax evasion. In addition, white-collar criminals may be charged with the facilitating crimes of making false statements, obstruction of justice, and perjury. False statements are those made to the government to conceal facts that are material to a government interest when the person making the statement is not under oath. Perjury entails deliberately making materially false or misleading statements while under oath. Obstruction of justice includes giving false information or withholding evidence from law enforcement authorities or harming or intimidating a witness or juror. White-collar criminals may be charged with one or more of these facilitating crimes through actions such as filing false reports with the Securities and Exchange Commission, lying to federal investigators about insider trading activities, concealing sources of income from IRS agents, shredding documents to avoid prosecution, bribing witnesses, and denying knowledge of foreign bank accounts during a federal hearing. But charging white-collar criminals with these crimes may pose a greater challenge in the future. As Mike France explains:

> For prosecutors the easiest path to a conviction traditionally has been to charge white-collar defendants with perjury, making false statements, or obstruction of justice. These comparatively minor crimes are much easier for jurors to understand than securities fraud or insider trading, and they don't require nearly as much heavy lifting to prove. That's why they were a potent weapon against Martha Stewart—who wasn't even indicted for the underlying allegations of insider trading that originally brought her to the government's attention. . . . But the government's tried-and-true strategy will have to be reconsidered in the wake of the Supreme Court's Arthur Anderson verdict. In a unanimous vote, the justices raised the standards for proving obstruction of justice.[7]

Crimes That Facilitate Primary White-Collar Crimes

Mail and Wire Fraud

Nearly every white-collar crime involves mail or wire fraud. Federal prosecutors frequently use mail and wire fraud statutes when prosecuting white-collar criminals because these statutes are flexible, straightforward, and easy to use, and they have been the subject of extensive judicial interpretation.[8] Acts of organizational crime and corruption may be prosecuted solely on the mail and wire fraud statutes, or the statutes may be used in conjunction with other statutes such as securities statutes or the Racketeer Influenced and Corrupt Organizations Act.

Prosecutors must demonstrate that the defendant engaged in a "scheme to defraud" by using the mail or the wires to make material misstatements or omissions with the purpose of defrauding, resulting in the victim's loss of money, property, or the deprivation of honest services.[9] The mail system can be used to commit a variety of frauds such as securities fraud, insurance fraud, Ponzi or pyramid schemes, extortion, and stalking. Since even wireless computers depend on telecommunications networks, computer crimes almost always involve wire fraud.

Mail and wire fraud raise interesting legal issues. Frauds must involve the misrepresentation of a material fact. A material fact is one that would entice a reasonable person to act on that fact. Telling a prospective buyer that the title to a used aircraft is free of any liens when the seller knows this statement to be false is misrepresenting a material fact. However, a realtor saying, "This property has the most scenic view in the world!" does not constitute fraud because most reasonable individuals realize that such remarks are sales hyperbole.

The use of truthful statements or photographs might be construed as fraud if such representations are deceptive. Suppose that the management of a resort hotel mails brochures (or places this information on a website) describing the establishment as an attractive seaside resort with luxurious rooms, an attractive pool, and an elegant dining establishment. In reality, the property is dirty, has poor security and maintenance, and has a restaurant and pool that have been shut down by local health officials. A reasonable person viewing the brochure would have concluded that the resort was of high quality. Only after the vacationing customer arrives at the resort would the fraud become apparent. The brochure was accurate on its face because it contained actual photographs, and the photographs gave no indication of a lack of cleanliness, inadequate security, poor maintenance, or closed facilities. Resort management, however, probably cannot rely on the defense that no fraud occurred because there was no misrepresentation of a single fact. Similarly, other acts of concealment or omission that occur through the mail or wires may also be regarded as illegal fraud.

The courts may rule that mail and wire fraud occurred even when their use is not central to the fraud. A used-car broker by the name of Schmuck rolled back the mileage on his vehicles before selling them to dealers. The dealers sold Schmuck's over-valued cars to customers during a fifteen-year period. The U.S. Supreme Court, in a sharply divided opinion and a five-to-four vote, ruled that the use of the mails need not be an essential element but simply "incident to an essential part of the scheme." In this case, dealers mailed change-of-title forms to the state, and this part of the sales transaction was sufficient to sustain a charge of mail fraud against Schmuck.[10]

Money Laundering

Both white-collar crimes and street crimes often involve the collection of large amounts of cash or other negotiable instruments. Money laundering encompasses a variety of methods that are used to "clean" money generated by criminal activities or to hide income and evade taxes. By cleaning "dirty" money from crimes such as drug trafficking, gambling, bribes, or theft, criminals avoid the attention of law enforcement. Money earned through legal means may also be laundered to avoid federal, state, or local income taxes. Although money launderers want to hide their illegal activities and evade taxes, they want to keep their money accessible. They may maintain control of their money by diverting it to a foreign bank account in a country that offers bank secrecy laws, tax advantages, electronic technology for ease of transfer, and safety from economic instabilities or government corruption. In 2004, several large U.S. banks were under investigation because of suspicious transfers to foreign accounts, breakdowns in money laundering controls, and questionable ties to banks in Eastern Europe and Russia.[11]

There are many ways to launder money. Since money from drug trafficking usually involves large sums in small bills, money launderers often try to consolidate their cash holdings into larger bills.[12] They may convert dirty cash into cashiers checks, Treasury notes, money orders, gold, or precious stones. Money launderers may use ingenious methods to move money out of the United States through electronic transfers, check-cashing services, money orders, stored-value cards such as debit cards, foreign currency exchanges, shell companies and trusts, casinos, double invoicing for goods purchased in foreign locations (with the excess money being placed by an accomplice in a foreign bank account), or purchasing goods in the United States and then shipping these goods to other countries where the goods are sold and converted to that country's currency.[13] Money has been laundered by eBay scam artists who hired unsuspecting individuals to transfer stolen funds through their personal accounts in the name of a charity. A California medical researcher was hired by a European nonprofit health care organization to forward charitable donations through her bank account to Western Union offices in Germany and Romania. She was told that the money would be used for AIDS research. In reality, she had been pulled into an international money-laundering scheme. When confronted by the police at her residence, she learned that at least some of the "donations" were actually payments from eBay customers. One customer complained to authorities that he had paid several thousand dollars to the woman's account for a set of high-end stereo speakers that he never received. The well-intentioned and trusting intermediary avoided arrest, but she had to personally repay approximately $25,000 to the bilked customers.[14]

The United States has enacted several laws to thwart money laundering activities, and these laws have become a staple weapon for federal prosecutors.[15] Money-laundering laws are also attractive to prosecutors because they carry harsh penalties. The most notable law is the Bank Secrecy Act (BSA) (1970). The BSA requires that a Currency Transaction Report (CTR) be completed by a bank for cash deposits or withdrawals in excess of $10,000 as well as for the purchase of money orders, cashiers checks, or traveler's checks in excess of $3,000 per transaction.[16] Financial institutions are expected to file a Suspicious Activity Report (SAR) if a person or group is thought to be engaging in money-laundering activities. Businesses with heavy cash transactions such as retail stores or grocery stores, however, are routinely exempted from CTR requirements.

Money laundering per se was not illegal until the Money Laundering Control Act was passed in 1986. This act makes it a crime to structure cash transactions to avoid compliance with the Bank Secrecy Act. One structuring activity known as "smurfing," involves the use of individuals (known by law enforcement as "smurfs") who purchase traveler's checks and other negotiable noncash instruments in amounts that will not trigger a CTR. The smurfs pass the negotiable instruments to another party who deposits the funds in a bank.

Additional legislation has been enacted since 1990 to combat money laundering, and the Bush Administration established a money-laundering strategy in 2002 that emphasizes detecting and prosecuting money launderers. The George W. Bush Administration's attack on money laundering was directed heavily at drug traffickers and terrorists, but it will also have an impact on white-collar crime. Nevertheless, the widespread use of banking and wire-transfer services, the growth of multinational businesses and international migration patterns, the use of nonfinancial institutions such as casinos and underground money launderers, and the ingenuity of money launderers to devise new ways of concealing and transferring cash will continue to pose a challenge for law enforcement.[17]

Prosecuting money launderers can be a formidable task. It must be demonstrated that persons involved with money laundering conducted or attempted to conduct a financial transaction that either: (1) they knew involved the proceeds of a felony, (2) would further the commission of a felony, (3) would disguise, conceal, or hide the source of the money, (4) would circumvent currency transaction laws, or (5) would move money illegally into or out of the United States.[18]

Income Tax Evasion to Avoid Revealing a Crime

Income tax evasion can be both a primary crime and a facilitating crime. It involves the willful underpayment of legal taxes through the failure to disclose taxable income or through the overstatement of income tax deductions (or a combination of these two methods).[19] In addition, white-collar criminals may attempt to avoid paying property taxes on real estate, automobiles, airplanes, works of art, jewelry, and other valuable assets that were purchased with money from both legal and illegal sources. Former Tyco CEO Dennis Koslowski was indicted in New York on charges of conspiring with art galleries and consultants to evade paying over $1 million in sales taxes on $13.2 million worth of artwork, including paintings by Monet and Renoir.[20]

Criminals usually engage in income tax evasion for two reasons. First, and most obvious, they want to limit their tax liability and pay less than their fair share of taxes (a primary crime). Second, they may want to conceal that they are engaging in illegal, but financially rewarding, activities (a facilitative crime). A crooked politician who receives several hundred-thousands of dollars in cash kickbacks may be hard-pressed to explain why his taxable income is so high. An identity thief who has accumulated substantial assets from his victims faces a similar dilemma. The solution for these criminals is to hide the income from law enforcement and tax authorities.[21]

White-collar criminals along with their accountants and attorneys may analyze existing tax laws, carefully looking for loopholes to exploit. Some common ways that white-collar criminals may engage in tax evasion are by failing to report a portion of their income, by maintaining a double set of accounting records, by making false entries in or alterations to accounting records, by concealing or destroying records, by filing false or frivolous income tax returns, by moving income to accounts where it will not be detected by tax authorities, by writing off personal expenses as business deductions, by stretching allowable tax exclusions and deductions beyond their legal limit, or by misrepresenting the own-ership of real estate or valuable property.

Income tax evasion charges may be precipitated by investigations that focused originally on other white-collar criminal activities. When prose-cutors do not have adequate evidence to prosecute a primary crime, they may still be able to prosecute the defendant for tax evasion. Prose-cutors may charge a white-collar criminal with tax evasion because of the stiff fines and prison sentences associated with this crime as well as the ease with which some cases of tax evasion can be proven.

Conspiracy

Many white-collar crimes cannot be carried out by one person alone. In crimes with two or more participants, conspiracy laws provide prosecu-tors with significant legal advantages and flexibility against white-collar criminals.[22] For this reason, conspiracy ranks among the most frequent of federal criminal cases.

One advantageous aspect of conspiracy charges for prosecutors is the incomplete (or inchoate) nature of the crime. Persons can be prose-cuted successfully for conspiracy even if the primary crime never reached fruition. A bank executive and an information systems adminis-trator may devise a scheme to siphon funds electronically from the bank's accounts. Once the plot is detected, these individuals may be charged with conspiracy even though no money was embezzled. If it can be established that the two individuals agreed to commit a crime (em-bezzle funds from bank accounts) and took action to set the crime in motion (had unauthorized access to individual accounts or disabled se-curity devices), then they can be prosecuted for conspiracy.

Mere knowledge of an illegal activity may not be adequate to demon-strate guilt in a conspiracy charge. Suppose that the owner of a camera shop sold surveillance equipment to individuals knowing that they would likely use the equipment to obtain pin numbers from customers using ATM machines. This knowledge, by itself, is generally not ade-quate to charge the camera shop owner with conspiracy. The shop owner would be embroiled in an illegal conspiracy, however, if he or she promoted the venture and had a stake in its outcome.

Another prosecutorial advantage of conspiracy laws is the government's ability to bring criminal charges against individuals who may have played a minor role in part of a larger conspiracy. A participant in a tax fraud scheme was held responsible for the actions of his coconspirator even though he was in jail during the time that his coconspirator was committing the fraud.[23]

The crimes discussed above facilitate a variety of primary (or object) white-collar crimes, explored below.

Primary White-Collar Crimes

Violations of Antitrust Laws

Antitrust violations are among the most economically devastating of primary white-collar crimes, and the origins of antitrust laws go back to the late nineteenth century with the passage of the Sherman Act. The primary forms of antitrust violations are price fixing among competing firms, bid rigging, and the creation of monopolistic conditions. Price fixing is an agreement among competitors (manufacturers, distributors, retailers) to maintain a specific price, establish uniform price discounts, adopt a standard formula for computing prices, standardize credit terms among competitors, or maintain minimum prices or predetermined price differentials.[24]

Bid rigging is an agreement among a group of competitors to take turns submitting the winning bids on contracts. This conspiracy allows competitors to eschew a competitive bidding process and to defraud the bidding customer into paying a higher price. Bid rigging may entail a conspiracy in which all but one competitor submits an unreasonably high or an overly restrictive bid. Price fixing and bid rigging enable competitors to reduce market competition while guaranteeing themselves a profit at the expense of consumers who are forced to pay higher-than-market prices.

The New York Attorney general's office charged Chicago-based insurance broker Marsh & McLennan Company with bid rigging and pay-to-play deals. Businesses seeking insurance often hire a broker to solicit bids from insurance companies. Marsh allegedly sought artificially high bids from some insurers as a guarantee that the preferred insurer would receive the business. Criminal charges against the company's top managers were avoided when Marsh chairman and CEO Jeffrey Greenberg resigned.[25]

Market allocation schemes are agreements among competitors to divide a market so that each competitor has its own monopolistic market. Monopolies allow a firm to set high prices and restrict output in ways that do not reflect market realities. Both of these violations restrict trade, defraud customers, inflate prices for consumers, and lead to diminished product and service quality. Over the past decade, the Antitrust Division of the U.S. Department of Justice has stepped up its enforcement actions against international cartels. One such cartel involved the manufacture and distribution of vitamins. Vitamin cartel members agreed on how much of a product each company would manufacture, which customers each company would serve, and the price that would be charged for the product.[26]

Accounting, Financial, and Corporate Fraud

Accounting, financial, and corporate fraud have become one of the most-publicized forms of white-collar crime.[27] This broad category of white-collar crime has two objectives. First, accounting fraud may be used to cover up the embezzlement or misappropriation of funds. A manager who is stealing money from his or her company may alter accounting ledgers and supporting documentation to conceal the crime. Second, financial fraud is used to mislead investors and regulatory agencies about the financial health and future prospects of a company.

In 2005, American International Group (AIG) was believed to have inflated its financial performance through the improper accounting of reinsurance transactions to bolster corporate reserves along with other questionable accounting measures. The two most glaring transactions involved General Re Corp., in which a $500 million loan was "dressed up on the books" as insurance premium revenues. Three companies that provided reinsurance to AIG were not completely independent, meaning that $1 billion in income since 1991 should not have been counted. AIG was also accused of delaying the accounting of expenses and misclassifying losses.[28] Ex-chairman Maurice "Hank" Greenberg and ex-CFO Howard I. Smith were charged in late May 2005 in a civil suit for manipulating financial results, hiding losses, propping up stock, and arranging "sham" deals.[29] AIG later agreed to pay a $1.64 billion settlement and change its accounting procedures.[30]

Qwest Communications International was accused by the SEC of accounting fraud between 1999 and 2002 when it allegedly generated more than $3.8 billion in false revenues and excluded $231 million in expenses. Qwest agreed to pay a $250 million penalty for frauds that included booking inflated results for its phone directory business.[31]

Financial fraud focuses on any of the following five objectives: (1) increasing revenues, (2) decreasing expenses, (3) overstating assets, (4) understating or hiding liabilities, and (5) distorting cash flow. The manner in which these deceptions take place can be exceedingly complex or amazingly simple. Accounting and financial fraud usually entail violating generally accepted accounting principles, establishing fictitious subsidiaries to boost revenues or hide liabilities, and using falsified documentation to support the numbers on puffed-up financial statements. Enron used a complex arrangement involving over three thousand special-purpose entities to inflate revenues and hide liabilities.[32] WorldCom, in contrast, violated simple accounting rules by amortizing, or paying off, hundreds of millions of dollars in current expenses over an extended period of time (thereby decreasing expenses and increasing profits on WorldCom's financial statements).[33]

Corporate fraud extends the idea of accounting and financial fraud even further by falsely portraying the future prospects and business plans of a corporation. Such fraud may take the form of lying about the company's future products or clients, plans for international expansion, acquisitions, or other strategies that would entice investors to purchase company stock. Other forms of financial and corporate fraud include selling worthless securities on sham companies and pump-and-dump schemes. In the latter scam, unscrupulous stock-market manipulators plant positive but false information about a company on Internet financial chat lines and then reap a handsome profit from the temporary stock price increase.

The major financial and corporate frauds since the late 1990s have been based, to a significant degree, on conflicts of interest that had evolved among corporations, top executives, investment banks, security analysts, financial rating agencies, and government regulators. For example, a firm normally hires an investment bank to make an initial public offering of stock. It is in the investment bank's interest for the stock to perform well on the market so that the client firm will maintain its business relationship with the bank. Security analysts employed by the investment bank provide investment advice to individual and institutional investors regarding the potential performance of various corporate stocks. There is an obvious conflict of interest when security analysts provide biased information to investors based on the investment bank's relationship with its client firms. The research analyst clearly has a greater financial loyalty to the investment bank and its client firms than it does to prospective investors. This conflict of interest was a primary factor in the demise of WorldCom.

Another major conflict of interest existed between accounting firms and their clients. Accounting firms providing both auditing and consulting services to the same client were pressured to overlook discrepancies during accounting audits or risk losing their profitable consulting work. These conflicts were a significant part of the Enron case, and the Sarbanes-Oxley Act of 2002 was directed largely at eliminating this problem.

Financial Institution Fraud

Financial institutions may be victimized by both insiders and outsiders. The classic crime against financial institutions is the trusted bank officer who embezzles several million dollars over many years or the bank robber who shoves a gun in the face of a horrified teller and demands that he or she hand over the contents of the cash drawers. Banks and credit-card companies now face more resourceful white-collar criminals who target them for embezzlement and fraud. For example, a technique known as "salami-slicing" has been used to divert large sums of money from banks by rounding off account amounts to the lowest cent and transferring the fraction of a cent to a special account. Although damage to a single account is miniscule, the perpetrator can garner huge sums of money by salami-slicing thousands of accounts repeatedly.

Financial institutions may also be victimized by commercial loan frauds, check frauds, credit card frauds, mortgage fraud, falsified loan applications, counterfeit money and securities, and ATM scams. The boom in the housing market led to a boom in real estate frauds. From 2000 to 2005, the FBI claimed that federally chartered banks reported nearly a five-fold increase in fraud incidents. Criminals used fake documents to obtain mortgages on homes they did not own, concealing their acts by taking advantage of overburdened mortgage companies and county deed offices. They also engaged in property flips by selling real estate back and forth among two or more buyers to inflate its value. Other criminals used courthouse listings to find owners who were facing mortgage foreclosures. Then, using a mountain of confusing paperwork, they duped the rightful owners into deeding over their homes. Equally despicable are the con artists who convince naïve and elderly homeowners with residences in need of repair that they will help them refinance and repair their property; the crooks then take the money from the refinanced property and never perform the work.[34]

Many of these crimes involve conspiracies among financial institution insiders and outsiders. A bank executive may commit fraud by teaming with real estate brokers or executives from other financial institutions. Loans to sham corporations, reciprocal loans to officers at competing banks, swapping bad loans to inflate bank assets, and misappropriating bank funds are among the many ways that banks, shareholders, and customers have been defrauded. These tactics were especially common during the savings and loan scandal of the early 1980s.

Fiduciary Fraud

A fiduciary is a person or entity that safeguards or invests the money or resources of others. Banks, pension funds, insurance companies, and unions are examples of fiduciaries. Fiduciary fraud occurs when the entrusted money is misappropriated or embezzled. Such frauds include investment scams, the pilfering of retirement monies, the failure of insurance companies to pay legitimate claims, and the savings and loan scandals of the early 1980s. The now defunct Bayou Securities LLC, a money-management firm, was being investigated in 2005 to determine the whereabouts of hundreds of millions of dollars in funds that were missing.[35]

Retirement programs are a fertile ground for fiduciary fraud. The large sums of money in these funds present a tempting target for unscrupulous fiduciaries. The Employee Retirement Income Security Act was passed in 1974 partially in response to the Teamster's Union central-states pension-fund scandal. Theft from employee 401(k) plans also appears to be on the rise. Employers may collect monies through payroll deductions and never deposit the funds in employee accounts. The problem is compounded by the fact that auditing is lax, and the number of federal investigators has not kept up with retirement-plan growth.[36] Municipal pension funds for employees of large cities may be especially vulnerable to fraud and mismanagement as illustrated by the irregularities in the City of San Diego pension-fund case. The fund was facing a $1.1 billion deficit and accounts that were riddled with errors.[37]

Insurance represents another avenue for fiduciary fraud. Individuals and organizations purchase property, health, liability, and other forms of insurance. Beneficiary scams involve the filing of false or inflated claims or intentionally destroying property in order to profit from an insurance claim. Since insurance represents a contract for the possible payment of claims in the future, a portion of the premiums collected must be set aside to cover these obligations. Insured individuals may discover that claims are not paid because the insurance company has mismanaged or stolen the premiums or that they have been cheated by a reinsurer who is unable or unwilling to pay claims.[38]

Insider Trading

Insider trading occurs when an individual obtains access to information about a corporation that is not available to outside investors and uses that information to reap a financial gain or to avoid a financial loss on trades made through a public stock exchange. A person who provides information is known as a tipper, and the recipient of the information is known as a tippee. Tippees can be prosecuted for insider trading if it can be shown that they bought or sold stock based on exclusive material information that they possessed at the time of the trade.[39] Insiders might be top managers, employees, persons who do business with the company (consultants, accountants, or attorneys), or someone who has a fiduciary relationship with the company.

The information transmitted from the tipper to the tippee must be material in nature, meaning that it must be significant enough to have affected the company's stock price had the information been available to the public. Material information might include details about a proposed merger, tender offer, proxy contest, the release of favorable financial reports, the imminent signing of major business contracts, changes in the top management team, or other extraordinary events. An example involving day traders, reported in the *Wall Street Journal*, follows.

> The stock market was falling sharply, but Mr. Amore outlined a surefire way for the recruits to earn profits at Whatley, the traders recall: electronically eavesdropping on traders at major Wall Street firms and rapidly buying and selling based on what the big boys were about to do. A large purchase of, say, Goodrich Corp. stock executed by Citigroup Inc.'s brokerage unit would almost certainly push the price up. Anybody with advance word could buy Goodrich stock first—and sell for a quick profit once the Citigroup trade was finished. . . . The brokers allegedly left phones off the hook to allow Whatley traders to listen in on in-house stock orders piped over a kind of speaker phone known as a "squawk box."[40]

Insider trading is regarded as a quintessential white-collar crime, but it is also viewed by some as a morally ambiguous and victimless crime. Insider trading might be regarded as simply another form of compensation for individuals who work in a corporation. Achieving a competitive advantage in a capitalistic economy is frequently obtained because a company has more information than its competitors. Insider trading, its supporters argue, is just another aspect of this competition. Others argue that insider trading is poorly defined and persons acting on inside information are often indicted for operating in the gray area between legal and illegal activity. Former Qwest Communications International, Inc., CEO Joseph Nacchio claimed that his sale of Qwest stock was not based on inside information. Nacchio claimed that the sales were part of a prearranged trading schedule aimed at maintaining a diversified portfolio and raising funds to pay taxes on the exercise of a stock option.[41] Advocates of decriminalizing insider trading claim that the cost of prosecuting inside investors often exceeds the damage caused by the crime.

Insider trading distorts the relationship between risk and rate of return that is fundamental to investments. There is generally an inverse relationship between these factors. Investors who are willing to assume more risk traditionally stand to make higher profits (or suffer greater losses) than will investors who opt for less risky investments. Insider trading, however, provides privileged investors with the best of both worlds: relatively high rates of return (or minimal losses) with low levels of risk.

The impact of insider trading is similar to playing poker against opponents who cheat. Rather than playing by the rules of the house, they play with a loaded deck, hide cards up their sleeves, or receive signals from accomplices who are watching the hands of opposing players. The card cheats gain an unfair advantage in the zero-sum game in which the gains of one player equal the losses of another player. Few people would play poker with a card cheat. Furthermore, if insider trading became widespread, it would erode the confidence of investors and discourage their participation in financial markets. For these reasons insider trading has been criminalized under the Security Exchange Act of 1934, the Insider Trading Sanctions Act of 1984, and the Sarbanes-Oxley Act of 2002.

Corrupt Acts of Public Officials

Corrupt acts of public officials as a category focuses primarily on the perpetrator of a crime rather than the nature of the crime itself.[42] Elected officials control the passage of legislation, command vast resources, and make important decisions that have profound social and economic consequences. Political appointees and civil servants are also in positions of specialized access and trust.

Corruption occurs when public officials use their position of power for personal gain. The state senator who enjoys a cozy relationship with an industry interest group, the governor who is a silent partner in a highway construction company, the city judge who accepts bribes from drug dealers, or the police officer who gives preferential referrals to certain ambulance and towing companies in exchange for a kickback are all examples of corruption within the public realm. While the scandals of Watergate, Iran-Contra, and ABSCAM represent the most flagrant episodes of corruption by prominent elected officials, the more pervasive problems occur among lower-ranking civil servants.

Acts of corruption differ among federal, state, and local officials because each has different opportunities on which they can capitalize. Table 2.2 summarizes the types of crime and corruption that might be committed by federal, state, and local politicians. Although there are differences among the levels, there is also a significant degree of overlap.

Table 2.2. Corruption among Public Officials

Crime and Corruption at the Federal Level
campaign fund-raising improprieties
bribes of federal regulatory inspectors
kickbacks in exchange for favorable treatment by public officials (e.g., ABSCAM)
favoritism in granting federal projects (schools, highways, research funding)
bid rigging
hidden business interests and conflicts between public officials and government
     agencies (secret sweetheart deals)
procurement fraud
payroll fraud
questionable criminal pardons
harassment of political enemies (IRS audits, FBI investigations, privacy violations)
perjury by public officials
misappropriation of public resources (lavish spending, diverting public resources to
     personal use, falsified expenses and billings)
sexual misconduct that diminishes the reputation of a federal public office
tax evasion
accepting lavish gifts from foreign dignitaries
embezzling funds
obstructing justice (e.g., destroying or tampering with evidence, intimidating or
     bribing witnesses)
mail and wire fraud
diverting funds from their intended use (e.g., HUD scandal that siphoned off and
     wasted money for low income housing)

Crime and Corruption at the State Level
campaign fund-raising improprieties
bribes of inspectors (agriculture, workplace safety, building and construction)
kickbacks in exchange for favorable legislative treatment and special access to public
     officials
bid rigging
hidden business interests and conflicts between public officials and government
     agencies
procurement fraud
payroll fraud
state police and corrections-department criminality and corruption
bribes of judges (gambling, narcotics, organized crime, extortion)
questionable criminal pardons
harassment of political enemies (illegal surveillance, tax audits, criminal investigations)
perjury by public officials
sexual misconduct that diminishes the reputation of a state public office
tax evasion
embezzling funds

misappropriation of public resources (e.g., using state vehicles for personal use,
    spending grant monies illegally)
mail and wire fraud
obtaining exorbitant honoraria for speeches and appearances
obstructing justice

Crime and Corruption at the Local Level
bribes by building and construction inspectors, tax assessors
bid rigging on municipal projects
kickbacks on procurement and construction contracts
bribing judges (gambling, narcotics, organized crime, extortion)
hidden conflicts of interest between local officials and private businesses
steering municipal-bond business to selected brokers
illegal or illicit gratuities received by city or county officials
police criminality and corruption (brutality, extortion, opportunistic theft, kickbacks
    from towing and ambulance services, shakedowns, fixing tickets, protection of illegal
    activities)
county and city jail criminality and corruption (e.g., using inmate labor for private gain)
perjury by public officials
embezzling funds (e.g., stealing licensing fees and traffic fines)
misappropriation and theft of public assets
submitting false vouchers or inflated or fictitious bills

Criminogenic Factors
- control of legislative proposals and votes that can be worth millions of dollars to
  private parties
- control of abundant resources (staff, expense accounts, vehicles)
- ability to influence other powerful people, both inside and outside the government
- conflicts of interest that are generated by the ability to divert resources and influence
  powerful people
- job characteristics: discretionary power, minimal direct supervision, and few controls
- constant temptations (bribes, sexual favors)
- asymmetric knowledge and proprietary information that is valuable to powerful
  individuals
- mismatch between power and income (police officers, tax assessors, local judges)
- opportunities for easy rationalization

Bribery, Gratuities, and Extortion

The corruption of public officials often involves a bribe, an illicit gratuity, or an act of extortion. Bribery involves offering, giving, or soliciting
anything of value in order to influence an official act by a government
official or to influence a business decision. One of the most newsworthy
acts of corruption by a public official during the early years of the
twenty-first century was the case of Randy "Duke" Cunningham. The

former eight-term U.S. congressman and decorated Vietnam-era fighter pilot served on the House Defense Appropriations Subcommittee where he used his position to influence government appropriations and contracts. Cunningham admitted to receiving $2.4 million in bribes and evading more than $1 million in taxes. He pleaded guilty to conspiracy, tax evasion, and mail and wire fraud. One of his boldest acts was the sale of his Del Mar Heights, California, home to the Washington defense contractor Mitchell Wade for $1,675,000, an amount well above the market value of the property. Wade tried to hide his identity as the buyer, never lived in the house, and sold it seven months later for $975,000. The loss that Wade took on the property amounted to a $700,000 bribe to Cunningham. The ostentatious former lawmaker also admitted to accepting vacations, jewelry, antiques, cash, and a Rolls Royce in exchange for helping defense contractors secure millions of dollars in contracts. Ironically, in an earlier campaign speech, Cunningham remarked: "I first ran for Congress because I was fed up with politicians who took advantage of our trust and put powerful special interests ahead of those who elected them." As part of the plea, he forfeited his $2.5 million California mansion and $1.8 million in cash and antiques. In sentencing Cunningham to eight years and four months in a federal prison, U.S. District Court Judge Larry Alan Burns said that he often sends destitute people to jail who commit crimes because they had no where else to turn. Judge Burns told Cunningham, "You weren't wet. You weren't cold. You weren't hungry. And yet you did these things."[43]

Section 201 of the federal criminal code makes it illegal to bribe a federal public official to influence an official act or for an official to take a bribe in return for an official act. The law defines "federal public official" to include elected officials, civil servants, and private-sector individuals who represent a governmental entity or who apply federal policy in some way. Official acts might include a governmental official favoring an industry group in a legislative vote, granting federal financial assistance to a community, dismissing a criminal charge against a favored client, or awarding a government contract to a private business. The payer of the bribe must give or offer the payee something of value or perceived value such as money, goods or services, jobs for family and friends, or private business opportunities. Like conspiracy, bribery may be an inchoate crime. That is, it is illegal to offer a bribe even if the bribe is never paid.

Gratuities, though illegal, are regarded as being less serious than bribes because they are not linked to a specific corrupt act. The line between bribery and illegal gratuities, however, is often unclear. A public official who accepts a ride on a corporate jet or who is presented with jewelry as a Christmas gift from a constituent is probably accepting a gratuity. Similarly, the senator who receives a gift of thanks for an act that has already been performed independent of the payer's influence is probably receiving a gratuity, not a bribe. A payment made after the corrupt act, however, may be regarded as a bribe if the agreement to make the payment preceded the corrupt act.

Darleen Druyan, a prominent U.S. Air Force acquisitions officer, was sentenced to nine months in prison after she admitted to steering billions of dollars worth of business to the Boeing Company in gratitude for Boeing's hiring her daughter, future son-in-law, and her. She saw to it that Boeing was improperly awarded a $4 billion contract and a favorable aircraft leasing deal. One puzzling aspect of this case is that Druyan "was viewed as so upright that the government considered bringing her in as an expert witness" during a 1980s corruption probe that nabbed senior Navy and Air Force acquisition officials.[44]

Extortion is an attempt to coerce a victim through physical or economic means to comply with the demands of the extortionist. The Hobbs Act of 1946 is the primary statute that prohibits extortion by force, threat, or fear and extortion under the color of law. Unlike bribery in which both the payer and payee benefit, extortion is one sided. As a result, it generally carries stiffer penalties than bribery.

White-collar criminals typically use economic pressure or the threat of adverse publicity, rather than physical threats, when they engage in extortion. The restaurant industry analyst C. Clive Munro wrote a series of glowing reports for prospective investors on CKE Restaurants, Inc. Munro then placed pressure on CKE to hire him as a consultant. When CKE ignored Munro's overture, Munro published critical and inaccurate assessments of the company, calling its customer traffic "anemic" and predicting that its "earnings growth will begin to slow." Munro then proposed a deal with CKE under which he would be paid to stop publishing reports that were critical of the company.[45] Munro pleaded guilty in a federal district court to one count of communicating interstate threats. He was sentenced to twenty-one months in prison

Union officials are engaging in extortion by force, threat, or fear if they threaten to call an economic strike unless the business owner makes a payoff to the union. A judge who agrees to fix a case in return for a fee from either the plaintiff or the defendant would probably be guilty of extortion under the color of the law. In some cases, defendants have been charged with both extortion and bribery because the distinction between the two was unclear.

Congress enacted the Foreign Corrupt Practices Act in 1977 (FCPA) in response to the widespread bribery of foreign officials by U.S. business executives. The United States, United Nations, and European Union (EU) have conventions designed to fight international bribery and corruption by businesses. In addition to the FCPA, Congress has passed antibribery and corruption laws such as the International Anti-Bribery and Fair Competition Act (which implements the provisions of the Office for Economic Cooperation and Development Convention on Combating Bribery of Foreign Officials in International Business Transactions), the International Anticorruption and Good Governance Act (which creates systems for the United States to promote good government and help other countries fight corruption), and the Traveler's Act (which is directed primarily at international organized crime).[46] As businesses became more multinational in nature and as developing countries became increasingly involved in foreign trade, the opportunities for bribery also expanded.

Lucent Technologies, Inc. became entangled in bribery allegations after it paid expenses for medical treatments, donations to a cancer research center, private jet transportation, and other amenities for Al-Johani, Saudi Arabia's telecommunications minister. Johani was responsible for paying out billions of dollars for government contracts to upgrade Saudi Arabia's telephone system. The lawsuit claimed that Lucent paid Johani between $15 million and $21 million from 1995 until early 2003. Lucent received more than $5 billion in contracts at Johani's behest.[47] Allegations of bribery have also been leveled at firms such as Monsanto and Halliburton. In seeking permission to sell genetically modified seed, Monsanto made $750,000 in payoffs in Indonesia over a six-year period, according to the SEC.[48] Halliburton became embroiled in bribery allegations over funneling money to Nigerian officials in return for multi-billion-dollar contracts to build energy facilities in the African country.[49]

Some foreign governments and their officials regard bribes and extortion as a normal way of life, and U.S. companies that pay millions of dollars to these officials view bribes as another cost of doing business. Such illicit activities, however, can cause human rights abuses, undermine social integrity, and disrupt the operation of free markets.

The antibribery provisions of the FCPA make it illegal for any company or its officers, stockholders, or agents to bribe a foreign official by offering anything of value for the purpose of obtaining or retaining an improper business advantage. Both direct bribes and bribes made to foreign elected officials, officers, departments, or agencies through intermediaries are illegal. Companies can make payments to officials if such payments are in accordance with the written laws of that country. Facilitating payments are allowed by the FCPA for required licenses, permits, processing governmental paperwork, mail service, inspections, utilities, or loading and unloading cargo.

Health Care Fraud

One of the fastest-growing white-collar crimes is health care or medical fraud. Common forms of health care fraud include providing unnecessary treatments to patients, double billing patients and insurance companies, rendering less expensive services but billing the patient for more expensive ones, fee splitting (obtaining kickbacks for referrals to other health care professionals), submitting fraudulent claims to health insurers so that insurers will pay for noncovered medical procedures (e.g., filing a claim for a hernia repair to cover the cost of a liposuction), self referrals (sending patients to facilities in which physicians have an undisclosed financial interest), distributing pharmaceuticals illegally, and sexually exploiting patients.[50]

A major consequence of health care fraud is that it inflates the already high cost of medical care. Some physicians, for example, send patient laboratory work to an inexpensive lab but bill the patient's insurance company at a much higher rate. A North Carolina dermatologist made nearly $200 profit off one lab test.[51] Health care fraud forces insurers to raise their group and individual premiums. Honest health care providers incur the added expense of complying with legislative and antifraud measures. These safeguards slow insurance payment processes and inconvenience patients and health care providers. False payments also steal health insurance benefits from patients whose policies have lifetime limits on health insurance coverage. Patients whose diagnoses have been falsified by dishonest health care providers may later find it difficult to obtain insurance coverage. Using cut-rate lab services also raises questions about the reliability of the test results and the dangers posed to patients whose lives depend on accurate lab work.

Health care fraud is attractive to white-collar criminals for several reasons. First, the U.S. health care industry is one of the largest industries in the world, with trillions of dollars in transactions. Second, the U.S. health care system is a complex network of patients, health care providers, and third-party funding entities. White-collar criminals have discovered how to hide their fraudulent activities within this complicated system. Third, consumer knowledge of proper medical practices and treatments is inadequate. Patients generally trust the information and advice given by health care professionals, and they are reluctant to question the legitimacy of their medical treatment. Furthermore, patients are not aware of the treatments or medications they received when sedated or anesthetized, giving dishonest anesthesiologists and surgeons the freedom to bill for services or medications that were not provided. Fourth, perpetrators know that the risks of being caught and prosecuted are low.[52] Former drug traffickers, for example, have discovered that medical frauds are a more lucrative and less dangerous way to make a living.

Some forms of medical fraud entail unnecessary physical risks for patients. One reprehensible form of medical fraud, quackery, occurs when a health care provider entices a patient to submit to treatments that are known to be ineffective or useless. Quacks posing as health care professionals have touted a cure for maladies such as sexual impotency, psychological problems, aging, and obesity. At best, quackery offers little help to those who throw their money away on worthless treatments. At its worst, the treatments cause more harm than good. Plastic surgery performed by incompetent physicians may actually hasten the aging process and diminish rather than improve the patient's appearance. Victims of terminal illnesses may resort to medical quackery in a desperate attempt to buy more time and, possibly, to find some peace of mind during their final months of life. The most despicable form of quackery, however, occurs when patients are induced to obtain useless medical treatments when legitimate treatments are still available.

Another physical risk to patients occurs when physicians order unnecessary surgeries, invasive testing, or drug therapies. Many jurisdictions view the needless use of such procedures in the same vein as the street crimes of assault and battery. That is, they regard the unnecessary removal of a patient's gallbladder no differently than if the surgeon had attacked the patient with a scalpel on a street corner. Few surgeons, however, face criminal charges for such actions.

Consumer Scams

Consumers may be enticed to purchase inferior products, pay money for products or services they fail to receive, or disclose personal information to a criminal who later uses the information to commit financial fraud or identity theft.

Many consumer scams are committed by freelance individuals who operate on their own. Home-repair scams, street hustlers, door-to-door salespeople peddling stolen or counterfeit goods, and imposters posing as bank examiners, law enforcement officers, or the disabled are examples of individual scam artists. Other scams are engineered by groups or organizations. These include vanity scam artists who peddle worthless weight loss and fitness products, unscrupulous mail-order businesses, and opportunistic automobile repair shops.

Consumer scams always involve a con (perpetrator) and a mark (victim). Some scams also involve other parties such as a roper (a person who entices the victim to participate in the scam), a shill (a person used to show how profitable a scam is by "winning" something of value from the con artist), and a heavy (a physically intimidating person who discourages the victim from complaining to the police).[53]

The U.S. Federal Trade Commission (FTC) released a consumer fraud survey in 2004 that queried 2,500 randomly chosen adults about their consumer experiences during the previous year. The FTC targeted ten specific types of fraud:

1. Paying an advance fee to obtain a guaranteed loan or credit card in violation of FTC rules (advance fee loan scheme). An estimated 4.5 million consumers made such payments but did not receive the promised loan or credit card.
2. Being billed for a buyers' club membership that the consumer did not agree to purchase. The consumer may be induced to

try the membership free for a period of time with the belief that if they fail to pay the fee at the end of the trial period, the membership will automatically expire. Unscrupulous businesses may use a negative option whereby the membership goes into effect and a fee is charged unless the consumer notifies the club that he or she wants to cancel the membership. The consumer may be notified of the negative option through an innocuous bulk mailing that is received and thrown away unopened.

3. Being persuaded to purchase credit card insurance as protection against the unauthorized use of credit cards. Consumers are told that they face high financial risks for the unauthorized use of their credit cards notwithstanding the fact that federal law limits consumer liability to $50 if a card is reported lost or stolen.

4. Credit repair frauds involve paying money to someone who promises to have unfavorable information removed from the consumer's credit report or who promises to establish a new credit history for the consumer using a false Social Security number.

5. Informing a consumer that he or she has won a prize and then inducing the consumer to pay a handling or shipping fee to receive the prize. Prizes typically include a product, vacation, or money. The prize is either not shipped or is actually a different prize of lower value. In some cases, the consumer must purchase a product or attend a lengthy sales presentation to earn the prize.

6. Being billed for Internet services such as access to a website that the consumer did not agree to purchase or did not receive. Small businesses were often enticed by a free trial period to participate in a web-based "yellow page" services. The businesses were billed for services not received.

7. Being enticed to participate in a pyramid marketing scheme. These schemes offer consumers a business or marketing opportunity in which they will sell a product or service and recruit others to sell. The scheme promises consumers income from both their sales and the sales of their recruits. Each new recruit pays a fee to participate in this business opportunity.

Pyramid schemes collapse under their own weight because participant income comes primarily from recruiting fees rather than from sales revenues. The program transfers money from those who have joined recently to those who have been involved for a longer period of time. Most participants never sell enough to recoup their initial fee.

8. Being billed for unauthorized Internet or telephone (pay per call) information services such as adult entertainment, gambling, or psychic hotlines.

9. Promising consumers the inside track on government jobs, usually with the U.S. Postal Service. Some of these frauds involve selling home-study courses that will improve their test scores on Civil Service examinations.

10. Enticing a consumer to purchase a business opportunity that includes equipment, information on customers and choice locations, and related services. The fraud may also include promises of a guaranteed amount of income with only a minimal amount of work.

The FTC also asked survey participants whether they had been billed for products or services that they had not agreed to purchase or products or services that they had agreed to purchase but did not receive. An estimated 4.6 million adults experienced this type of fraud. In addition, 13.9 million consumers were estimated to have had their long distance telephone service provider switched without their authorization (a practice known as slamming).[54]

Telemarketing Fraud

The telephone represents a major crime medium. Many of the consumer crimes discussed here are initiated with a telephone call to the victim. Fraudulent telemarketers dupe victims through the sales and deals that should sound too good to be true. Phony charities and religious causes use telemarketers to appeal to the good side of human nature as they scam their victims. Telemarketers often offer free prizes or vacation packages that require a shipping fee or deposit to be paid by the victim's credit card. The credit card number is then used for credit card fraud or identity theft. Boiler room operators entice gullible investors to hand over thousands of dollars for worthless securities and promising business opportunities. After an individual has been swindled, the same telemarketer claiming to represent a recovery firm may offer to retrieve the stolen money for a fee, leading the victim to be bilked a second time.

Employee Theft

Both white-collar and blue-collar employees engage in various forms of employee theft. Thefts may occur at loading docks, storage facilities, office suites, or retail sales areas. According to the University of Florida 2004 National Retail Security Survey, employee theft accounted for 47 percent of inventory shrinkage ($14.6 billion out of a total of $31 billion annual inventory shrinkage), whereas shoplifting accounted for 34 percent of shrinkage and administrative error and vendor fraud accounted for 15 percent and 5 percent respectively. The average dollar loss per employee theft incident was $1,238, while shoplifters netted over $621 per incident.[55] Merchandise that is easy to remove and conceal such as electronic devices, compact disks, jewelry, and designer clothing are especially attractive to employee thieves. Items that can be easily sold and converted quickly to cash are also popular.

Employee theft goes well beyond the theft of merchandise from retail outlets. A former BMW Manufacturing employee of five years was charged with grand larceny for allegedly stealing 270 Mark IV navigational units from the automobile plant over a two-year period. The units, valued at $1,800 each, were then sold online at heavily discounted prices. The employee was arrested after BMW discovered a $486,000 inventory shortage.[56] At the upper end of the professional spectrum, a Yale University professor was forced out of his job after being accused of double billing Yale for about $150,000 in business travel expenses.[57]

Employees may convert company assets such as automobiles, computers, or customer lists to their private personal or business use. They may steal cancelled or unused checks from mail rooms or offices, sell proprietary information to competitors, submit fictitious bills payable to phony vendors (owned and operated by the employee), steal cash from cash registers or customers, falsify time sheets or submit false claims for overtime pay, make personal purchases with company funds, or burglarize company property after hours.

Employees steal for a variety of reasons. They may have a legitimate need for money or merchandise, or they may steal to support a drug habit or alcohol problem. In some cases, employees feel a sense of entitlement and they regard theft as another form of compensation that is owed to them by the organization. In other cases, certain thefts become part of the organizational culture and are condoned by co-workers and even supervisors.[58]

Computer Crime

Computers have opened up new routes for committing old crimes. Sabotage, embezzlement, fraud, counterfeiting, identity theft, stalking, and distributing child pornography have long been criminal acts. The use of computers, however, has made these crimes easier to commit and more pervasive.

Computers provide almost unlimited opportunities for white-collar criminals. A Massachusetts entrepreneur allegedly sabotaged the website of a Los Angeles company in retaliation over a rebuffed business proposal.[59] A German student planted a computer virus that spread throughout the world. Businesses have used delay-of-service techniques that make it impossible for a competitor's customers to place orders online. Similarly, some businesses have repeatedly accessed a competitor's website to run up their website costs.[60] A criminal living in Los Angeles can assume the identity of a stranger living in New York by using personal information that can be obtained easily on the Internet. A drug cartel may use computer technology to transfer millions of dollars to a Caribbean-nation bank. A bank manager can hack into the system of a large bank and salami-slice her way to hundreds of thousands of dollars from bank customer accounts. A computer-savvy entrepreneur in Asia may use computer technology to manufacture and sell pirated software, music, and movies at a fraction of their normal retail price. Nigerian scammers and their ubiquitous e-mail pleas and promises of easy riches can lure gullible individuals into helping them smuggle money out of the African country. Victims of this scam have been coaxed into sending money, revealing bank account information, and (occasionally) traveling to the African country where they have been prosecuted by the authorities, held for ransom, and even killed. Similarly, Internet scam artists posing as bank personnel try to entice bank customers into sending confidential personnel and financial information to a bogus bank website under the guise of "reinstating" their accounts.

Some computer-based criminal operations are extensive. A spammer in Europe was arrested after he amassed a fortune selling fake college degrees, phony hair-growth products, and medications without the required prescriptions. The FBI seized $4.2 million in assets from Christopher Smith (aka "Rizler"), whose eighty-five-person organization sent more than one billion e-mail advertisements. Smith made approximately $18 million from his overseas operation.[61] Buzz words such as "spamming," "phishing," and "pharming" are among the latest terms that are used to describe various types of computer fraud.

Computer hackers are lifting passwords from personal computers and emptying online brokerage accounts, as the following unfortunate case describes:

Arriving home from a five-week trip to Belgium and India on Aug. 14, a jet-lagged Korukonda L. Murty picked up his mail—and got the shock of his life. Two monthly statements from online brokerage E*Trade Financial Corp. showed that securities worth $174,000—the bulk of his and his wife's savings—had vanished. During July 13–26, stocks and mutual funds had been sold, and the proceeds wired out of his account in six transactions of nearly $30,000 apiece. Murty, a 64-year-old nuclear engineering professor at North Carolina State University, could only think it was a mistake. He hadn't sold any stock in months.

Murty dialed E*Trade the moment its call center opened at 7 a.m. A customer service rep urged him to change his password immediately. Too late. E*Trade says the computer in Murty's Cary (N.C.) home lacked antivirus software and had been infected with a code that enabled hackers to grab his user name and password. The cybercriminals, pretending to be Murty, directed E*Trade to liquidate his holdings. Then they had the brokerage wire the proceeds to a phony account in his name at Wells Fargo bank. The New York–based online broker says the wire instructions appeared to be legit because they contained the security code the company e-mailed to Murty to execute the transaction. But the cyberthieves had gained control of Murty's e-mail too.[62]

The crime of invading home personal computers and stealing funds from brokerage accounts is on the rise. According to Towergroup, consumers have an estimated $1.7 trillion worth of assets online. Online stock thieves often work out of Eastern Europe and have graduate degrees in finance or banking. Companies such as Ameritrade are responding by offering customers a program that scans personal computers for malicious code when they log onto the Internet. Consumers have been urged to shield access to their personal computers through antivirus software, spyware, and tough-to-crack passwords. Investor alerts identify specific problems that account holders are likely to encounter. These alerts also discourage the use of public computers and unknown sites offering free games and music downloads.[63]

Identity Theft

Identity theft occurs when a perpetrator assumes the identity of another individual for the purpose of opening credit card or telecommunications accounts, passing bad checks, obtaining loans, using the other person's educational or professional credentials to obtain a job, or avoiding criminal prosecution. Identity thieves obtain the information needed to assume someone's identity by hacking into corporate or governmental databases, stealing mail, rummaging through trash receptacles, burglarizing storage areas containing backup files and tapes, and stealing laptop computers containing confidential information. Other methods used by identity thieves include stealing personal documents (birth certificates, social security cards, driver's licenses), pulling personal information from Internet sites, gaining access to improperly stored information (credit card, personnel files, medical records, client files), using information that is in the public domain (property records, real estate transactions, legal proceedings, "Who's Who" listings), eavesdropping on cellular telephone calls, and gathering information from marketing surveys or sweepstakes applications.

Identity theft has become a crime of enormous proportions, primarily because of the growth in the use of computers and the Internet and the pervasiveness of credit and debit cards. In October 2004, the massive databank at ChoicePoint, Inc. was accessed by an identity thief. As Evan Perez and Rick Brooks reported in the *Wall Street Journal*, "ChoicePoint,

Inc. has 19 million data files, full of personal information about nearly every American adult. In minutes, it can produce a report listing someone's former addresses, old roommates, family members and neighbors. The company's computers can tell its clients if an insurance applicant has ever filed a claim and whether a job candidate has ever been sued or faced a tax lien."[64]

The episode at ChoicePoint was the subject of nationwide concern as the company attempted to trace the intruder's electronic footsteps and to determine how many files had been compromised. Similar incidents of data loss or theft have occurred at Bank of America, Time Warner, LexisNexis, and DSW Shoe Warehouse.[65]

Banks, schools, federal agencies, local division of motor vehicle offices, telephone companies, merchants, credit card companies, credit reference agencies, data-brokerage firms, and payment processing agencies all possess information that can be extremely valuable to identity thieves as well as to individuals who sell personal information to these thieves. Identity theft occurs when this information is not protected adequately or when it is given inadvertently to unscrupulous individuals. Surprisingly, however, a great deal of identity theft is done by family members or others who personally know the victim.[66] Parents with poor credit histories have used their children's identities to secure loans and credit cards. Furthermore, many cases of identity theft involve imaginary rather than real people; the identity thief creates and uses the identity of a nonexistent person.

The impersonal and nonviolent nature of this crime makes it attractive to criminals who prefer to operate in a nonconfrontational mode with their victim. Identity thieves can fleece a victim without ever coming into face-to-face contact. "And since the crime is all done remotely," comment the *Newsweek* reporters Steven Levy and Brad Stone, "modern ID thieves suffer little of the risk that [Willie] Sutton shouldered a half century ago when he robbed banks with a machine gun."[67]

The U.S. government has passed several laws to deter and control identity theft. The most prominent of these acts is the Identity Theft, Assumption and Deterrence Act. The Act provides severe penalties for individuals who misappropriate the personal information of another person to commit a federal or state felony. Corporations such as Microsoft have developed PC operating systems and Internet browsers that help individual computer users and businesses identify themselves online, exchange data, and guard against software that can steal personal information.[68] Some companies are now offering identity-theft resolution services as part of their employee benefit packages. Resolution services range from advising employees on how to resolve identity-theft problems to helping them clear their name and repair credit problems.[69] In an almost unprecedented move, the U.S. Social Security Administration is beginning to allow some identity-theft victims to change their social security numbers.[70]

Bodily Injury or Death from Unsafe Products

A less-obvious form of white-collar crime is the manufacture and sale of unsafe products. Consumers may purchase products or services that can cause bodily injury, illness, or death. Tobacco products, fast foods, pharmaceuticals, sunglasses, personal-hygiene items, recreational devices such as bicycles and trampolines, as well as clothing and electrical appliances are among the items that have harmed consumers. Certain products may be dangerous because of design flaws, mistakes made during the manufacturing process, and the failure of manufacturers to warn consumers about possible hazards.

Manufacturers, sellers, or leasers are strictly liable for product safety. If the user of a product suffers personal injury, property damage, or death, the liability of the manufacturer, seller, or leaser does not depend on demonstrating negligence or the intent to do harm. One of the most-publicized products liability cases involved the Ford Pinto. Ford positioned the Pinto as a low-cost automobile for first-time car buyers and for families wanting an inexpensive second car. The Pinto's design problem was based on the improper positioning of the vehicle's fuel tank that made it susceptible to a fiery explosion from a rear-end collision.

Another products liability problem is the use of substandard or defective parts. Aircraft manufacturers in the United States must use parts that meet exacting FAA standards. If FAA-approved parts are not used, the aircraft is not deemed to be airworthy under federal law. The FAA's exacting specifications have created a black market for less-expensive, bogus aircraft parts. Mechanics may unknowingly purchase and install these parts in aircraft with disastrous consequences.

Other products liability cases involve accusations of false marketing claims or the sale of products without providing adequate information to consumers on their safe and proper use. Much tobacco litigation has centered on the alleged suppression of research results on the harmful effects of tobacco as well as the inadequate warnings to consumers about the hazardous effects of tobacco use.

The design, manufacture, and sale of unsafe products raise several issues:

1. What product or service safety standards are most appropriate? Nearly all products and services present at least a minimal degree of danger. How far should businesses go to ensure that their products and services are safe, and what tradeoffs between design costs, manufacturing costs, and safety are optimal?
2. How much advice and warning should consumers receive with respect to the dangers of a product or service? Some products come with voluminous operating manuals that few consumers are likely to read carefully.
3. Where do we draw the line between manufacturer liability and consumer negligence when a product is misused? Consumers have been known to abuse products and to exceed product limits. Should aircraft manufacturers, for example, be liable for the death and destruction caused by an incompetent pilot who blunders into a thunderstorm?[71] Should parents hold the manufacturer of a trampoline liable because their unsupervised preteen children were injured while jumping onto the device from a second-story window?[72]
4. Is it fair or practical to expect a company to anticipate all of the possible dangers that might be inherent in a product or service?
5. For how many years from the time of sale should the designer or manufacturer be subject to liability?
6. Finally, where do the designers and manufacturers of a product cross the line between negligent activities (civil wrongs) and criminal activities?

Environmental Crimes

Environmental crimes create damage to the ecosystem by depositing toxic substances into the system (pollution) or by misusing scarce natural resources (resources depletion). These crimes cause birth defects, cancer, respiratory and other illnesses, and they destroy wildlife, upset delicate ecological balances, create unpleasant odors, and cause unsightly damage to communities and natural areas. Environmental abuses occur because white-collar criminals realize that it is less expensive and more expedient to release hazardous substances into the air or water than it is to comply with federal or state environmental laws and properly dispose of these substances. The greatest costs of pollution often fall on residents of low-income areas, especially minorities and immigrants who have little political clout and who are more likely to purchase lower-cost residential land near industrial areas (a condition referred to as environmental racism). Citizens of third-world countries are also likely to be victimized by environmental crimes because firms in industrialized nations may seek to transport and dump toxic waste illegally with the assistance of corrupt officials in these countries.

Some white-collar criminals have few reservations about dumping waste into rivers, landfills, sewer systems, or other convenient spots. Others attempt to dispose of hazardous wastes by allowing toxic chemicals to leak from transport containers or storage tanks. Perpetrators also know that there are clandestine ways of dumping hazardous waste, making it difficult for authorities to detect its presence or to identify its source.

There is a thriving black market for certain illegal toxic substances such as chlorofluorocarbons (CFCs) that were used in automobile air-conditioning systems built before 1995. CFCs have been linked to the depletion of the ozone layer and to an increase in the incidence of skin cancer. White-collar criminals have discovered a burgeoning market for the coolant because owners of older automobiles do not want to spend several hundred dollars retrofitting their vehicles with environmentally friendly cooling systems. According to the National Institute of Environmental Health and Safety, "Contraband CFCs are so pervasive they have at times rivaled cocaine as among the most profitable illegal imports crossing U.S. borders. . . . A 30-pound cylinder of colorless, odorless CFC-12 bought in China for US$40 can be sold on the U.S. black market for up to $600."[73]

The time between when an environmental crime is committed and when the damage is discovered (if it is, in fact, ever discovered) can be months or years. This time lag makes it difficult to identify and prosecute the culprits. The fact that air and water contaminants can travel vast distances before being detected also makes successful prosecution difficult. Criminals who dump medical waste in the ocean, for example, count on its vast size to shield them from detection. When caught, most companies get away with merely paying fines, cleaning up contaminated sites, and making restitution to communities or individuals who suffered damage; criminal charges against executives and managers who commit environmental crimes are rare.

Another form of environmental crime is the misuse and destruction of natural resources through illegal forestry activities and hunting. Rainforests are destroyed by illegal logging activities. Exotic and endangered wildlife species are either killed or captured because of their high market value. According to the U.S. Department of Justice, "a single rhinoceros horn can earn one destitute poacher several hundred dollars, equivalent to a year's salary in some African countries. The same horn, ground up and used as a perceived remedy for impotence and other ailments, can fetch half a million dollars in Asia. Illegal wildlife trading generates at least $10 billion a year."[74]

Bodily Injury and Death of Employees

Occupational safety and health violations expose employees to dangerous conditions in the workplace that can lead to bodily injury, illness, or death. As with water and air pollution, perpetrators of these crimes are motivated by the belief that noncompliance with federal and state occupational safety and health regulations is less expensive than compliance. The result is that workers are subjected to traumatic injuries and occupational diseases. Injuries or death from moving machinery, falls, vehicle accidents, electrical shock, and exposure to substances that cause cancer or respiratory ailments (asbestos, dust, radioactivity, and beryllium) are among the most common hazards.

The long-lamented problem with occupational safety and health laws is their spotty enforcement and light civil penalties. Furthermore, many companies simply view Occupational Safety and Health Administration (OSHA) fines as another cost of doing business rather than as an incentive to improve workplace safety. Criminal charges (including murder and manslaughter) have been brought against managers who have purposefully exposed workers to life-threatening situations. Demonstrating mens rea (criminal intent) in such cases, however, can be difficult.

When workers are killed on the job by the gross negligence of management, the maximum charges are likely to be involuntary manslaughter, a crime that results in little or no jail time.

Prosecutors are frustrated by the time lag between the cause of an occupational illness and its appearance. An employee exposed to a carcinogenic substance, for example, may not be diagnosed with cancer until years later. Legal counsel for the company can then argue that intervening events such as the employee's use of tobacco, poor diet, or exposure to other toxic substances caused the disease. In other cases, management may blame the injured worker for not following safety procedures. Furthermore, it may be impossible to pin the responsibility for workplace hazards on a specific manager or group of managers. High turnover among managers and poor record keeping all make it easier for managers and corporations to shirk responsibility for occupational injuries and diseases.

The Salient Features of White-Collar Crime

White-collar crimes defy simple definition and categorization. The crimes discussed here often overlap and are complex, making them difficult for criminologists and law enforcement agencies to analyze. The criminologist Marcus Felson has developed a white-collar crime classification scheme that is both straightforward and encompassing. The four categories of crime and corruption in Felson's scheme are: (1) the illicit transfer of money and other resources, (2) misinforming others, (3) manipulating others, and (4) endangering the health and safety of others.[75]

The illicit transfer of money and resources is fundamental to white-collar crime. Money and resources may be stolen in several ways: theft, embezzlement, misappropriation, conversion of company property to personal use, and the sale of proprietary information. The first method is the theft of something that has not been entrusted to the care of the perpetrator.[76] An office employee who enters her employer's warehouse and steals valuable computer components is committing an act of theft. A salesperson who creates a fictitious company and then alters his company's master vendor account so that he can bill his employer for services that were never rendered is also committing an act of theft.

Embezzlement is the term that describes the theft of money or resources that have been entrusted to the perpetrator. One example of embezzlement is the mailroom employee who steals checks from incoming mail and then alters and cashes the checks. Another example is the convenience store manager who accepts money from a customer, fails to record the sale or provide the customer with a receipt, and pockets the cash. Similarly, the jewelry store manager who substitutes fake diamonds for real diamonds and then sells the authentic ones to a rogue gem dealer is also committing embezzlement.

A misappropriation occurs when money or other resources that are intended for the exclusive business purpose of the organization are used for the personal benefit of the perpetrator. An executive who uses the company aircraft for a weekend boondoggle is a prime example. A crackdown by the Securities and Exchange Commission on undisclosed executive perquisites shows that the use of corporate jets for vacation and leisure travel has been on the rise. The CEO of a Midwest company, for example, allegedly spent $832,000 of company funds for free personal use of the company's airplane. During this time, his annual salary was reported to be $930,000.[77] One of the most egregious examples of misappropriation was the activities of the Rigas family who ran Adelphia Communications Corporation. Prosecutors at the Rigas's conspiracy and bank and securities fraud trial contended that the family treated the company like "their own ATM machine."[78]

Corrupt televangelists have diverted donations from members of their flock to fund lavish personal purchases with tax-exempt monies. Illicit charities have siphoned money from funds that donors thought was intended for a needy group or worthwhile cause. Misappropriation may also occur when an employee uses company assets such as proprietary computer software or customer lists to further a personal business.

The illicit transfer of resources may include selling proprietary information to competitors. Corporations guard information on which they have built core competencies or have attained a competitive advantage. This information may pertain to the design and manufacture of a product, the development of specialized technology such as computer software and information systems, or the formulation of strategic plans that will affect a company's stock price.

Acts of illicit transfer permanently deprive the rightful owner of the resource. An employee who removes a laptop computer from his employer's office and then sells it and pockets the proceeds is committing an illegal act. If the employee takes the computer home to catch up on his work and later returns it, no law has been broken (although the company may have a policy against removing property from the premises). Many acts of larceny (theft, embezzlement, burglary, robbery) entail a conversion process in which the thief sells the stolen merchandise for cash or exchanges it for other property. The conversion process may also involve altering the cash or merchandise through money laundering, physical conversion (e.g., removing diamonds from a bracelet and selling them separately), or transporting the stolen merchandise to a distant location.

Some acts of organizational crime and corruption involve providing false or misleading information to victims. As noted earlier, there are two forms of deception: overt lies (lies of commission) and untold truths (lies of omission). The insurance agent who tells an elderly client that she needs to purchase health insurance coverage because Medicare will no longer cover her hospital bills is committing a lie of commission. The middle-aged Illinois farmer who purchases sight unseen a parcel of land in Florida that was touted by the real estate agent as a tropical paradise (if you happen to be a swamp-dwelling sand crane, water moccasin, or alligator) has been victimized by a lie of omission.

Another form of misinformation is falsifying the authenticity of securities, monetary instruments, or merchandise. Producing and passing counterfeit checks, securities, currency, and important documents is done with the intent of misleading someone to believe that these documents are real. False social security cards and birth certificates are also used by criminals to commit credit card fraud and identity theft.

An age-old form of misrepresentation is lying about the quality or performance of a product. The market for fitness and weight loss products attracts hucksters who tout everything from special belts with a low electrical charge that turns midriff fat into hard abdominal muscle to weight loss creams, metabolism-boosting pills, and exercise and diet programs that transform a sedentary person into a well-conditioned athlete. Internet dating services may guarantee "matches made in heaven," employment agencies may place clients on "the job of a lifetime," and a warranty purchased on a used car may come with "complete bumper-to-bumper protection." All of these promises are easy to make and difficult to keep.

Counterfeit products may entail the illicit transfer of resources (stealing a legitimate brand name) misinforming others (consumers who un-knowingly purchase a counterfeit item), and endangering others (coun-terfeit designer clothing made with a flammable material). There is a multi-billion-dollar market for products such as fake jewelry, watches, handbags, designer clothing, and household appliances. Even entire au-tomobiles and motorcycles have been counterfeited.[79]

Music, movie, and software piracy is a multibillion-dollar industry in Asia. In China, Shanghai police seized 210,000 pirated DVD movies. Some of the movies were copied illegally in theaters with camcorders and then recorded by DVD replicators.[80] In summer 2005, the U.S. Supreme Court ruled in favor of copyright holders and against two com-panies that distribute peer-to-peer (P2P) music and films. The Court's ruling will not eliminate illegal copying, but it may encourage more users to acquire music and movies through legitimate online resources.

Rolex watches, Gucci handbags, Calvin Klein apparel, and Microsoft software are among the more popular pirated items. In many cases, con-sumers purchase these items knowing they are counterfeit. A woman may buy a fake Kate Spade bag at a fraction of the original price because she plans to use it only for special social occasions, and she is willing to accept its inferior quality and poor durability. In other cases, consumers have unwittingly purchased counterfeit items such as name-brand sun-glasses that provide no protection against harmful ultraviolet rays or poorly constructed and dangerous electrical appliances that have fake Underwriters Laboratory labels.[81]

Counterfeiting and piracy violate copyright and patent laws. Rightful copyright and patent owners lose millions of dollars in revenues. Legiti-mate manufacturers are forced to spend money to protect their written works, music, and products from copyright and patent infringement.

Misinformation may take the form of making false promises or claims about a service. A common example of misrepresentation are private employment agencies that advertise attractive positions, collect fees from clients after guaranteeing them interviews with Fortune 100 firms, and abscond with their clients' money. Another such misrepresentation are travel agencies that promise all-inclusive services as part of a vaca-tion package and then fail to deliver these services or provide services that are of an inferior quality.

Tricking customers into purchasing a product or service that they do not need is another age-old form of misrepresentation. One ubiquitous scam is telling an automobile owner that his or her vehicle needs expensive repairs when the necessary repairs are actually minor. Many a crooked automobile mechanic, for example, has made expensive repairs to an air-conditioner when all that was needed to fix the problem was a new fuse.

Misrepresentations made by professionals such as physicians, attorneys, or professors are regarded as being especially serious. One almost expects to be lied to by a used-car dealer who is out to make a quick buck on a car with a mileage rollback and hidden mechanical problems. But the characteristic that sets professionals apart from other occupational groups is that they are supposed to subordinate their personal and financial interests to the interests of their clients and the public. Some of the most reprehensible examples of misrepresentation occur when an attorney jeopardizes his client's position because of secret conflicts of interest, when a realtor misrepresents the condition of a property to a client, or when a researcher falsifies scientific results to achieve breakthrough results that will advance her career.

The news contains plenty of harrowing stories of individuals in positions of trust who have violated their sacred duties by taking advantage of those who are vulnerable, such as one of the most reprehensible and publicized of these criminal and corrupt acts, the sexual misconduct of pedophile clergy.

Three factors appear to be at the heart of manipulative conduct with regard to white-collar criminals. First is the presence of asymmetric information or power, which means that one party, in this case the corrupt professional, has more knowledge or power than the victim. Insider trading is a classic example of asymmetric information. The crooked attorney who engages in securities fraud with an equally crooked banker likewise has an informational edge over trusting investors who pour their savings into this scheme. Workplace sexual harassment has long been viewed as having its roots in an asymmetric power relationship, primarily between male supervisors and female subordinates.

Second, certain groups are more prone to manipulation than others. Children and the elderly are most often cited as being especially susceptible because of their cognitive vulnerabilities. Children generally lack the neurological development and life experiences to be suspicious and distrusting of adults who may try to harm them. The elderly, while long on life experiences, may be plagued by diminishing mental capacities associated with the onset of dementia. Many elderly people have lived in high-trust environments, and they are often ill prepared to deal with modernity and its white-collar criminals. Furthermore, the elderly have poor memories and are easily confused, impairing their reliability as witnesses if the criminal is caught and prosecuted.

Third, certain mental and emotional states can cause otherwise savvy individuals to become easy prey for criminals. People suffering from depression or loneliness can be seduced by ingratiating scam artists who pretend to have a romantic interest. Lothario scam artists look for vulnerable individuals who are seeking a romantic companion and marriage. After a whirlwind courtship and, possibly, a marriage ceremony, these con artists manage to steal or embezzle sizeable amounts of money, and they often leave their victims saddled with a mountain of debt. Other criminals seek out individuals who have recently lost loved ones or who have experienced a personal tragedy. Home repair scam artists descend on hurricane and tornado ravaged areas. These criminals befriend distraught and confused homeowners, assess the damage to their homes, offer reasonable repair rates, and then disappear with the cash advance.

As noted previously, examples of some of the most egregious white-collar crimes include the sale of unsafe products, forcing workers to toil under dangerous conditions, and emitting hazardous wastes into the ecosystem. Although white-collar crimes are regarded as being nonviolent in nature, many cause physical damage to humans, water supplies, wildlife, natural habitats, and the atmosphere and ozone layer. These crimes illustrate how white-collar criminals can be equally or in some cases more dangerous than street criminals.

Conclusion

This chapter covers a wide spectrum of crimes and corrupt acts ranging from minor pilfering and misappropriation to crimes that have a major impact on the personal safety and financial well-being of the public. White-collar crimes consist of: (1) primary crimes such as financial fraud, embezzlement, occupational safety and environmental health crimes, and (2) the facilitating crimes of money laundering, conspiracy, mail and wire fraud, and tax evasion. We can also categorize these crimes using Felson's description of white-collar crime: (1) the illicit transfer of money and other resources, (2) misinforming others, (3) manipulating others, and (4) endangering the health and safety of others. The salient characteristics proposed by Felson encompass all white-collar crimes, and one or more of these characteristics can be found in each of the crimes discussed here.

3

White-Collar Criminals: Risks and Rationalizations

Perpetrators of organizational crime and corruption act with fore-thought. They assess the potential risks and benefits of their acts. If they are confronted with their misdeeds, they often offer elaborate rationalizations to mitigate the impact of their crimes. This chapter discusses the major types of white-collar criminals, how they decide what crimes to commit, how they assess the risks and benefits of their crimes, and how they cope psychologically with their decisions.

Three Types of White-Collar Criminals

One method of classifying both white-collar and street crime is by examining characteristics of the perpetrator. Crimes may be analyzed by examining factors such as the perpetrator's mode of operation and crime victim as well as their race, age group, educational level, occupation, and socioeconomic status. Weisburd, Waring, and Chayet offer an innovative way of classifying white-collar criminals based on the frequency of their crimes and on the ways in which the crimes were instigated. Their scheme focuses on three types of offenders: (1) crisis responders, (2) opportunity takers, and (3) opportunity seekers (chronic offenders).[1]

First are crisis responders. Many individuals who have been prosecuted for white-collar crimes have had little or no previous contact with the criminal justice system. These individuals usually have a stable work and family history. They may have distinguished military records, college degrees, be active in church affairs, and come from highly respected families. When they are arrested for a white-collar crime, friends and acquaintances react with disbelief and find it incomprehensible that a pillar of the community could have committed such an egregious act.

Crisis responders, as the name implies, commit white-collar and other crimes because of financial exigencies or personal tragedies. They may claim that they were faced with insurmountable or "nonsharable" problems from gambling debts, unpaid medical bills, problems with the IRS, or a past-due mortgage.[2] A Pennsylvania woman, for example, was charged with embezzling more than $618,000 from her employer over a twelve-year period. She claimed she was the target of an extortion ring that was linked to her gambling debts.[3] Other crisis responders may reason that their white-collar crimes were committed to serve a higher cause such as protecting a business from financial ruin. They often rationalize their acts by stating that the pressures of the moment temporarily clouded their otherwise good judgment, and they are quick to reassure their victims or prosecutors that it will never happen again.

Crisis responders may be further classified into three categories. First, there are individuals whose illegal behavior may represent an aberration in an otherwise law-abiding lifestyle. They may learn their lesson or never again feel the need to commit an act of theft, embezzlement, or fraud. Second, there are white-collar criminals who commit acts in response to a crisis more readily because they have committed previous illegal acts that have gone undetected. Third, there are some crisis responders who, having gotten their first taste of crime in response to a crisis, may subsequently decide to commit other illegal acts. That is, their initial crisis sets the stage for subsequent criminal behavior.

Weisburd, Waring, and Chayet's second main type of offender is the opportunity taker. Most occupations provide some degree of specialized access to money, resources, or people. A classic example is the purchasing agent who accepts gratuities or offers of a kickback from a vendor. Another example is a corrections case worker who succumbs to the sexual advances of a manipulative inmate. Still another example is a politician who is offered a bribe by a lobbyist representing an industry group that is anxious to see a proposed environmental bill killed.

At some point in their careers, many professionals and managers have the opportunity to engage in a criminal or corrupt act. The vast majority resist these temptations because they either believe such behavior is wrong ("How could I live with myself if I accepted a bribe?"), or they believe the risks are too great ("I could never endanger my family, destroy my professional reputation, or risk going to jail for a mere one-hundred grand!"). For managers with a corrupt bent, however, the perceived benefits of a crime outweigh these risks.

Opportunity takers are different from crisis responders in that they feel no immediate financial or personal pressure to do something illegal. The once-in-a-lifetime opportunity to make easy money and improve their lifestyle is too good to resist. Some opportunity takers may stop after committing a single crime ("I'm not a crook, after all!"). Others will commit additional crimes if future opportunities arise. Their crimes may start as small unethical acts that are easy to rationalize. An attorney, anxious to meet a monthly law-firm billing goal, may work on an account for three hours and bill the client for four hours. The rationalization for inflating the number of billable hours might be based on the attorney's belief that his or her client is unethical and has deep pockets. If the overbilling of clients continues, the attorney may soon regard this behavior as an acceptable practice (normalization of deviance).

There are numerous professionals and managers who are willing to take moderate risks in exchange for a financial windfall. Some of the executives at Enron, WorldCom, Tyco, and Adelphia appear to be classic opportunity takers. These individuals had no personal financial crises. To the contrary, they had successful careers and plenty of money. Yet the opportunity to siphon off millions of dollars from their firms was golden, especially when they considered the low risk of prosecution white-collar criminals historically have enjoyed.

Weisburd, Waring, and Chayet's third main type of criminal is the opportunity seeker. Habitual criminals spend a great deal of their lives circulating through the criminal justice system. These individuals view crime as a way of life, and they seek criminal opportunities and victims much in the same way that a legitimate business person seeks new markets and customers. Many career street criminals have arrest and conviction records for dozens of crimes. Furthermore, they may have committed additional crimes for which they were never arrested. Habitual criminals frequently suffer from antisocial personality disorder, and efforts to rehabilitate them are almost always unsuccessful. They are a primary reason that jails and prisons were built.

A milder counterpart to the habitual criminal also exists among professionals and managers. Opportunity takers include the counterfeiter who sells fake Super Bowl tickets to eager fans, the computer buff who repeatedly hacks into bank computer systems to steal money, or the deposed university president who has a history of misappropriating public funds, income tax evasion, and money laundering.

Opportunity seekers who commit white-collar crimes are constantly assessing the costs and benefits of illicit opportunities. These individuals may fall into one of four categories.

The first opportunity seeker may be part of an organized crime operation. An attorney whose sole client is an organized crime syndicate may spend his working days brokering deals with corrupt judges, accountants, and union officers.

The second opportunity seeker may use his or her occupation or business interests as a front for illegal activity. Illegal activity provides greater financial rewards than the legal occupation, yet it is not part of a more permanent and highly structured organized crime operation. A manager of a heating and air conditioning firm may use his legitimate business as a front for laundering money. The true purpose of making trips to the homes of customers is to pick up money generated through criminal activities. Money is then funneled through the legal business operation to avoid the attention of law enforcement or the IRS. The heating and air conditioning company may also install and service appliances for customers who have no idea that they are doing business with a criminal enterprise.

The third type of opportunity seeker may hold a legitimate position and commit white-collar crimes on the side whenever an opportunity presents itself. An insurance agent may operate a legal business, but she also helps certain clients commit arson and insurance fraud from time to time. A retail clothing store manager may occasionally pilfer merchandise and sell it to fences as a means of supplementing his income. He then writes off the missing merchandise as inventory shrinkage.

How Do Perpetrators Decide What Crimes to Commit?

White-collar criminals can select from a smorgasbord of crimes (recall Table 2.1). The type and frequency of an individual perpetrator's white-collar criminal activity is a function of their personal preferences, motivation, opportunities, propensity for risk, and ability to rationalize their actions.

Personal preference plays a major role in how most criminals choose certain crimes. Some white-collar criminals stick with one type of crime such as medical fraud. Others commit a range of white-collar crimes but abhor the notion of committing a violent crime such as assault or robbery. Still other white-collar criminals will commit crimes in the streets as easily as crimes in the suites. They have no specific crime or victim in mind. Instead, they will commit any crime that appears to have a high probability of payoff and a low probability of apprehension.

Criminals may also exhibit preferences for certain victims. One white-collar criminal may have no reservations about embezzling hundreds of thousands of dollars from a large bank, but this same individual cannot fathom taking advantage of an elderly person. Another criminal may not hesitate to bilk a low-income elderly victim out of her life savings, but he would be fearful of embezzling money from his employer. Still another white-collar criminal has no problem cooking the books to defraud her company's shareholders (a corporate crime), but she would be appalled at the thought of stealing merchandise (an occupational crime) from the discount retail store chain where she is the chief financial officer.

Some criminals favor certain technologies, locations, or industries. One criminal may use computers as the primary technology for crime, while another is skillful at real estate fraud. Criminals also exhibit preferences for the location of their crimes. A scam artist may operate only in neighborhoods where residents are of a certain income level, race, or ethnicity. Another thief may ply his trade primarily in mail rooms where he steals checks from incoming mail. Some white-collar criminals limit their activities to one industry or occupation. An example would be the life insurance agent who convinces his clients to replace their current policy with a newer policy. The replacement policy, while no better than the client's previous life insurance policy, enables the agent to generate additional sales commissions. This practice is known as "churning." The technologies, locations, or industries selected by criminals may depend on their particular skills as well as the places where they feel most comfortable committing crimes.

A question that is of interest to criminologists, managers, and security specialists is: How are individuals drawn into white-collar crimes and what role does socialization play? The speed with which an individual moves into the realm of white-collar crime varies. Incrementalism is a form of socialization that entices individuals to commit minor criminal or corrupt acts followed by increasingly serious acts.[4] For example, as Moore, Tetlock, Tanlu, and Bazerman write:

> in one year, an auditor might decline to demand that the client change an accounting practice that is at the edge of permissibility. The next year, the auditor may feel the need to justify the previous year's decision and may turn a blind eye when the client pushes just past the edge of permissibility. The following year, the auditor might endorse accounting that clearly violates GAAP [generally accepted accounting principles] in order to avoid admitting the errors of the past two years, in the hope that the client will fix the problem before the next year's audit. By the fourth year, the auditor and client will both be actively engaged in a cover-up to hide their past practices. . . .
>
> Faced with the choice between a guaranteed loss of income and status on the one hand and the chance of a more severe penalty (and the chance that one might never be punished) on the other, people tend to opt for the risky option.[5]

Incrementalism leads to the normalization of deviance; actions that were once viewed as corrupt or illegal become normal and acceptable. The above scenario describes a form of "moral seduction" that entices a perpetrator one step at a time into deeper involvement with white-collar crime.

Group dynamics also play a role in how perpetrators are socialized into crime. Although some white-collar criminals act alone, many white-collar crimes involve conspiracies or alliances among co-workers. Police officers have long adhered to the "blue code of silence" to protect corrupt fellow officers. Similarly, politicians, executives, and other powerful individuals occasionally form alliances to facilitate criminal or corrupt activities. These conspiracies have been described as social cocoons composed of a subculture of individuals in an organization who adopt deviant social norms and modes of behavior. Anand, Ashforth, and Joshi explain:

Once a social cocoon has formed, corruption may be facilitated through the following steps: (1) veterans model the corrupt behavior and easy acceptance of it, (2) newcomers are encouraged to affiliate and bond with veterans and develop desires to identify with, emulate, and please the veterans, (3) newcomers are subjected to strong and consistent information and ideological statements such that they view corrupt acts in a positive light, and (4) newcomers are encouraged to attribute any misgivings that they may have to their own shortcomings (particularly naivete) rather than to what is being asked of them.[6]

Being socialized into the world of white-collar crime is similar to entering a swimming pool filled with cool water. Once the initial chill wears off, the water feels fairly comfortable as long as the crime remains undetected and unpunished.

Motivations of white-collar criminals vary in level and type. When considering the motivations of criminals, two factors should be considered: the motivation to lead a criminal lifestyle and the motivation to commit a particular crime. Crisis responders and opportunity takers do not pursue a life of crime, but their level of motivation to commit a particular offense may be high under certain circumstances. The former may be highly motivated to capitalize on an opportunity to embezzle if they are in dire financial straits. Opportunity seekers, in contrast, have accepted crime as a way of life even though they may not regard themselves as criminals. Their motivation to commit a particular crime may vary, depending on their assessment of its potential risks and benefits.

White-collar criminals are motivated by both economic and noneconomic factors. The opportunity to reap large sums of money through theft, fraud, or kickbacks is an obvious motivator for most white-collar criminals. Although they have a normal positive utility for money (more money is preferred to less money), they may have an abnormal marginal utility for money (the incremental value of additional money remains strong even when they already possess substantial wealth). White-collar crime also involves psychological and social factors. A criminal may obtain a dark sense of satisfaction because he has pulled the wool over the eyes of regulators and auditors or he has gotten away with embezzling money from a cold and uncaring employer. Some white-collar criminals may enjoy increased status and respect among their coconspirators after having planned and pulled off an intricate scam.

Opportunity is a necessary condition for crime. Even the most habitual, impulsive, and irrational criminal cannot commit a crime unless opportunities (no matter how risky) are available. As discussed in the introduction and chapter one, organizations and society provide opportunities for crime. Lax security procedures, the presence of cash and other valuable assets, unsupervised work environments, a climate where bribes are tolerated, computer and copier technology, the presence of potential victims, and Internet access provide opportunities for illegal acts.

Criminals also encounter threats. The presence of potential witnesses, security guards, electronic surveillance, accounting controls as well as organizations that are willing to see to it that white-collar criminals are prosecuted all serve as deterrents for white-collar criminals.

White-collar crimes have been depicted as crimes that are committed within a commercial establishment and where the primary motive is financial gain. Because white-collar crimes are thought to be economically motivated, they have been distinguished from crimes of passion. The supposedly economic and passionless nature of white-collar crimes has led to the use of rational choice theory to explain the behavior of corporate criminals.[7] Rational choice theory has its origins in economics, and the theory is based on the idea that criminals take a calculated and deliberate approach to criminal acts. The theory assumes that:

1. People make choices about how they want to spend their time, energy, and resources. They must decide whether to work legally, illegally, or not work at all.[8] Some criminals may engage in all three activities at different times, or they may combine illegal and legal occupations simultaneously.
2. Criminals have a solid grasp of reality. They are not psychotic. Some criminals, however, may have personality disorders, or they may exhibit impulsive behaviors that create the appearance of irrationality to observers.
3. Criminals recognize that their crimes impose costs (and risks) and provide benefits. The decision to commit a crime requires that criminals assess these costs and benefits. Criminals hope to

profit from their crimes while avoiding detection and punishment. Table 3.1 summarizes the major benefits and costs of white-collar crime.

Table 3.1. Benefits and Costs for the Perpetrators of White-Collar Crime

Benefits	*Costs*
cash	criminal sanctions
assets	adverse civil court judgments
psychological thrill or satisfaction	administrative law sanctions
social approval of criminal peers	loss of license, banishment
improved status and career opportunities	ostracism, damaged reputation
improved organizational performance	loss of self-esteem
	loss of legal profits
	loss of leisure time

Although rational choice theory makes sense intuitively, it does not provide complete insight into criminal and corrupt behaviors because the term "rational" is subjective. Except in very simple decisions with complete and perfect information, rational behavior is a matter of degree rather than an either-or proposition.[9]

The decision to commit a white-collar crime does not lend itself to simple analysis. White-collar crimes are complex and even the most meticulous perpetrator does not have complete information about the probabilities, costs, and benefits of the crime. There are frequent media accounts of crimes that seem "senseless" or "stupid." Yet, at the time the crime occurred, the crime may have seemed to be a logical choice to the criminal. Complex decisions involve a phenomenon known as bounded rationality. The term was coined by the Nobel laureate Herbert Simon to describe how decision makers cope with incomplete information. Even when information is abundant, the human mind can process only a limited amount of it. Saddled with these constraints, a criminal's assessment of the risks and rewards of a crime are far from perfect.

There are several explanations for seemingly irrational crimes. First, the criminal may lack intelligence or be impulsive. The man who robbed a convenience store while wearing a high school letter jacket with his name emblazoned on the front suggests as much. The motorist who attempted to flee from police at night by turning off his lights but continuing to use his turn signal as well as the man who tried to elude police by hiding in a tree only to be betrayed by his ringing cell phone both are deserving of time on *America's Dumbest Criminals*. Street criminals are more likely to face stressful situations requiring immediate action while they are on the run, and their judgments may be impaired by alcohol or drugs. White-collar criminals, however, are usually able to plan their crimes in a stress-controlled environment that enables them to exercise better judgment.

Second, the criminal may have underestimated the likelihood of being identified and prosecuted. Criminals are often superoptimistic, and this attitude is reinforced each time they commit a crime and avoid apprehension. Yochelson and Samenow explain,

> superoptimism differs from the confidence experienced by the noncriminal. Confidence, like superoptimism, is based on anticipation of success. The noncriminal expects success only after he has appraised what is needed to achieve it in a responsible endeavor. His confidence is warranted by responsible considerations rather than pretensions and unrealistic expectations. Thus, the layman is often astonished at the chances that the criminal takes. In fact, observers have concluded that the criminal must *want* to get caught, or he would not assume such risks. The noncriminal views everything as loaded against the criminal, whereas the criminal sees everything stacked in his favor. The superoptimism may appear "crazy" or "stupid" from the noncriminal's perspective, but it is warranted by the criminal's ability to cut off deterrents, by his past successes, and by his carefully thought out scheme.[10]

Stephen Glass, the journalist who fabricated facts, quotes, and stories while working for the *New Republic*, seemed overly optimistic that he could perpetuate his frauds and avoid detection indefinitely. In an interview with CBS correspondent Steve Kroft of *60 Minutes*, Glass said,

> My life was one very long process of lying and lying again, to figure out how to cover those other lies.
>
> Like a stock graph, there's going to be exceptions in this. But the general trend of the stories is that they started out with a few made up details and quotes. And granted a few too many, of course. But a few. And then they progressed into stories that were completely fabricated. Just completely made up out of whole cloth . . .

I remember thinking, "If I just had the exact quote that I wanted to make it work, it would be perfect." And I wrote something in my computer, and then I looked at it, and I let it stand. And then it ran in the magazine and I saw it. And I said to myself what I said every time those stories ran, "You must stop. You must stop." But I didn't.

I loved the electricity of people liking my stories. I loved going to story conference meetings and telling people what my story was going to be, and seeing the room excited. I wanted every story to be a home run.[11]

Stephen Glass's story not only exhibits an unrealistic optimism that he could avoid detection indefinitely but it also illustrates how a small act of corruption can escalate to serious levels.

Third, the criminal may have overestimated the costs or underestimated the benefits of the crime. Criminal history is replete with cases in which a victim is murdered during a robbery that nets little or no money. The perpetrator is apprehended, convicted of capital murder, and sentenced to death. When the execution is carried out, the press usually emphasizes the senseless nature of the crime and the steep price paid by the perpetrator for the few dollars netted. White-collar crimes too involve distorted cost and benefit estimates. The career of a South Korean scientist was destroyed overnight amid allegations that he had falsified the results of his research on a major development in stem cell research.[12] If the allegations against him are true, it has difficult to imagine how he planned to perpetuate this fraud knowing that other scientists would attempt to replicate his work. Absent a serious mental problem, this case also illustrates how a white-collar criminal may underestimate the likelihood of getting caught as well as the impact of a minor crime on one's career. Criminals must make a priori assessments of the impact of their crime, but unfortunately, the real costs and benefits become apparent only after the crime has occurred.

Fourth, the decision to commit a crime is often a linked decision. Linked decisions are those that have an impact on subsequent decisions. That is, an alternative selected today affects future available alternatives.[13] After Stephen Glass wrote his fraudulent stories, he compounded his problems as he attempted to cover his lies through the creation of fake notes, the use of false voice mailboxes and business cards of phantom sources, reference to nonexistent organizations (e.g., one story referred to a made-up group, the National Assembly of Hackers), and accounts of meetings that never took place. He finally reached the point where his web of stories, sources, and documentation became so entangled that even he became confused: "I'm juggling so much at this point and I just made so many more lies on top of what's in my story I can't even remember what's in my story."[14]

Various forms of embezzlement and financial fraud often create linked decisions; once the crime sequence begins, additional illegal measures are necessary to conceal or perpetuate the devious acts. A criminal who is accused of income tax evasion is put in the position of committing additional crimes such as obstruction of justice, lying to federal prosecutors, and perjury. Since many crimes involve linked decisions, the perpetrator's ability to realistically assess the costs and benefits of a white-collar crime becomes exceedingly difficult.

Fifth, the concept of secondary deviance must be considered when discussing decisions to commit a crime. Secondary deviance is a concept developed by the sociologist Edward M. Lemert during the early 1950s.[15] Secondary deviance begins when a person commits deviant acts such as a white-collar crime and is punished for the crime. According to Lemert, an individual may commit several acts that are punished by subsequently harsher penalties. After being labeled as a deviant or a criminal, the perpetrator responds by committing additional deviant acts. These acts increase the level of stigmatization against the perpetrator to the point where he or she accepts the deviant role or reputation and behaves in accordance with this role. Thus, one risk that crisis responders and opportunity takers encounter when they enter the realm of white-collar crime is the possibility of being stigmatized or labeled to the point where committing additional crimes or acts of corruption becomes easier. One possible example of secondary deviance is a university president who was fired for misappropriating funds. He subsequently became involved in tax evasion, money laundering, and an illegal visa racket. Once he was labeled as a criminal, he continued pursuing illegal activities. It should be noted, however, that it is difficult to demonstrate secondary deviance empirically. Furthermore, the concept may be more applicable to street criminals than to white-collar criminals. Because of their social standing, wealth, and conventional appearance, the latter group may be able to avoid the stigma of their crimes.

Some percentage of any population will refuse to engage in illegal or corrupt acts under any circumstances. These individuals cannot be corrupted no matter what temptations are present. One example would be someone who refuses to accept a cash bribe even if her family is destitute and lacking the basic necessities of life.

Some otherwise law-abiding individuals have a threshold for corruption, and they may be lured into committing a criminal act once they perceive that the benefits are sufficiently high. Crisis responders who are desperate for a way out often have few legal alternatives. During the savings and loan scandal of the early 1980s, some savings and loan managers resorted to high-risk and ruinous financial activities in a last-ditch effort to save their institutions from insolvency.

White-collar criminals who are regarded as crisis responders may have legal ways in which they can extricate themselves from trouble, but they find the illegal solution to their problem more appealing. A manager facing personal bankruptcy (and all of its attendant financial, legal, and social problems) may decide that a more palatable way out of his financial disaster is to embezzle cash or accept a kickback. Similarly, the CFO of a company that has experienced a severe downturn in sales and profits may elect to falsify financial statements, risking fraud and other criminal charges, rather than incurring the wrath of shareholders and a loss of confidence by prospective investors. Opportunity seekers may view the risks associated with different crimes in the same manner as an investor assesses the risks of various stocks within a portfolio, picking and choosing among the best alternatives. Furthermore, some opportunity seekers experience psychological pleasure from a criminal lifestyle and the risks associated with committing serious crimes.

Psychological Coping Mechanisms Associated with White-Collar Crimes

Board members, executives, managers, politicians, and others who violate white-collar criminal statutes rarely regard themselves as criminals. Instead, they are more likely to view themselves as misunderstood but law-abiding citizens. White-collar criminals use a variety of ego defense mechanisms to reduce the anxiety associated with their crimes.[16] The first line of defense for almost all criminals is to deny their misdeeds.

When evidence of their guilt is strong, other rationalizations will likely be used. The term "misunderstanding" is a staple of the criminal's lexicon. Specifically, they adopt an innocent posture to reduce the severity of legal repercussions and to maintain their self esteem and social status.[17]

Cognitive dissonance is the negative or uneasy feeling that people have after they have engaged in a questionable act or decision. When people assume a large mortgage on an expensive home, agree to a risky business venture, or commit an illegal act, they may have dissonant feelings. Since dissonance is uncomfortable, people use a variety of psychological ploys to reduce it. They may describe being mortgaged to the hilt as a "wise investment decision" or that their risky business venture will benefit the community. Criminals too use psychological ploys to reduce dissonance before, during, and after committing a crime.

The claim that eliminates the most cognitive dissonance for a white-collar criminal is to state and, perhaps to believe, that they are innocent of any wrongdoing. The denial-of-wrongdoing defense is often the initial response of CEOs and board members when trouble surfaces. Some perpetrators deny culpability even in the face of overwhelming evidence to the contrary. The defense strategy during the trial of Kenneth Lay and Jeffrey Skilling was simply to deny that any wrongdoing occurred at Enron. Instead, their attorneys blamed the energy company's fall on adverse newspaper reports, short-selling investors, and a market panic that caused Enron shares to plummet. Even after a Houston jury convicted Lay and Skilling on a total of twenty-six federal conspiracy and fraud charges, both former CEOs steadfastly maintained their innocence. Once confronted with the incontrovertible facts of the crime, however, executives and managers often resort to other rationalizations.

Denying knowledge of a crime or act of corruption is one step removed from denial of wrongdoing. Board members, CEOs, and top-level managers almost always claim that they are unaware of any malfeasance in their organizations, and they usually lay the blame at the feet of their subordinates. The age-old, "ignorance of the law is no excuse," still holds true for both white-collar and street crimes. But ignorance of the facts surrounding a crime may be a legitimate defense for a defendant facing criminal charges.[18] Top executives and corporate board members have routinely pled ignorance, claiming they had no knowledge of or were kept in the dark about fraudulent activities.

A variation of the denial of knowledge defense is the executive's excuse that he did not have the professional expertise to detect a white-collar crime. Kenneth Lay's codefendant, Jeffrey Skilling, told a nationwide audience watching the *Larry King Live* show that he was not an accountant and could not have known that Enron's financial statements were in error. When King asked Skilling whether he was required to take accounting courses while a Harvard MBA student, he simply reiterated that he was not an accountant. Being asleep at the switch or ignorant may be poor management, but it is not necessarily a crime.[19]

In large multinational enterprises, one cannot expect a CEO to be aware of everything that occurs. Top managers spend a great deal of their time formulating strategies and meeting with influential business people, industry groups, and politicians. They cannot oversee the daily activities of vice presidents, division managers, facility supervisors, and staff personnel. HealthSouth's Richard Scrushy, who was acquitted of criminal charges, never attended any of the meetings where executives devised ways to inflate earnings as part of an alleged $2.7 billion accounting fraud.[20] But the hands-on management style of Bernard Ebbers may have contributed heavily to his conviction. Scott Sullivan, WorldCom's former CFO, claimed during Mr. Ebbers's trial that the CEO micromanaged nearly every aspect of WorldCom's business from arcane financial issues to the length of employee smoking breaks.[21]

Perpetrators of white-collar crime are usually trusted individuals who may go to great lengths to hide their misdeeds from top management. The transgressions at Enron, WorldCom, and Arthur Andersen took place over a period of several years before problems surfaced that led to the downfall of these companies. It is difficult to know when the corporate boards and top management teams became aware of these illicit activities and what steps they might have taken to control the damage.

A critical issue surrounding major white-collar crimes is the extent to which top executives should be held responsible for crimes committed during their time at the corporate helm. One extreme view is that CEOs are earning multimillion-dollar salaries, and they should be held responsible for all that goes on in their corporations, both good and bad. The "honest-but-ignorant" defense strategy may succeed, however, because significant evidence of an executive's knowledge about or participation in a wrongdoing is required before determining guilt. Speculation or moral judgments about what a CEO or board knew or should have known is the stuff of editorial pages, not legal proceedings.

One of the issues that will continue to plague the prosecution of white-collar criminals is establishing adequate evidence of guilt beyond a reasonable doubt. This burden may be relatively easy to meet when prosecuting those who were directly involved in committing the crime. Accountants who construct fraudulent financial statements, doctors who bill health insurers for services never rendered, office managers who order the shredding of documents to obstruct justice, and brokers who buy and sell stock immediately after receiving inside information all have first-hand knowledge that a crime was committed. Proving that corporate executives knew about the commission of a crime, however, may be exceedingly difficult. A strategy increasingly used by prosecutors is to first indict those closest to the crime (perhaps a middle-level manager) and then agree to drop or reduce the charges in exchange for information that will lead to the prosecution of higher-level managers or the CEO.

Since fraud is a key element in many white-collar crimes, determining whether the parties acted with an intent to defraud becomes critical. The former Enron prosecution team member and University of Texas law professor Samuel Buell described the complexity of assessing the intent of those accused of fraud in the following legal commentary about the case:

> One way to understand the legal requirement would be to consider how the defendants might argue that there was no "intent to defraud." One argument is to say there was no fraud (i.e., Enron was a great company killed by an irrational run on the bank). . . .
>
> But even if there was a fraud in the sense that people were deceived about Enron, that doesn't automatically mean that the defendants had the "intent to defraud." The other argument the defendants will make is that they didn't have this bad thought in their heads called "intent to defraud." . . .
>
> [W]hen we talk about "intent to defraud" in the criminal law, we usually mean something more general like "bad purpose" or "awareness of wrongdoing." We look for this consciousness of wrongdoing in fraud cases because norms about what's permissible

vs. what's out of bounds in commercial conduct are so dependent on context (the used car dealer can do lots of things the securities offeror cannot).

So look for this trial . . . potentially to turn on small pieces of evidence that might tell a great deal about the extent to which the defendants were thinking *at the time of their conduct* that they were engaged in something wrongful. Often, this telling kind of evidence takes the form of efforts to conceal some important fact about a defendant's conduct from others, in a way that indicates the defendant feared reprisal or rebuke for what he or she was doing. . . .

A little evidence can be very telling in this regard.[22]

A white-collar criminal may claim that he was experiencing a personal or financial crisis. Uninsured medical expenses, gambling debts, past-due mortgage or automobile payments, credit card debts, victimization by extortion, or an expensive drug habit are among the reasons cited by white-collar criminals who are apprehended for committing acts of theft or embezzlement. Acts of organizational crime and corruption are also attributed to family crises, work-induced stress, psychological problems, and romantic entanglements that impaired the perpetrator's otherwise sound judgment. White-collar criminals who use personal and financial reasons to explain or justify their actions almost always make it clear that their illegal behavior represents an aberration. They may claim that personal pride made it difficult for them to seek help through legitimate channels. What remains unknown, however, is whether the offense for which the perpetrator is caught is actually the first offense or whether the crime is the only visible link in a chain of undetected crimes. The crisis excuse also ignores the fact that others facing insurmountable personal problems did not resort to crime.

Some white-collar criminals such as the aforementioned crisis responders and opportunity takers mitigate their actions by claiming that they encountered a situation that was too good to resist. Once the opportunity presented itself, they may bolster their rationalization by claiming that they are "only human" and made a serious misjudgment during a weak moment. The local politician who accepts a bribe from a construction firm, the manager who cannot resist acting on an inside stock tip, or the retail grocer who agrees to help drug dealers launder money are all examples of criminals reacting to a golden opportunity. These white-collar criminals hasten to add that they had always been law-abiding citizens, and they will never again succumb to such temptations.

Persons who steal or embezzle money and misappropriate other organizational resources often claim they were merely borrowing, and they had planned to make restitution to the organization before being caught. An embezzler may claim that she was using company funds to obtain a temporary loan to cover past-due debts and that she intended to replace the money on her next payday. If she cannot make restitution, she may commit additional crimes to cover her tracks (the linked decisions noted earlier). Lapping, for example, is a scheme in which an employee steals the receipts from one customer and uses subsequent payments by other customers to cover the theft. After stealing the money paid by Customer A, the employee uses Customer B's payment to cover Customer A's account and then uses Customer C's payment to pay Customer B's account, and so forth. Lapping schemes can be perpetuated for months or even years.[23]

The deserving-victim excuse has long been a staple in the criminal's repertoire of rationalizations. White-collar criminals may justify their actions by stating that the organization has cheated customers and employees, engaged in financial fraud, or perpetrated environmental crimes. Since the organization is bad, the rationalization goes, it too deserves to be victimized. Some health care providers may have no compunction about committing Medicaid fraud because they view Medicaid recipients as somehow less worthy than people who do not receive these benefits. Similarly, physicians who overcharge the Medicare program do so because they believe Medicare rates are too low and the federal government is taking unfair advantage of medical professionals.

Individuals who commit crimes against their organizations may rationalize their actions by stating that they are seeking revenge against the organization or an authority figure in the organization. Employees may claim that they have a score to settle because their supervisor failed to respect their dignity or publicly humiliated them. The crime may be directed at the supervisor or at the employee's department, facility, or organization. From a white-collar crime perspective, planting a computer virus, deleting computer files, or disclosing proprietary information might constitute an act of revenge directed at an authority figure.

After a group of managers resigned from their positions at a technology-based firm and were hired at a competing firm, their previous employer sued them for violating a noncompete agreement. The managers retaliated by going public with information about criminal and corrupt actions at their former company.[24]

When employees believe they have not been rewarded adequately because of low compensation, being passed over for a promotion, or a lack of individual recognition, they may engage in theft or embezzlement. If the employee is caught, he may claim that he was evening the score and collecting past due debts that were owed to him by the organization. This rationalization harkens back to J. Stacy Adams's equity theory from chapter one. When employees find themselves in an under-reward situation (i.e., their outcome-input ratio is less than the ratio of a referent other), they either attempt to increase outcomes (e.g., stealing from their employer) or decrease inputs (e.g., working less). In situations where decreasing inputs is difficult (because of a regimented work environment) and increasing outcomes is unlikely (the supervisor refuses to grant a pay raise), employees may engage in illegal or corrupt acts to achieve equity.

Some white-collar criminals claim that their crimes have minimal impact on the victim or society. Suppose that a warehouse employee steals $1,000 worth of merchandise from his employer, a discount retailer. He might claim that his theft could not possibly hurt the store chain whose annual sales are in the hundreds of billions of dollars. Similarly, a person manufacturing and distributing counterfeit compact disks may point to the fact that the recording artists are multimillionaires who will not be harmed by the loss of a few dollars.

The minimization rationalization is especially devastating because single organizational crimes and acts of corruption are usually not egregious. The low economic impact of many individual white-collar crimes (e.g., stealing small amounts of supplies, inflating travel vouchers by 10 percent over actual expenses, or shortchanging each customer by one dollar) makes this rationalization convenient, and it enables criminals to engage in these small transgressions repeatedly. The cumulative effect of these crimes, however, can be devastating as individuals continue the small thefts and, possibly, encourage other employees to do likewise. Furthermore, seemingly insignificant acts can entice perpetrators to escalate their crimes (sometimes slowly) into more serious ones. The escalation occurs because perpetrators are encouraged by their ability to escape detection and punishment for these crimes.

Saying there is no readily identifiable victim is an age-old rationalization and is a variant of the "no body, no murder" defense. White-collar criminals may believe they have committed no wrongdoing if a victim does not come forward or if a victim cannot be identified. According to the UCLA sociologist Jack Katz, "to assess the incidence and consequences of common crimes like robbery, one can survey victims and count arrests in a research operation that may be conducted independently of the conviction of the offenders. But individual victims cannot authoritatively assert the existence of tax cheating, consumer fraud, insider trading, price fixing, and political corruption; when prosecutions for such crimes fail, not only can the defendants protest their personal innocence, but they can deny that *any* crime occurred."[25]

If several companies are discovered conspiring to engage in price fixing, they might argue that no one was harmed because the crime was not completed. What the perpetrators ignore is the significant economic impact that would have occurred had the companies put their antitrust scheme into motion.

Suppose a corrupt judge dismisses a DUI case in exchange for sexual favors from the defendant. If his escapade is discovered, he might argue that the crime was victimless by saying that the woman cooperated willingly in exchange for leniency. The judge, of course, would be ignoring the psychological impact on the defendant as well as the possibility that it might encourage her to drive while intoxicated in the future.

Police officers patrolling a night beat in an urban area may be encouraged by the owner of a twenty-four-hour diner to stop by for free coffee. The owner is willing to provide this service because it costs him almost nothing, and it establishes a police presence at his restaurant that discourages loitering and petty crime. The police may soon up the ante by asking for more than free coffee. Free coffee becomes free doughnuts, free doughnuts become free meals, and free meals for two officers become free meals for the officers' friends. A small courtesy may be allowed to bloom into an act of corruption by police officers who are eager to mooch.[26] Not only is the well-intentioned diner owner obligated to provide free meals but also nearby businesses that offered no amenities to the police are left unprotected as the officers spend more time eating and less time patrolling. Since the diner owner initially offered the free coffee, he is not likely to be viewed as a victim (but perhaps as a deserving victim).

Crimes such as financial fraud also lend themselves to the no-victim rationalization. If several top executives conspire to boost the price of a company's stock by falsifying financial statements, the subsequent losses endured by investors can be explained plausibly by a downturn in economic conditions and other factors outside of the executives' control. By spreading or diffusing responsibility to other people or to other conditions, white-collar criminals can convince themselves that they are innocent of wrongdoing.[27]

A final variation of the no-readily-identifiable-victim excuse is the criminal's claim that he bears no personal animosity toward his victim or that his crime was "just business." During a prison interview with an A&E correspondent, an identity thief described how he stole personal financial information from a Baltimore man's mailbox and then assumed his identity and pilfered his bank accounts. The thief hastened to add that his crimes against the man were "nothing personal."[28] This tactic dehumanizes the victim, and it is typical of how criminals with antisocial personality disorder view their victims as objects rather than as people.White-collar criminals who pirate software or steal proprietary information may believe that their misdeeds are not serious because they have not stolen something tangible. A small business owner who finds nothing wrong with downloading, copying, and selling music files and movies might be appalled at the idea of stealing cash directly from an artist or author. Some unscrupulous professors have no compunctions about selling complimentary copies of textbooks to book buyers. Textbook publishing companies routinely supply educators with books to examine for possible classroom adoption. When these complimentary copies are sold to book buyers, the author receives no royalty income and the publisher receives no sales revenues. Educators also justify this practice by noting that they did not solicit copies of the books from the publisher. Similarly, journalists who fabricate stories, researchers who falsify data, and managers who take the ideas of others and present them as their own may also use this rationalization to mitigate the psychological impact of their actions.

A white-collar criminal may claim that even though he or she broke the law, the actions were justified by a higher cause. In Mario Puzo's book, *The Godfather*, crime boss Don Corleone justified his family's involvement in gambling and prostitution by stating that these are vices that people want but that are forbidden to them by the government. At the same time, he refused to expand his family business into drug trafficking because he perceived it as socially harmful. Terrorists invoke a high religious and political purpose to justify their brutality. Savings and loan managers who engaged in desperate and illegal dealing and risk taking in an attempt to bail their firms out of financial insolvency (or to hide impending insolvency from customers and regulators) frequently invoked the rationalization: "It is better to break the law than to have the institution go bankrupt." Automobile executives have placed profits and shareholder interests above the safety of human lives to justify manufacturing affordable, profitable, but unsafe automobiles.[29] "White-hat" computer hackers have justified their illegal entries into restricted governmental and proprietary computer systems by claiming that they did not intend to harm the system or steal information. Rather, they wanted to warn administrators of security weaknesses so that the system security could be improved.[30]

Even the most despicable criminal can behave in a conventional manner much of the time. Serial killers such as Ted Bundy (the Florida and Pacific Northwest killer of young girls), John Wayne Gacy Jr. (the Chicago-area killer of teenage boys), Dennis Rader (the Kansas BTK Killer), and Gary Ridgway (the Washington state Green River Killer) held jobs, participated in civic activities, and treated friends and coworkers with respect. Committing brutal acts less than one percent of the time, of course, was more than sufficient reason, however, to execute them (Bundy and Gacy) or to imprison them for life (Rader and Ridgway).

White-collar criminals are often pillars of their communities. They may participate in fund-raising efforts for social causes, serve as benefactors for educational institutions or foundations, and give their time generously to church groups and volunteer organizations. The acquitted HealthSouth chief Richard Scrushy mounted a righteous rejoinder as he preached the gospel in Birmingham, Alabama, churches while awaiting the jury's verdict on charges of conspiracy, fraud, money laundering, and violation of the Sarbanes-Oxley Act.[31] Enron CEO Kenneth Lay was involved in many charitable and civic events in Houston, and WorldCom CEO Bernard Ebbers was the quintessential good neighbor and Sunday school teacher in his Mississippi community. John Rigas and his sons,

who were accused of misappropriating funds at Adelphia, were respected and magnanimous citizens of Coudersport, Pennsylvania, while
Sam Waksal of ImClone was a popular New York City socialite.

Friends, business associates, and the media focus on the incongruity
between the good deeds and the serious crimes of white-collar offenders. The criminals themselves draw on the support and strength of their
loyal friends and business associates to soften the belief that they are
criminals. The fact that the good outweighs the bad (at least in the criminal's mind) makes the white-collar criminal feel as though he or she is
off the hook and has little to fear. Prosecutors and judges often appear to
view exemplary deeds as mitigating factors either when deciding
whether to prosecute or when imposing sentences on convicted white-
collar criminals. The "good deeds offset bad deeds" excuse is related to
the "not me" fallacy of criminal behavior. Law-abiding citizens feel little
kinship with criminals. Yet the difference between the two groups is
often smaller than it is perceived to be. Law-abiding citizens are capable
of bad deeds and criminals are capable of good deeds.

Ironically, organizations with a checkered past were called on to help
in the aftermath of Hurricane Katrina. Goldstar EMS was in the midst
of an FBI investigation for Medicaid fraud and faced a $1.3 million IRS
tax lien when the Federal Emergency Management Agency (FEMA)
needed help. Rather than getting bogged down in the red tape of
screening and approving contractor backgrounds, the Bush Administration turned to both legitimate and rogue organizations for help in rebuilding the Gulf Coast. According to a Goldstar EMS attorney, "It
would be pretty sad for the government to say that we won't use Goldstar because they are being investigated, so we'll leave people to die in
the streets."[32]

White-collar criminals may claim that they were forced to engage in
criminal or corrupt behaviors because of restrictive governmental regulations, strict organizational policies, or unreasonable pressures to
achieve goals. A research scientist may falsify experimental data to expe-
dite the approval of a new pharmaceutical because he perceives FDA
standards to be unreasonable, and because he believes people are in
desperate need of the drug. The white-collar income tax evader may
claim that she was entrapped by a complicated tax code that breeds
"mistakes."[33]

Because of looming deadlines and the need to sell newspapers, an enterprising journalist may find it easier to manufacture facts that will grab reader attention than to go through the drudgery of digging up the real, but mundane, facts that are worthy only of being buried on the back pages. Similarly, research analysts at investment banks might claim that they were pressured into providing glowing assessments of client company stock even when such positive evaluations were not warranted by financial and market realities.

This rationalization enables the white-collar criminal to assume the role of victim rather than perpetrator. It allows them to shift attention from their own shortcomings to the shortcomings of a governmental agency, industry, or organization. They may bolster their rationalization and further divert attention from their misdeeds by calling for governmental, industry, or organizational reforms.[34] What white-collar criminals astutely ignore is that others managed to deal with a less-than-perfect system without resorting to crime or corruption.

White-collar criminals often believe that nonviolent crimes are not truly crimes. Individuals who commit acts of fraud, embezzlement, or environmental pollution are viewed as being different from street criminals by both the white-collar criminals themselves and by society. White-collar criminals may refer to their crimes in euphemistic terms. They may refer to a fraud or insider trading conviction as "that stock deal." Rarely do they refer to their actions as a crime.

Some white-collar criminals may claim that they adhered to the letter of the law even though the spirit of the law was clearly violated. The chief financial officer who conspires to commit financial fraud and mislead investors may claim that GAAP were not violated. Instead, she may point to the fact that GAAP contain ample gray areas that can be interpreted broadly, notwithstanding the fact that federal prosecutors viewed the principles more strictly than she. It was her honest difference of opinion with federal prosecutors (rather than her dishonesty or her gross incompetence) that led to her conviction for conspiracy and securities fraud.

The fact that white-collar crimes are not violent, that they can be explained using euphemistic language, and that they involve subjective interpretations of the law all enable the white-collar criminal to rationalize and reduce the psychological discomfort associated with these acts. What white-collar criminals may not realize is that violent criminals use the same rationalizations. The abusive husband who threatens to kill his wife and verbally taunts her does not regard himself as violent; in his mind, the violent abusers are the husbands who bludgeon, stab, or shoot their spouses.[35] When interviewed, a convicted rapist who tried to beat his victim to death euphemistically described the need to clear up the frivolous case against him so that he could be released from prison and resume a normal life. Violent criminals frequently blame their troubles on plea-bargaining accomplices, vindictive police officers, politically motivated prosecutors, incompetent defense attorneys, biased judges, and ignorant jurors. White-collar criminals do the same.

White-collar criminals find solace in the fact that they did not act alone and that other executives and managers share their guilt. By being part of a corrupt group, the perpetrator is able to diffuse responsibility and to believe that no crime was committed, notwithstanding a criminal statute to the contrary. The most egregious use of this rationalization might have been by the guards and officers who worked in the Nazi death camps.

Deviant behaviors such as white-collar crime do not occur in isolation. Individuals who face conviction and punishment for white-collar crimes are quick to cite the fact that their colleagues and the organizational culture encouraged their corrupt behavior. They may claim that top management engaged in illegal acts themselves or that they looked the other way when such acts were committed by employees, suppliers, or customers. In other instances, white-collar criminals rationalize and shift blame by saying that their corrupt superiors coerced or tricked them into committing illegal or corrupt acts.

Most white-collar crimes involve conspiracies or at least the knowledge by other persons that illegal activities are taking place. The rationalization of "I'm not the only one," is a way of normalizing deviant behavior. Phrases such as "You have to go along to get along," "Boys will be boys," "The boss knows best," and "I was just following orders," have also been used to explain the normalization of deviance with respect to organizational crime and corruption. A variation of the "others do it" rationalization is: "All of our competitors cheat, so we have to do it too." Automobile dealers may use this excuse to legitimize rolling back the odometer mileage on preowned vehicles. College coaches may complain that it is impossible to recruit blue-chip athletes unless under-the-table payments are made in violation of NCAA regulations. Firms that generate hazardous waste may justify illegal dumping as a means of containing costs in a corrupt and highly competitive industry.

If something is normal, the logic goes, then how can it be bad? Deviance, a concept referred to extensively by sociologists, has been viewed from several perspectives. An absolutist theory of deviance is influenced by religious doctrine. If a belief or behavior is contrary to religious teachings, it is regarded as deviant. The absolutist theory has become less relevant in explaining deviance in organizational life because of the increasing religious and cultural diversity in the workplace. Objectivist theory is based on the establishment and violation of societal norms. People act in social situations in ways that test and alter the boundaries set by these norms. The extent to which someone strays from societal norms is a measure of deviant behavior. Subjectivist theory places emphasis on society's reaction to certain behaviors.[36] During the late-nineteenth century, the ruthless and monopolistic business tactics of robber baron industrialists were tolerated to a greater extent than such tactics would be tolerated today. Similarly, discriminatory workplace practices that were condoned by the racist and sexist prejudices of the first half of the twentieth century had become morally unacceptable and illegal by the early twenty-first century.

Although the term "deviance" has a negative connotation, deviance can also be beneficial. Durkheim argued that deviance (such as organizational crime and corruption) encourages society to re-examine what behaviors are good and bad, and this examination facilitates changes in norms.[37] Criminal behaviors are, by definition, a form of deviance that society has decided not to tolerate. Yet, some crimes have a high degree of moral ambiguity. White-collar crimes contain greater moral ambiguity than street crimes. Most people agree, for example, that robbing a convenience store is morally wrong, but society is less certain about the morality of white-collar crimes such as insider trading, stock parking (transferring stock ownership to a third party to conceal an illegal activity), or certain kinds of fraud. Persons working in the criminal justice system view persons who use illegal drugs as criminals. Some health care professionals, however, believe that drug abuse and addiction should be decriminalized. In their opinion, users of illegal drugs should be given treatment that eliminates or diminishes drug abuse and dependency. By doing so, the jail and prison population would be reduced and the multibillion-dollar drug trafficking industry in the United States would largely disappear.

Organizational crime and corruption can be viewed in a similar vein. If white-collar criminals fail to regard their behavior as deviant, then they will have fewer reservations about committing such crimes. If the criminal justice system supports this view, then little effort will be made to prosecute these crimes with fervor.

Linking the Psychological Coping Mechanisms to Perpetrators and Crimes

The selection of a particular psychological coping mechanism probably depends on whether the perpetrator is a crisis responder, opportunity taker, or opportunity seeker. Furthermore, the selection of coping mechanisms is likely to be affected by the perpetrator's personal characteristics, type of crime or act of corruption, and the stage of the crime. Crisis responders will likely focus on psychological coping mechanisms that place them in the role of being a victim rather than a perpetrator. They want to be portrayed as the person who made just one mistake. Rationalizations such as: "I had no other choice," "The system made me do it," "I broke the law, but I'm not a criminal," "I'm really a good person who made a stupid decision," or "I plan to make restitution," best fit crisis responders.

Opportunity takers might use the same rationalizations, especially if they have never before been accused of a crime and they want to convince either their superiors or their prosecutors that they are really crisis responders. In addition, opportunity takers may have a tendency to view the organization or other victims as ignorant, gullible, greedy, and deserving of their fate. Rationalizations such as "Those idiots were practically begging me to steal from them" (golden opportunity), "This company does not care about its employees, so when I saw that no one was watching, I put the merchandise in my trunk" (deserving victim, revenge, or restoring equity), "I substituted these cheap parts for the more expensive ones, billed the company for the more expensive parts, and pocketed the difference. No one is the wiser, and I earned an easy $4,000" (no real victim and minimizing the impact).

Opportunity seekers view crime as a business, and if the white-collar criminal suffers from antisocial personality disorder, they may spend little time rationalizing their misdeeds because they feel no remorse for what they have done. Habitual criminals often view the world as a corrupt place, and they believe that crime is just another normal activity (normalization of deviance and "others do it too"). Some criminals, especially those involved with organized crime, accurately see themselves as providers of goods and services that people want but which are not available to them through legal channels (crime has a social benefit). Criminals who make their living counterfeiting popular merchandise or pirating software, music, and movies would likely use the "minimization of impact" and "nothing tangible stolen" rationalizations. Lying comes easily to most habitual criminals. When confronted with their crimes, they are quick to invoke the denial of culpability or knowledge strategies.

As noted previously, top executives who are accused of white-collar crimes usually insist that they had no knowledge of the crime, and they often shift blame to their underlings. Shortly after his federal indictment during summer 2004, the former Enron CEO Kenneth Lay agreed to appear on *Larry King Live*. King's interview with Lay illustrates some of the rationalization tactics used by CEOs who face charges of malfeasance. It is quite likely that Lay's legal counsel advised him not to appear on the show. Nevertheless, a humble, contrite, and articulate Lay spent nearly an hour before the television cameras. His forthright demeanor and seriousness of purpose seemed to be one of wanting to set the record straight for the benefit of the American people.

During the early minutes of the interview, Lay made it clear that he had never before been accused of a criminal act. He then claimed that even though some former Enron employees, investors, and others probably held grudges against him, the vast majority of people he and his family had encountered were cordial, understanding, and sympathetic to his plight. He used his heretofore clean record and his perception of the way others supposedly viewed him as validation that he was not a bad person. Lay expressed deep sorrow for the Enron employees who lost their jobs and retirement savings and conveyed the impression that he too felt their pain. This tactic was his way of possibly obscuring the difference between being the perpetrator and being the victim. He reinforced this position with the comment that he, like many other Enron employees, had lost a large percentage of his wealth and that much of his remaining funds would be spent on his legal defense. Lay admitted that criminal behavior had probably occurred at Enron, but he pointed the finger elsewhere and claimed no knowledge of these acts. Throughout the interview, Lay portrayed himself as a solid citizen and devoted family man. Toward the end of his hour with Larry King, he emphasized that he was a son of a Baptist minister, and all human beings eventually answered to a higher power. This rationalization seemed to reinforce his "I'm a victim, not a criminal" posture. Less than two months after he was found guilty of multiple counts of fraud, Lay died suddenly of an apparent heart attack. His unexpected death may have been triggered by the stress of the federal court verdict and the prospect of being incarcerated for the rest of his life. While those who had lost their jobs and life savings had mixed reactions to his death, Lay's family could certainly be regarded as victims in this tragedy.

Conclusion

White-collar criminals—whether they are crisis responders, opportunity takers, or opportunity seekers—make decisions based on the amount of risk they are willing to take to reap the benefits of a crime. Criminologists have studied the thought processes and behaviors of criminals in an attempt to understand why some people break the law while others do not. Criminals are usually rational thinkers, although they may appear, at times, to be impulsive and careless. It is probably safe to say that criminals usually have a higher propensity for risk taking than noncriminals.

With the exception of persons with antisocial personality disorder (i.e., sociopaths or psychopaths), criminals experience dissonant feelings as they plan, execute, and deal with the aftermath of a crime. The array of rationalizations, psychological coping mechanisms, and excuses discussed here represent some of the strategies that criminals use to justify their actions and convince themselves and others that they are not really bad people and should not be judged harshly.

4

The Elusive Impact of White-Collar Crime

Assessing the impact of white-collar crime is complicated. Most accounts of organizational crime and corruption focus on its economic costs rather than psychological and social repercussions.

The multibillion-dollar estimates of the economic impact of white-collar crime are rough, at best, for two reasons. First, as described by the *New York Times* writer Stacy Horn, we do not have a comprehensive national database on white-collar crime,

> but what is most shocking is that we don't know how many more Bernard Ebberses are out there. We have no idea if white-collar crime is going up or down.

> In contrast, police departments across the country must report annually to the Federal Bureau of Investigation every murder and nonnegligent manslaughter in the jurisdiction—not to mention every rape, robbery, aggravated assault, burglary, larceny-theft, and car theft. The bureau incorporates this information, along with arrest statistics into a crime reporting program, which is published in a report called "Crime in the United States." As a result, we know, for instance, that the murder rate in New York City is going down.

> But we don't know how many white-collar crimes have been committed or how many arrests have been made in connection with those crimes. If you call the state attorney general's office, the F.B.I. or the Security and Exchange Commission, no one will be able to tell you how many white-collar crimes were committed in

any year, or provide any arrest statistics. The investigators there could be doing a great job, but they might also be concentrating on a few, select cases for years, letting countless others go by.

Granted, the S.E.C. publishes the number of cases it is working on in its annual report, but this number is meaningless without knowing the total number of crimes committed. What good would it do to know that the New York Police Department arrested 50 murderers if you don't know the total number of murderers?

No one is auditing the agencies charged with white collar crime the way the Department of Justice and the F.B.I. audit the police. And because the bodies of white collar crime victims are not piling up at the morgue, there is little public pressure to do so.

This should change. As devastating as murder is for the victims and their loved ones, it's a contained crime. Significant time, money and manpower are spent tracking down murderers, even though statistically, they are not likely to kill again. But the effects of corporate crime are felt worldwide, sending ripples throughout the economy in the form of decreased investment and product development. Such fraud can send innocent hard-working people, like Enron's 21,000 employees, into poverty or financial distress.

We need to have the same fix on white collar crime that we have on murder.[1]

Second, even if a comprehensive, up-to-date database existed, many (if not most) white-collar crimes are either not detected or not reported to a law enforcement agency. The lack of a comprehensive national database and chronic underreporting make it difficult to assess the economic impact of white-collar crime. We can be safe in estimating that the major forms of organizational crime and corruption discussed here—medical, consumer, and financial fraud along with theft and misappropriations by employees, corruption by public officials, identity theft, and computer crimes—all have multibillion-dollar impacts on the U.S. economy alone. Widely published dollar amounts on the economic devastation of certain white-collar crimes are, at best, rough estimates. Not to be overlooked, however, is the fact that crime also provides benefits to certain individuals and organizations.

Table 4.1. The Economic Costs of Selected White-Collar Crimes

Industry	Type of Crime	Estimated Cost (Year)	2005 Adjustment
all	employee theft	$435 billion (1996)	$542 billion
health care	overcharges, services not rendered, kickbacks	$3.7–$5.0 billion (1995)	$4.7–$6.4 billion
entertainment	bootlegging	$2.3 billion (1995)	$2.95 billion
telemarketing	con artists, sweepstakes, telephone scams	up to $40 billion (1995)	up to $51.3 billion
all consumers	fraud in general	$45 billion (1991)	$64.6 billion

Source: Cohen 2000, 295.

Examples of the Economic Costs of White-Collar Crime

The economic costs of major white-collar crimes provide a starting point for discussing the impact on individuals, organizations, and society. Table 4.1 uses economic estimates for selected crimes taken from earlier studies and adjusts them to the 2005 price index.[2]

The Moral Ambiguity of White-Collar Crime

Added to the uncertainty of measuring the impact of white-collar crime is its inherent moral ambiguity. Even most habitual criminals agree that murder, sexual assault, robbery, burglary, and grand theft are wrong. Bribery, tax evasion, obstruction of justice, money laundering, conspiracy, perjury, insider trading, financial fraud, software piracy, and counterfeiting goods, however, are not universally regarded as hard-core crimes. Although white-collar crimes such as these are illegal according to statutory, common, or administrative law, the morality of such crimes has been subject to debate.

There are several factors that contribute to the moral ambiguity of white-collar crime. White-collar crimes often involve multiple participants with varying degrees of culpability. Some parties to a crime will play an integral role in its planning and execution, whereas others may participate without realizing that they are part of a larger criminal conspiracy. A secretary who obediently shreds important financial documents is following orders from his or her more culpable supervisor.

Some white-collar crimes are halted before significant harm is done. A conspiracy to commit a real estate fraud may be discovered before it can harm buyers. Likewise, a shipment of pirated software that is confiscated before it can be sold precludes harm to the company that holds the copyright on the product.

Actions that constitute white-collar crimes may be embedded in legal activities that are socially beneficial. The physician who defrauds the Medicare program may also be a concerned and caring advocate for her elderly patients.

The specific harms and victims of white-collar crimes may be difficult to identify. It is often challenging to discern the actual harm caused or the identities of victims hurt by offenses such as antitrust violations, bribery of politicians, and financial fraud.

As mentioned in previous chapters, white-collar crime does not usually result in immediate violence, and its victims are sometimes viewed as opportunistic and greedy individuals who have been outsmarted by their perpetrators.[3]

Moral ambiguity has softened the public's perception of the seriousness of white-collar crime. If white-collar crimes are viewed in a less-serious vein than other crimes, then several things may happen. Such crimes may go unpunished. Corporate management may handle internally incidents of embezzlement or fraud to avoid the public exposure of a criminal investigation.

The economic and social impact of these crimes may be underestimated. As noted, criminologists and social scientists cannot assess crimes that go undetected or unreported.

Fewer resources are allocated to the prevention and prosecution of white-collar crime because they are often not as newsworthy or dramatic as violent crime.

Moral ambiguity breeds confusion among executives, attorneys, accountants, and the public as to what behaviors are appropriate (and legal) and what behaviors are inappropriate (and illegal). Under what circumstances can aggressive business practices, hardball negotiations,

zealous advocacy for one's clients, tax avoidance, and creative accounting lead to criminal prosecution?[4]

The outcome of white-collar criminal trials may become less pre-
dictable, and the penalties imposed on those convicted may vary sub-
stantially from one case to another.[5] White-collar crimes often involve
legal and technical factors that are not fully understood by judges and
juries who lack specialized training in accounting, medicine, finance, or
environmental issues. The following is a case in point:

> In March 2004, Jamie Olis, a former tax-planning executive at
> Dynergy, was sentenced to 24 years in jail with no prospect of
> parole, for his role in Project Alpha, an accounting fraud that inflated
> the Texan energy company's cashflow by $300m [million]. On Octo-
> ber 31st, an appeals court, though upholding the conviction, threw
> out the sentence, concluding that Sim Lake, a Houston judge, had
> greatly overstated the losses caused by Mr. Olis.
>
> . . . Judge Lake had based the sentence on the $105m loss to a big
> shareholder, the University of California Retirement System (UCRS),
> that he said was due to Dynergy restating the results to correct its
> dodgy accounting.
>
> . . . But according to the [appeal court's] ruling, even under the
> [overturned federal sentencing] guidelines Mr. Olis got the wrong
> sentence, as he was not responsible for most of the loss. Among
> other things, the court's loss calculation had ignored the fact that
> UCRS bought its shares at the top of the market, that both the
> overall market and shares of similar firms had since fallen. . . . The
> appeals court suggests that at least $100m of UCRS's loss cannot
> be attributed to Mr. Olis.[6]

Assessing the Impact of Organizational Crime and Corruption

The costs and benefits of organizational crime and corruption are oppo-
site sides of a coin. In the short term, the victim bears the brunt of the
costs, and the perpetrator reaps the primary benefits. With time, the
costs and benefits spread and encompass a larger number of individuals,
organizations, and segments of society.

Individual Costs

Individuals may lose most of their life savings or retirement funds to white-collar criminals. They may have to pay higher taxes or prices because of the residual effects of crime. Individuals lose the benefits of higher-quality schools, parks, museums, and other social goods as public funds are shifted to fighting crime. Other individuals may be inconvenienced by tighter regulatory and security measures that are established once the government clamps down on certain crimes. Still others may suffer bodily injury, illness, or death from environmental hazards or unsafe products.

A notable example occurred in the wake of the Enron scandal that led to the demise of both Enron and its accounting firm, Arthur Andersen. Thousands of employees at each firm lost their jobs, and Enron employees aged in their fifties and sixties faced a future with depleted retirement accounts and little financial security:

Roger Boyce was looking forward to retirement from Enron's Minneapolis Gas Pipeline group in 2000. . . . His Enron stock was worth more than $2 million on paper. With that nest egg and other investments, Boyce anticipated a comfortable retirement that he'd spend traveling and funding his six grandchildren's college educations. . . . That didn't happen. At 71, he works fulltime in the summer months doing business consulting at a pool and spa company. Much of his savings evaporated in Enron's financial collapse in 2001. . . .

Dale and Darlene Roberts are still waiting for closure. In 2001, Dale earned $3,000 a month as a field mechanic at Enron in Oklahoma. The Enron stock in his 401(k) account was worth roughly $50,000. . . . Within months the couple lost it all: his job and the money in the stock. Dale was laid off, and the couple got by on $1,200 a month in unemployment until that ran out after six months. Darlene, a hairdresser, was disabled and couldn't work. Dale was out of work more than two years. . . . The family house was briefly put into foreclosure, but they sold one of their cars to make payments. . . . They also sold belongings such as tools and went to their local church for basic food supplies. It was humiliating, she [Darlene] says, to get a chicken, canned goods, toilet paper and soap from strangers.[7]

A less-obvious individual cost is that former employees of scandal-ridden firms may find it difficult to obtain employment elsewhere. Some former Enron employees who had nothing to do with the company's massive fraud found doors closed to them when they applied for jobs.[8] Persons who have been tried and acquitted of white-collar crimes continue to suffer even after they have been cleared of wrongdoing. Former Reagan-administration secretary of labor Raymond J. Donovan was charged with making illegal payments to a union official when he headed a New Jersey construction firm. Upon his acquittal, Mr. Donovan asked out loud in the presence of the media as to the office he should contact to restore his good name. Similarly, once cleared on fraud charges, Richard Scrushy made it clear that he intended to re-claim his post as CEO of HealthSouth. HealthSouth's new management team made it equally clear that they did not want him back. "Under no circumstances will Mr. Scrushy be offered any position within the company by this management team or by this board of directors," said HealthSouth chairman Robert May after a Birmingham, Alabama, jury acquitted Scrushy on all thirty-six criminal counts in the $2.7 billion accounting fraud.[9] May's position was bolstered by Scrushy's later conviction on state fraud charges.

Innocent family members of accused and convicted white-collar criminals also suffer. Anthony Elgindy, a convicted stock felon, was facing a possible twenty-year prison term that would separate him from his young family. "After the arrest, Mrs. Elgindy was suddenly a single parent with three sons—at the time, 10, 8, and 5—who were alternately angry and withdrawn. The situation has been particularly tough for their youngest son, Samy. On a recent family visit to the New York jail, Samy sat on his father's lap and told him, 'Daddy, if I could stay here with you, I would,' Mrs. Elgindy recalls."[10]

Organizational Costs

When an organization is damaged by a white-collar crime, it may be forced to raise prices, lose its competitive advantage, lay off employees, terminate business relationships, downsize operations, or go out of business. Enron and Arthur Andersen's suppliers and vendors undoubtedly suffered due to the backlash from these white-collar crimes. The city of Houston lost tax revenues as former Enron and Arthur Andersen employees fled town. The U.S. Supreme Court reversed and remanded the criminal conviction that contributed heavily to the downfall of Arthur Andersen, although this vindication will not resurrect an accounting firm that once employed 90,000 people worldwide.[11] Citigroup and J.P. Morgan agreed to settle claims of damages in the wake of Enron for a combined $4.2 billion, while plaintiffs continued to pursue other defendants.[12] WorldCom's bond underwriters agreed to a collective settlement of approximately $4 billion for their lack of due diligence and failing to disclose sufficiently the risks to investors before bond offerings were made.[13]

A defunct organization's clients and customers may be hurt because they are forced to purchase products and services from other firms at higher prices or on less-advantageous terms. At the pinnacle of Enron's success in 1998, Kenneth Lay donated $1 million of stock to his alma mater, the University of Missouri-Columbia, to endow the Kenneth L. Lay chair in economics. The University immediately sold the 16,500 Enron shares and, by the time Lay was convicted of federal conspiracy and fraud charges in 2006, the endowment had grown to $1.8 million. In trying to renege on the donation, Lay first asked that the money be redirected to help Hurricane Katrina evacuees in Houston (where he lived), and then one of his attorneys asked the school to return the unspent endowment to offset Lay's legal fees. Although the fate of the endowment has yet to be determined, the fallout from Enron's collapse and Lay's felony conviction may have cost the university a chance to add a distinguished economist to its faculty.[14] Even when the organization avoids bankruptcy and remains intact, the publicity generated by a white-collar crime usually causes key financial measures and the price of a company's stock to decline, causing a loss of wealth for investors.[15] Other forms of white-collar crime lead to increased insurance premiums, beefed-up security forces and surveillance technology, and shrinkage caused by theft from loading docks, warehouses, and retail areas.

Societal Costs

When a segment of society is victimized by white-collar crime, state and federal jurisdictions must foot the bill for criminal investigations, trials, and the incarceration of white-collar criminals. Environmental crimes may damage large expanses of air, land, and water causing real estate values to plummet and diminishing the quality of life in communities near the polluted sites. Crime forces the diversion of tax dollars toward the criminal justice system and away from beneficial public services such as hospitals, parks, or educational programs. The major crimes committed by executives at Enron, WorldCom, Tyco, and Adelphia have raised questions about the integrity of capitalism. In the wake of these scandals, investors are likely to be distrustful of financial markets, and they are likely to be fearful of being victimized by companies that cook their books, misrepresent their business plans, or engage in insider trading.

Table 4.2 summarizes some of the economic, psychological, and opportunity costs of white-collar crime.

It is not always easy to separate the societal, organizational, and individual costs of crime. The direction in which societal, organizational, and individual costs flow varies from one white-collar crime to another. The savings and loan scandals of the early 1980s first affected the individual financial institutions, followed closely by the individual savings and loan company investors, and eventually the tax payers who were forced to help bail out insolvent firms. Identity theft first hurts the individual whose good name and credit rating have been misappropriated, followed by financial institutions and credit reporting agencies entangled in the fraud, and then by a society that enacts legislation and institutes measures to reduce identity theft. Environmental crimes first damage individuals and their communities, followed by the governmental agencies (societal level) that must clean up the polluted site and investigate and prosecute the offenders, followed by organizational stakeholders who pay for the actions of a negligent few.

Societal, organizational, and individual costs often overlap. It is difficult to sort out where these costs begin and end, and it appears that the government, organizations, and individuals often bear these costs simultaneously. Figure 4.1 illustrates some of the complexities associated with pinpointing the impact of white-collar crime costs. The type of crime is listed along with a partial sequence of the crime costs and its aftermath. Whether individuals, society, or organizations are affected is noted beneath each stage description.

Some regions, industries, or segments of the population pay higher crime costs. Heavily populated states such as California, Florida, and New York have a higher prevalence of white-collar crime. Industries

Table 4.2. The Costs of White-Collar Crime

Societal Costs	Organizational Costs	Individual Costs
Legislative and regulatory costs (SEC, EPA, OSHA)	Loss of money and merchandise	Higher taxes and less efficient use of tax dollars to offset the societal costs of crime
Investigatory, prosecutorial, and incarceration costs	Increased insurance costs or the inability to insure business operations	Increased consumer prices to offset organizational costs and effects of crime
Diminished public trust in corporations and executives	Loss of business and asset productivity	Inconveniences associated with regulatory and security measures
Reduced activity in financial markets	Increased security costs	
Damage to ecosystems	Regulatory compliance costs imposed on firms not involved with criminal or corrupt activities	Loss of property, retirement assets, and investment values
Diversion of public funds from good public programs (schools, hospitals, recreation) to bad public programs (criminal courts, prisons, environmental cleanup)	Firms that abide by federal and state laws are placed at a competitive disadvantage against firms that do not comply	Bodily injury, illnesses, posttraumatic stress, and psychological damage from crime victimization
Criminals forego the opportunity to engage in activities that are legal and beneficial in favor of activities that are illegal and harmful to society	Loss of public and consumer confidence in an industry or firm	Reluctance to invest in financial markets
	Bankruptcy or business failure	Unpleasantness associated with living near environmental pollution and the loss of enjoyment of wildlife and recreational areas
Loss of integrity in the capitalistic economy and a reduction of competitive and market opportunities	Lawsuits by stakeholders in the wake of financial scandals	Diminished opportunities for individual consumers, suppliers, vendors, and employees (both current and prospective)

with more competitive markets and organizations in which authority is dispersed, as well as the presence of flexible work schedules, low levels of supervision, valuable merchandise, high degrees of computer technology, and pressures to meet exceptionally demanding goals offer fertile environments for white-collar crime. Customers doing business with firms in retail sales, the health care industry, automobile sales and service, and telemarketers are especially susceptible to the costs of organizational crime and corruption.

FINANCIAL FRAUD

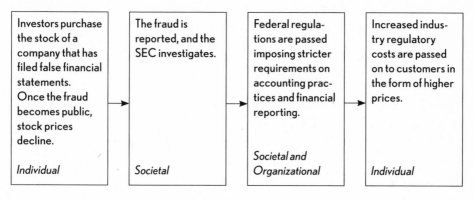

MEDICAL FRAUD

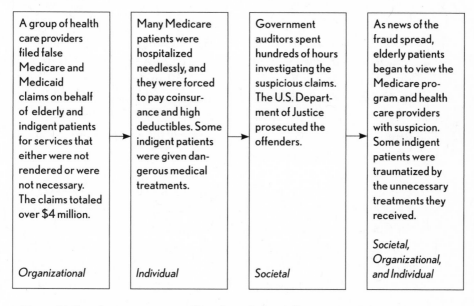

Figure 4.1. Partial impact sequences of hypothetical white-collar crimes

Some consumer frauds such as home repair and sweepstakes-prize scams impose a disproportionately high cost on the elderly. Securities fraud is likely to affect individuals with ample savings accounts, whereas identity theft victims are usually middle-class individuals with good credit histories. Victims of environmental crime are often members of

racial or ethnic minorities living in low-income areas near industrial facilities or waste disposal sites.

The High-Calorie White-Collar Crime Revisited

Recall the case of Robert Ligon, the sixty-eight-year-old health-food executive who was sentenced to fifteen months in prison for labeling and
selling regular doughnuts as low-fat doughnuts. He sold the doughnuts
(as well as cookies and cinnamon rolls) nationwide for three years. The
label on his company's "carbo-coated" doughnut claimed that it contained three grams of fat and 130 calories, whereas the chocolate glazed
doughnuts actually had eighteen grams of fat and 530 calories. Ligon
purchased the full-fat doughnuts from the Cloverhill Bakery in Chicago
for twenty-five to thirty-three cents each and resold them as low-fat
doughnuts for a dollar each. Suspicious customers filed complaints with
the Food and Drug Administration (FDA) claiming that the doughnuts
had a great taste but caused them to gain weight and left grease stains
on napkins. The FDA raided Ligon's office and packaging facilities and
seized 18,720 doughnuts, along with cinnamon rolls and the fraudulent
labels.[16]

This almost laughable crime does not appear to be especially serious.
There are, however, several costs associated with it. First, customers
paid nearly four times the price of a regular doughnut for a tasty, but
fake, diet doughnut. Second, customers on restrictive, low-fat diets were
exposed to a serious health hazard. Third, honest competitors in the
bakery business were placed at a competitive disadvantage, and they
probably lost a significant amount of revenue because of Ligon's dishonest practices. Fourth, consumer confidence was shaken; many consumers familiar with Ligon's fraud will be more suspicious of authentic
low-fat snacks, and the sales of these products may suffer. Consumer
frauds such as these may also lead to greater FDA scrutiny and impose
higher regulatory costs on law-abiding businesses in the diet-food industry. Fifth, Ligon's suppliers, vendors, and employees suffered from the
demise of his company. Finally, taxpayers bore the costs of investigating
Ligon's activities, prosecuting him for consumer and mail fraud, and incarcerating him for fifteen months.

Psychological and Social Costs

All crimes impose psychological damage. Violent crimes such as murder, rape, and robbery can cause a lifetime of psychological devastation to victims and their families. Victims who perished in the fiery Ford Pinto crashes lost their lives, and their families suffered enduring trauma.[17] Individuals who lost their life savings in consumer, investment, and real estate scams will likely bear permanent psychological scars. Even victims of minor property crimes experience emotional trauma. A friend who was the victim of a minor crime told me that she felt violated and vulnerable after thieves stole the wheel covers from her Mercedes. Such psychological pain can be magnified many times for victims of financial and credit card fraud, environmental crimes, occupational safety and health violations, medical fraud, and major consumer scams.

White-collar crime victims are frequently forced to spend time and energy dealing with the aftermath of a crime. Identity theft victims may spend months trying to repair their damaged credit histories. Victims of consumer, financial, and real estate fraud must work with (sometimes uncooperative and uncaring) law enforcement and governmental agencies in an attempt to track down the perpetrators. Victims of financial crimes may be plagued with self-blame, and they may have to deal with the resentment of family members who view them as greedy, gullible, or stupid. Psychological damage of this sort may lead to substance abuse, increased susceptibility to physical illnesses, or suicide.[18] Environmental crimes may force residents of polluted areas to abandon their homes. Employees injured because of occupational safety and health violations must endure the hassles of dealing with workers' compensation, social security disability, and health insurance claims. All of these time-consuming inconveniences impose psychological and social costs.

We live in a high-trust society. When we consult a financial advisor, physician, insurance agent, or attorney, we expect to receive professional advice that places our interests over the personal interests of the professional. When we take our automobile to a mechanic for services or repair, we expect the mechanic to perform only the necessary work and to do so at a fair price. When we use public transportation, we assume that pilots, drivers, operators, and attendants are well trained, attentive, and free from the influence of alcohol or other drugs. We expect corporations to act responsibly and not to engage in anticompetitive practices, deceptive advertising, financial fraud, or pollution of the ecosystem. We expect teachers, ministers, social workers, and psychologists to behave professionally and ethically. When these expectations are not met, both the economic and the psychological costs to the victim can be severe.

It is easy to understand the psychological trauma of those who are victimized directly by white-collar and street crime. But the psychological effects of crime go well beyond the immediate victims. Persons who are not direct victims also suffer because they are exposed to media accounts of crime. During the early years of the twenty-first century, newspapers and business periodicals featured an almost daily diet of white-collar crime stories. Society becomes increasingly impaired as our trust in major institutions such as corporations, government agencies, and churches is destroyed. People become reluctant to participate in financial markets. They grow suspicious of honest retailers, real estate agents, and sales people. Others view health care professionals with greater skepticism. Still others withdraw from school and church activities and, perhaps, avoid making financial contributions to worthwhile causes and charities. Finally, crime and corruption by high-profile politicians and executives sends a message that corruption is acceptable in the routine activities of daily life.[19] In short, organizational crime and corruption creates a level of cynicism and distrust that is hard to measure but difficult to reduce in the short term.

The Benefits of Organizational Crime and Corruption

Individual Beneficiaries

Crime provides benefits to certain individuals. The obvious beneficiary of crime is the criminal, especially if the crime goes undetected, unreported, or unpunished. Even when a criminal or corrupt executive is punished, it is possible that he will realize a net gain from his actions. A once-revered telecommunications industry analyst produced hyped-up research reports that touted a seemingly never-ending growth potential for telecommunications firms. The corrupt and conflict-laden relationships among research analysts, investment banks, financial rating agencies, and companies such as WorldCom, led to the loss of trillions of dollars from the financial markets. Stock prices vastly exceeded the true value of the firms, and investors were misled into buying stock whose prices ultimately crashed as the NASDAQ lost 4,000 points over a three-year period.

Upon his resignation, the analyst received a multi-million-dollar settlement from his firm. His bargain with the federal government enabled him to avoid criminal charges in exchange for a substantial fine and banishment from the securities business.[20] After paying the fine, he appeared to be free and clear with tens of millions of dollars at his disposal and a lifetime of financial security.

Most white-collar criminals do not enjoy such an embarrassment of riches. They may supplement their income and enhance their lifestyles modestly through small acts of theft or embezzlement. Others may swindle their way to larger fortunes only to let their extravagant lifestyles betray them. After such white-collar criminals are prosecuted, their ill-gotten wealth is often confiscated or forfeited in the criminal proceedings. Other major figures such as Bernard Ebbers of World-Com, Dennis Kozlowski of Tyco, John and Timothy Rigas of Adelphia, or Jeffrey Skilling and Andrew Fastow of Enron face stretches in prison where their residual wealth will be difficult to enjoy.

Additional individuals that benefit from crime are those who purchase and resell stolen goods, those who buy stolen goods at a discount price, and entrepreneurs who are in the business of dealing with criminals and crime (e.g., attorneys who represent criminal defendants as well as consultants, investigators, or security guards who offer personal services). Shareholders may benefit (at least for a short time) from corporate crimes such as antitrust violations or false advertising. Professors who conduct research on crime and teach courses in criminology or criminal justice are also indirect beneficiaries of crime, as are the journalists and freelance writers who earn their living turning out thousands of stories and dozens of books about crime. Furthermore, persons who simply get entertainment from reading about or following criminal cases can also be regarded as receiving some benefit from crime.

Organizational Beneficiaries

Organizations too benefit from crime. In the private sector, the security industry generates billions of dollars in revenues. Private companies provide security guards and a plethora of surveillance devices and other technology designed to reduce criminal activity. Prisons in some states are operated by for-profit private firms. Insurance companies indemnify potential crime victims against acts of theft, embezzlement, and fraud by charging premiums that enable them to turn a profit from these criminal acts. Accounting firms have capitalized on the Sarbanes-Oxley Act by recasting their auditing and antifraud services.[21] The news media and publishing houses profit from articles and books written about white-collar and other forms of crime. White-collar crime has also resulted in the creation of private enterprises such as the National White Collar Crime Center and other agencies dedicated to studying white-collar crime.

In the public sector, the criminal justice system exists solely because crime is regarded as a major social problem. Police forces investigate crimes and arrest suspected criminals. Prosecutors charge criminals with offenses, and judges and court personnel are given the task of conducting trials. State departments of correction and the Federal Bureau of Prisons are responsible for housing convicted felons during their period of incarceration. Upon release, criminals are supervised by probation and parole agencies. Thus, crime results in the creation of thousands of local police jurisdictions, jails, and courts as well as state and federal governmental agencies such as the FBI, IRS, and the U.S. Department of Justice. These organizations spend billions of dollars employing hundreds of thousands of personnel.

The public and private sectors have formed a symbiotic relationship in dealing with crime. Private-sector firms provide a wide array of goods and services to public-sector criminal justice agencies. These goods and services include personnel, food, clothing, transportation, office supplies, utilities, security technology, facilities, and consulting services.

Given the low rates of detection, arrest, conviction, and imprisonment of white-collar criminals, it can be argued that white-collar crime does not benefit the public criminal justice system and supporting private enterprises to the same degree as street crime. But because of the extreme complexity of some white-collar criminal cases, extensive investigations and lengthy trials may consume a great deal of criminal justice resources. Furthermore, there appears to be a trend toward harsher sentences for those convicted of serious white-collar crimes that could increase the role played by corrections, parole, and probation agencies in dealing with white-collar crime.

Benefits to Society

White-collar crime and corruption can be viewed as a form of economic activity in that it involves the illegal procurement of cash through theft, embezzlement, or fraud; the illegal acquisition of assets that can be converted to cash; the use of bribes or extortion to obtain cash or assets that can be converted to cash; or the illegal conservation of cash or assets through fraud or noncompliance with federal and state tax laws. Money generated by criminal activities is spent by criminals and their associates. These expenditures increase aggregate demand for goods and services, boost economic activity, and benefit society. Of course, this discussion of economic benefits ignores the more serious costs of crime. For that reason, costs and benefits must be considered simultaneously.

Linking the Costs and Benefits of White-Collar Crime

As noted, the costs of white-collar crime are distributed unevenly across individuals, organizations, and society with individuals ultimately bearing the cost burden of these crimes. It should be apparent by now that nearly every individual and organization can demonstrate that some cost has been imposed on them by white-collar criminals. Society also assumes huge costs associated with white-collar offenses.

This chapter also illustrates that certain individuals and organizations benefit from criminal activities. We might dichotomize the beneficiaries of crime as illegal beneficiaries (criminals and their coconspirators) and legal beneficiaries (the criminal justice system, attorneys, and private companies that do business with the vast criminal justice system).

When analyzing the costs and benefits of white-collar crime, it becomes apparent that the costs of such crimes are widely diffused, touching nearly every person, organization, and sector of society. But the benefits of white-collar crime and corruption are restricted to a smaller segment of individuals and organizations.

The following examples illustrate possible relationships between the costs and benefits of white-collar crime.

Example One: Employee Pilferage of Merchandise from a Warehouse

Suppose that a small group of first-line supervisors pilfers electronic equipment such as televisions, DVD players, and automobile radios from a warehouse where they work. Over a period of a year, they steal $100,000 worth of equipment. If the equipment is kept and used by the employees, some economists who study the impact of crime would claim that the thefts represent a simple transfer of wealth from the organization to the employees. That is, the employees' gain equals the company's loss, with no corresponding gain or loss to society.

This analysis ignores the fact that the organization will eventually have to replace the stolen merchandise, write it off as a business loss, or both. These measures will reduce the company's net profits (by increasing expenses) and reduce its net worth (by decreasing assets). Employee theft could eventually diminish the value of the company's stock, and it could force it to offset the loss by raising prices. If the demand for electronic goods is inelastic (e.g., a 5 percent price increase reduces product demand by less than 5 percent), then the company may be able to pass the economic loss to its customers. If the demand for electronic goods is elastic (e.g., a 5 percent price increase reduces product demand by more than 5 percent), then a price increase will result in a net loss of revenues. The company may also respond to this crime by taking additional measures that will raise its costs. These measures include improved employee screening during the hiring process, additional security personnel and surveillance technology in the warehouse, and tighter inventory controls.

The first-line supervisors who stole the merchandise may keep it for their personal use, or they may sell it to another party (a fence or a consumer). Suppose that over the course of a year, they sell the merchandise to a fence for a total of $60,000. The fence, in turn, sells it to customers at a price well below retail, receiving a total of $80,000 (a $20,000 profit). Not only have the employee thieves and the fence profited but also the electronic equipment manufacturers will now have the opportunity to sell replacement merchandise to the company. Replenishing inventories has a positive effect on the economy. Furthermore, companies that perform applicant background checks, security firms, and accountants stand to profit from this scheme as the company takes measures to reduce theft in the future.

The winners in this scheme include the thieves, the fence, the customers who bought the merchandise at a bargain price, the original equipment manufacturer, the security and accounting firms hired by the victimized company, and the economy. The losers are the company where the merchandise was stolen, its shareholders, and other retailers who lost an opportunity to sell electronic equipment to customers at the regular price.

Example Two: Bribing a Foreign Government Official

Suppose that a U.S.-based company desiring to open a facility in a third-world country meets with excessive bureaucratic demands and red tape imposed by five low-level government officials. It is suggested to company executives by these foreign government officials that if the company pays each of them US$10,000, the burdensome restrictions will disappear. Executives of this multibillion-dollar corporation promptly pay the $50,000 bribe. This practice violates the Foreign Corrupt Practices Act (FCPA), and possibly other laws and treaties.

The most obvious cost to the company is the $50,000 bribery payment. For a Fortune 100 firm, this cost is miniscule. But company executives soon discover that this payment is only the first of many installments required to maintain the cooperation of an expanding network of corrupt government officials who are eager to reach into the firm's deep pockets. The escalating costs of the bribes and fears of a federal investigation force the company to withdraw its business interests from the country.

The costs associated with this debacle are significant. They include the amount of bribe money already paid and the opportunity costs of losing access to the country's favorable labor conditions or unique natural resources. The company will have to relocate its business to a less-corrupt country or abandon its expansion plans altogether. Citizens of the politically corrupt country will lose the opportunity to improve their economic condition and quality of life. The company's withdrawal might arouse the suspicions of U.S. Department of Justice officials and lead to an investigation into possible FCPA violations. Even if executives avoid prosecution after the investigation has been completed, the adverse publicity will hurt the company's stock price. Other corporations and investors will be hesitant to participate in foreign direct investment activities with this corrupt country, and its tarnished reputation will hurt honest business people and citizens who are anxious to do business with a multinational enterprise.

Example Three: Cooking the Books and Cashing In

A computer software company files false financial statements that overstate the firm's net worth, profit margins, and cash flow. Investors eagerly purchase stock in this seemingly healthy enterprise before the Securities and Exchange Commission discovers that the firm's books have been cooked. During the time the stock prices were peaking, some of the company's top executives exercised over $10 million in stock options. As knowledge of the SEC's investigation became public, the firm's stock prices fell by nearly 30 percent, and investors suffered $500 million in losses.

The obvious cost here is the $500 million loss to investors. On closer examination, one could argue that the loss to some investors was simply a loss of paper wealth rather than of real wealth. An investor who purchased $100,000 worth of this firm's stock immediately before the price plummeted did indeed lose approximately $30,000. But the investor who purchased the stock two years ago when it was worth only 50 percent of its peak value—immediately before the financial fraud became public news and the stock price dropped—would (arguably) still have earned a modest profit. Viewing the cost of the crime in this manner might not provide consolation to longer-term investors who, in all likelihood, would still be seething over the bad financial news. Employees nearing or at retirement age who were holding large percentages of the company's stock in their retirement portfolios would suffer regardless of whether the loss is viewed as a paper loss or as a real loss.

News of the financial fraud will damage the reputation of the company, and investors and customers may decide to steer clear of the firm. If executives responsible for the fraud are forced to resign, they and their attorneys might demand generous severance packages, further harming the company's financial position. The board of directors may simply want to exercise damage control by putting this unfortunate incident to rest. Prosecutors may decide that the evidence needed for criminal convictions is inadequate, and the costs and risks of a criminal trial are too great. Rewarding illegal and corrupt behavior with severance pay and amnesty from criminal charges appears reprehensible. But this strategy may be preferable to years of expensive criminal trials and civil suits.

The beneficiaries of this financial fraud are the executives who pocketed profits from their stock options and severance packages, the attorneys who collected legal fees from the executives, and the firms that picked up lost business opportunities from their corrupt competitor. This financial fraud is a classic case of how the costs of white-collar crime are diffused widely, whereas the benefits are concentrated among a few.

Moral Intensity of White-Collar Crime

Delineating and measuring the costs and benefits of organizational crime and corruption are not easy. This problem is compounded by the moral ambiguity that surrounds white-collar crime. Not only is our assessment of the costs and benefits of white-collar crime clouded by an incomplete data base and imprecise methods of measurement but also there are divergent views as to how severe these crimes are.

In addition to looking at costs and benefits, another way of judging the severity of white-collar crime that encompasses both its economic and social impacts is through the concept of moral intensity. People judge criminal and other behaviors subjectively. Their reactions to a particular white-collar crime may range from amusement (e.g., a scam that defrauds a greedy and unethical investor) to outrage (e.g., a fiduciary fraud that depletes the retirement savings of thousands of employees).

Moral intensity consists of six components: (1) the magnitude of consequences, (2) social consensus, (3) the probability of effect, (4) temporal immediacy, (5) proximity, and (6) the concentration of effect.[22]

1. The magnitude of consequences associated with a white-collar crime is the sum of the harms or benefits to victims and beneficiaries. It is essentially what has been discussed so far in this chapter. Thus, the ethical impact and seriousness of a particular crime or act of corruption is high when its magnitude of consequences is high. The magnitude of consequences of embezzling $1 million dollars from a bank is greater than the magnitude of

consequences of embezzling $400,000 from the same bank. Similarly, the 1989 Exxon *Valdez* massive oil spill off the Alaskan coast had a higher magnitude of consequence than would an oil spill that was confined to one acre of land.

Assessing the magnitude of consequences of crimes that inflict significant psychological and social damage is more difficult than assessing crimes in which the impact is mainly economic. Victims of sexual harassment often experience severe psychological trauma even when the economic consequences are negligible. Compare this psychological damage to the damage inflicted by sweepstakes officials who mislead consumers into traveling to Florida thinking they had won a multimillion-dollar prize. Although the obvious loss was the money they paid for transportation and lodging, the humiliation of being taken for a fool was probably the more damaging aspect of this fraud. It would be difficult to compare the magnitude of consequences of these two cases because psychological trauma is a more subjective and personal reaction, whereas an economic loss can be expressed in dollars.

2. The social consensus surrounding an organizational crime or act of corruption is the extent to which people agree on its seriousness (or lack of seriousness). It is related directly to moral ambiguity. People have divergent views, for example, on the morality of magazines such as *Playboy* and *Penthouse* that contain photographs of nudity. That is, the social consensus surrounding such soft pornography is low. Some people oppose soft pornography on the grounds that it is demeaning to women and corrupting to youth. Others enjoy reading these publications or regard them as harmless. The social consensus surrounding child pornography, however, is high because of an overwhelming public sentiment that children must not be exploited and viewed as sexual objects.

Some people view Martha Stewart's insider trading charges and subsequent lies to federal investigators as a serious offense, whereas others view her crimes as minor. Thus, acts such as insider trading and misleading investigators to hide one's wrongdoing for minor offenses have a low degree of social consensus. The degree of social consensus surrounding the Enron, and WorldCom cases is much higher than for the Martha Stewart case. Citizens probably view the actions of Kenneth Lay, Jeffrey Skilling, Bernard Ebbers, and Scott Sullivan as egregious because their decisions had a multibillion-dollar impact on financial markets, destroyed large companies, and caused thousands of employees to lose their jobs.

3. The probability of effect is the likelihood that a white-collar crime or act of corruption will cause subsequent harm. A white-collar crime is generally perceived to be more serious when the probability of harm from the act is high.

Suppose a distraught middle-aged woman commits suicide after being jilted by a smooth-talking con artist who proposed marriage, squandered her life savings, and walked out of her life. Most people would assign a high probability of effect between the con artist's actions and the woman's suicide. Similarly, the probability of effect was high between the illegal actions of corrupt savings and loan officers and the subsequent collapse of these institutions during the early 1980s.

Product liability cases often turn on the probability of effect component of moral intensity. To what extent can the survivors of a person killed in a motorcycle accident blame the manufacturer in a wrongful death suit? A motorcycle in the hands of an inexperienced, impulsive, and risk-prone driver can be extremely dangerous. The case may hinge on the court's opinion as to whether the motorcycle dealership should have known that it was selling this vehicle to someone who would prove to be incompetent and negligent. A Texas aircraft manufacturer wisely refused to allow an inexperienced student pilot to fly his newly purchased high-performance single-engine airplane from the factory. The probability of effect of an accident would have been high had the customer been allowed to take possession of the aircraft.

4. Temporal immediacy pertains to the length of time between an organizational crime or corrupt act and the onset of damages. The more immediate the damage, the more serious the crime or act of corruption is perceived to be.

The temporal immediacy component of moral intensity is especially relevant when examining occupational and environmental crimes. As noted, the time lag between the exposure to toxic substances in the workplace and the onset of an occupational illness may be years. The same can be said of the time lag that occurs between an environmental crime and its impact on people or wildlife.

Temporal immediacy is an important component of moral intensity for at least two reasons.[23] First, temporally distant events, both good and bad, are perceived as being of less consequence than current events. An industrial accident that claims the lives of twenty workers today is regarded as being more serious than having twenty workers die over the next ten to fifteen years due to exposure to a carcinogenic substance in the workplace. Second, as the time interval increases between a crime and its consequences, mitigating factors reduce the moral intensity of the crime or corrupt act.

5. The proximity component of moral intensity refers to the nearness of a white-collar crime or act of corruption. In general, events that occur close to home are regarded as being more serious than similar events that occur in a distant place. Not surprising, a white-collar crime affecting the residents of a community will have a higher degree of moral intensity to them than a crime affecting residents several hundred miles away. The financial fraud and bankruptcy of Carolina Investors caused many blue-collar workers in Pickens County, South Carolina, to lose their modest life savings (they now expect to recoup eighteen cents on the dollar). This fraud led to the trial, conviction, and imprisonment of several prominent business people and a former high-ranking state official. For the citizens and media in the northwest corner of South Carolina, the revelation and subsequent legal events of this crime generated substantial news coverage throughout 2004 and 2005. Most people had a family member, friend, or acquaintance that was affected by this fraud. Residents of Missouri, in contrast, probably knew little or nothing of this crime. If they happened to read about the events surrounding the Carolina Investors case, they probably viewed it as being of lesser consequence and quickly forgot about it. Of course, if a similar crime occurred in their Missouri community, they would likely regard it as quite serious.

Proximity also means how closely people identify with the crime victims in question. People tend to assign a higher degree of moral intensity to crimes that victimize individuals with backgrounds similar to theirs. The elderly might regard crimes against other elderly people as being more serious than similar crimes against middle-aged individuals. Bank executives might view financial frauds against other banks as being more serious than frauds against nonfinancial institutions. The victim of a workplace injury might find OSHA violations by a company to be a more egregious offense than would an employee who had never been hurt on the job.

6. Concentration of effect pertains to the amount of damage caused by an organizational crime or act of corruption divided by the number of people affected. Committing a $1 million tax fraud against the United States government is regarded as being less serious than committing a $1 million financial fraud against ten middle-income investors. A $5 million salami slicing fraud that cheats thousands of bank customers out of several cents each is viewed with more leniency than a computer fraud that extracts $5 million from several hundred customers of a federally uninsured local bank.

To summarize, moral intensity has a bearing on how acts of organizational crime and corruption are perceived, and moral intensity also has a bearing on how people behave when faced with an ethical dilemma. There is a positive relationship between each of the six components of moral intensity (magnitude of consequences, social consensus, probability of effect, temporal immediacy, proximity, and concentration of effect) and the level of moral intensity experienced by a crime victim or observer. That is, moral intensity increases whenever one or more of these factors increase , and the inverse is also true. Furthermore, it is likely that some of these factors overlap. Magnitude of consequences and temporal immediacy may overlap with concentration of effect and proximity respectively.

Moral intensity is perceptual and varies from one person to another. It is probably affected by factors such as a person's race, gender, educational level, religious background, salary, and personal values.[24] Discussing moral intensity in general terms is easy, but measuring it in any precise way poses a challenge to criminologists and other social scientists.

A Twelve-Factor Test for Organizational Crime and Corruption

Moral intensity provides an indicator of an act's ethical seriousness when viewed from an individual perspective. Organizations, however, need a more specific set of guidelines for assessing the seriousness of a criminal or corrupt act. Managers can evaluate the following twelve factors when assessing the issues associated with white-collar crimes and other acts of misconduct:[25]

1. disruption to the workflow;
2. loss or damage to products and equipment;
3. creation of safety hazards;
4. bodily injury to customers, employees, and others;
5. acceptability of the conduct given the employee's professional background and position in the organization;
6. whether a state or federal law was violated;
7. extent to which organizational resources were misappropriated;
8. impact on the morale of co-workers and customers;
9. extent to which the individual's behavior can be corrected;
10. degree to which minor incidents might be a danger signal for more serious problems;
11. extent to which an individual's actions damage the reputation of the organization or industry; and
12. extent to which the incident undermines management's authority to maintain discipline and decorum in the workplace.

A Description of the Twelve-Factor Test

1. *Disruption to the workflow* measures the extent to which an act causes productivity to halt or slow down. *Example*: An OSHA inspector discovers that production workers are exposed to high levels of asbestos. This finding results in an entire facility being shut down for over three months to allow for

asbestos removal. Had management complied with OSHA regulations and spent $1 million for a renovated facility instead of setting up shop in the asbestos-laden older facility, the loss of production would have been avoided and a significant amount of money saved.

2. *Loss or damage to products and equipment* measures the extent to which the organization loses the use of products and equipment. The ultimate loss would occur if these resources were stolen. *Example*: Retail outlet employees steal thousands of dollars worth of merchandise by depositing the merchandise in the store dumpster and retrieving it after hours.

3. *Creation of safety hazards* measures the extent to which employees, customers, and others are exposed to safety hazards. The presence of a safety hazard, even though no one was injured, can create a major legal liability to the organization that can lead to administrative enforcement action, fines, and bad publicity. *Example*: The workers exposed to asbestos in the first example suffer no current health problems, but the harmful effects of this exposure are manifested in several years.

4. *Bodily injury to customers, employees, and others* assesses the extent of an injury as well as the degree and length of disability associated with the injury. These damages can be severe for occupational and environmental crimes as well as for the design, manufacture, and sales of unsafe products. *Example*: Exposure to asbestos in the above examples causes respiratory problems or cancer for several of the production workers.

5. *Acceptability of the conduct given the employee's professional background and position in the organization* addresses whether executives, managers, supervisors, and employees can be expected to exhibit different levels of professionalism depending on their organizational position, education, and professional qualifications. These varying degrees of professionalism should have a bearing on the acceptability of their conduct. *Example*: A CPA would be expected to understand what constitutes accounting fraud, whereas a clerk who is asked to shred accounting documents would not be expected to have an understanding of this complex subject.

6. *Whether a state or federal law was violated* deals with the

severity of an action that violates a state or federal law and can be assessed in terms of its potential legal penalties. *Example*: Financial fraud of the magnitude committed by WorldCom executives would carry more severe penalties than an isolated case of insider trading in which an employee netted less than $100,000 in unfair profits. Whether the violation is classified as a misdemeanor or a felony is also a useful measure of its severity.

7. *Extent to which organizational resources were misappropriated*. The money metric is a direct measure of the seriousness of a misappropriation. Accounting and financial fraud are among the most egregious of misappropriations because they may diminish or destroy a firm's net worth, profitability, liquidity, and shareholder value. Ambiguous situations arise when business resources are converted to personal use. Cases of low severity include an employee who occasionally uses a company car, office equipment, or laptop computer for personal benefit. At the other extreme are situations such as the Tyco case in which millions of dollars in assets were used for private purposes. *Example*: An executive throws lavish parties in which both clients and personal friends consume thousands of dollars in expensive food, entertainment, and other amenities. The question becomes how much of this money was spent for business purposes and how much money was spent for personal benefit.

8. *Impact on the morale of co-workers and customers*. Some white-collar crimes and acts of corruption have a negative impact on those who witness these acts. The seriousness of an action can be measured in part by the extent to which trust is eroded and working relationships are damaged. *Example*: An executive extracts sexual favors from a manager as a condition for the promotion. Other employees are upset that access to a prestigious position was based on sex rather than on merit. Working relationships between the employees and the manager become strained, and their respect for both parties is diminished significantly.

9. *Extent to which the individual's behavior can be corrected*. Some problems are the result of misunderstandings and can

be corrected easily, whereas other problems have deep-seated origins and are extremely difficult or impossible to correct. *Examples*: (1) The manager who inadvertently allows confidential customer information to be leaked to outsiders will not likely make the same mistake again once he or she understands the magnitude of the problem. (2) An employee who has been caught stealing on several occasions, however, may have a problem that will require psychological intervention over a lengthy period of time.

10. *Degree to which minor incidents might be a danger signal for more serious problems.* Seemingly innocuous actions might be a harbinger for more flagrant acts. *Example*: The manager who pads a travel expense account might later engage in a more serious fraud or act of embezzlement.

11. *Extent to which an individual's actions damage the reputation of the organization or industry.* Organizations often suppress information surrounding a white-collar crime for fear that the adverse publicity will harm business. *Examples*: (1) A private psychiatric hospital would likely try to keep the media from learning about a sexual affair between a staff psychologist and a patient. (2) The securities industry has probably suffered significant damage to its reputation with investors in the wake of recent Wall Street scandals.

12. *Extent to which the incident undermines management's authority to maintain discipline and decorum in the workplace.* Once a white-collar crime or act of corruption has occurred, the credibility of the offending executive or manager may have been damaged irreparably. The loss of trust may make it difficult for managers and employees to work together effectively. *Example*: Board members and executives may refuse to work with executives who have been indicted for financial fraud.

Applying the Twelve-Factor Test

The twelve-factor test is useful for making an in-house assessment of the severity of organizational offenses, including white-collar crime and corruption. Two hypothetical examples follow to demonstrate the application of the twelve-factor test (as shown in tables 4.3 and 4.4).

Example One: County Political Corruption

A town mayor and two county council members in a small Midwestern county were involved in an illicit bid-rigging and equipment-purchasing scheme. Each of these individuals held a secret financial interest in three separate farm-equipment dealerships. The dealerships colluded by taking turns submitting inflated bids on the purchase of road graders, tractors, and mowing machines. Two dealers would submit very high bids, and the lowest bidder submitted a proposal that was well above the sale price that one would expect in a normal competitive bidding process. The mayor and two council members also used county employees and resources to perform work for their private farming operations. An equipment dealer in a neighboring county reported these suspicious activities to the state attorney general.

Table 4.3 applies the twelve-factor test to this case.

Table 4.3. Applying the Twelve-Factor Test: Example One

1. Disruption of workflow	Yes, county employees and equipment were diverted from their intended use
2. Damage to products and equipment	No
3. Creation of safety hazards	Only to the extent that farming work is more dangerous than the jobs normally performed by county employees
4. Bodily injury	No
5. Acceptability of conduct	The professional and political stature of these three individuals indicates that they knew these actions were clearly unacceptable
6. Violation of state or federal law	Yes
7. Extent of misappropriation	This case represents a gross misappropriation of labor resources over an extended period of time, and taxpayers were forced to pay thousands of dollars to cover the rigged and inflated price of the equipment
8. Impact on morale	Many county citizens and employees will be outraged by this scandal
9. Correctability of behavior	The mayor and council members will not likely have the opportunity to commit these violations again
10. Danger signal for further crime	Yes, especially if they are not prosecuted

Table 4.3. (*continued*)

11. Damage to the organization	Yes, many will view the county government as corrupt
12. Undermining authority	Yes, citizens, county workers, suppliers, and vendors will lose respect for these three individuals; the loss of respect will likely make effective working relationships impossible

Example Two: Exposing Workers to Occupational Hazards

Employees working in a pipe foundry were ordered by plant managers to perform maintenance and repair work that exposed them to dangerous moving machinery, toxic fumes, and excessive heat. Safety devices on some machines were removed and, in other cases, workers were required to perform maintenance on equipment that continued to operate. Many workers were forced to work without hard hats, masks, eye protection, or steel-toe shoes. Seventeen workers suffered a variety of injuries during a one-year period. Others were exposed to hazardous substances that could eventually lead to cancer or respiratory illnesses.

Plant management warned injured workers not to file workers' compensation claims. A disgruntled former employee contacted his U.S. Congressman who then contacted the Occupational Safety and Health Administration. OSHA inspectors secured an injunction to have the plant shut down.

Table 4.4 applies the twelve-factor test to this case.

Table 4.4. Applying the Twelve-Factor Test: Example Two

1. Disruption of workflow	Lost productivity from worker injuries and mandatory shutdown of the plant
2. Damage to products and equipment	No
3. Creation of safety hazards	Yes, one of the most egregious aspects of this case
4. Bodily injury	Yes, seventeen individuals were injured, and others were exposed to future occupational illnesses and disease
5. Acceptability of conduct	Managers and first-line supervisors undoubtedly knew (or should have known) of the dangers imposed on workers
6. Violation of state or federal law	Yes

Table 4.4. (*continued*)

7. Extent of misappropriation	None
8. Impact on morale	Employee morale will suffer immensely as the result of actions by plant management; they will view managers as uncaring and motivated strictly by economic rather than humanitarian concerns
9. Correctability of behavior	Management's behavior can be corrected with proper training, but they should be terminated and held criminally and civilly liable for their actions
10. Danger signal for further crime	Probably not, now that management's actions have been detected and addressed, plant managers have demonstrated a disregard for the value of human life—if they escape responsibility, management may at some point in the future commit similar acts
11. Damage to the organization	Yes, the publicity generated from this scandal will undoubtedly have a negative impact on the corporation's public image
12. Undermining authority	A new management team with an enlightened attitude about safety will probably be able to operate the plant and command the respect of employees

The twelve-factor test is especially useful for assessing the impact of occupational crimes, collective embezzlement, and corporate crimes. It is less useful for assessing the impact of freelance criminals operating outside the confines of a formal organization or assessing the impact of organized crime groups. When management detects an occupational or organizational crime or act of corruption, the twelve-factor test serves as a useful guide for deciding whether to discipline, terminate, or press charges against the employee. The test combines economic and social factors that can be tailored to a specific organization. Management may also place variable weights on the twelve factors. Exposure to bodily injury, for example, may be of significant consequence in a manufacturing plant but of little consequence in a financial institution. Similarly, a disruption to the production flow is more likely to have a major impact on an automobile manufacturer or an airline but less impact on a library or a real estate office.

Once the twelve factors have been assessed, management may consider mitigating factors. These might include an employee's exemplary work history, the employee's being drawn into an illicit act by a superior, or the deterioration of the employee's physical or mental health.

Conclusion

Measuring the costs and benefits associated with organizational crime and corruption can be a difficult task. Mark A. Cohen summarizes these difficulties:

> Economic/white-collar crimes such as fraud, theft of services, and antitrust violations, are notoriously difficult to quantify because victims often do not know they have been subject to a criminal offense. Even for those crimes in which victims are aware of their losses, there is no central government survey or reporting mechanism to tally these crimes or their costs. Government regulatory or enforcement agencies often collect these figures and may report them as they see fit. However, it is often difficult to verify their methodology and to know if any figures can be compared in a meaningful way. Most estimates of the cost of economic crimes are based on either surveys of potential victims to ascertain their experiences or collection of government data on prosecutions.[26]

The costs of organizational crime and corruption have several additional problems. There may be a tendency to focus too much on the costs of crime while ignoring the fact that crime also benefits certain individuals and organizations. White-collar crime has a deleterious impact on individuals, organizations, and society, but it also has at least short-term benefits to the perpetrator, and it creates employment and economic opportunities for law-abiding citizens. Next, the lack of a common metric makes it difficult to compare the economic impact of crimes with their psychological and social impacts. Attempts to place a monetary value on human suffering are almost always met with criticism. An additional problem is that it is difficult to categorize and distinguish among the costs of white-collar crime. How do we separate direct and indirect costs or tangible and intangible costs? When is it appropriate to focus on the aggregate, average, and variable costs associated with crime? Table 4.1 summarizes aggregate costs, but the value of this information is diminished unless we know something about the average cost of a particular category of white-collar crime and the degree of variance in crime costs. Finally, white-collar crimes are plagued by moral ambiguities that exceed those of other crimes such as robbery, burglary, or sexual assault. Even when there is agreement that a particular criminal or corrupt act is wrong, there may be a great deal of debate on the extent of its wrongness.

Despite all of these difficulties, criminologists and other social scientists should continue to develop and refine measures of white-collar crime. Attempts to improve sampling methods and to sharpen the definition and categorization of crimes and their costs will be useful. Measuring the absolute economic impact of a particular crime provides little insight into its importance. If employee theft and fraud amounts to over $500 billion a year in losses, then it is easy to conclude that this is a major social problem. But this estimate does not tell us how employee theft and fraud compare with other white-collar crimes, and it does not tell us how these crimes compare with other issues such as drug abuse, prostitution, or environmental crimes.

5

Responses to White-Collar Crime

Society and organizations have responded to social problems such as white-collar crime in a multitude of ways. Measures taken by society and organizations to control organizational crime and corruption have two objectives: to increase the costs and to decrease the benefits of white-collar crime.

Points of Attack on Organizational Crime and Corruption

Crime can never be eliminated. Even if legislators made jaywalking a capital crime, a few individuals would continue to jaywalk. But it may be reduced, and criminologists have long studied methods of prevention. These methods include reducing the opportunities for crime, inculcating moral and ethical principles into people so that they will know right from wrong and behave accordingly, instilling the fear of punishment into those who might commit crimes, and rehabilitating criminals so they will become law-abiding citizens.[1]

Societal and organizational responses to white-collar crime can be viewed as points of attack designed to change human behavior. Points of attack might start with parents who teach their children right from wrong. Another point of attack might be found in school classrooms where civic responsibility and ethics are taught. Organizational structures, job designs, security technology, accounting and inventory controls, and human resource management policies are common organizational points of attack against white-collar crime. Legislative and regulatory measures and their associated enforcement mechanisms represent societal points of attack. Table 5.1 summarizes the key points of attack against white-collar crime.

Table 5.1 Points of Attack on White-Collar Crime

Societal Points of Attack

LEGISLATIVE, JUDICIAL, AND REGULATORY
- Passage of new laws designed to reduce specific white-collar crimes
- Increased emphasis on enforcing existing laws designed to reduce white-collar crime
- Providing additional resources to detect, investigate, and prosecute white-collar crime
- Stricter enforcement of white-collar crime laws (fewer plea bargains, heavier fines, lengthier prison sentences)
- Shifting accountability and liability from the corporation to corporate boards, CEOs, auditors, and members of the financial community and holding them personally responsible for acts of malfeasance
- Taxing executive perquisites (corporate aircraft, entertainment, gifts, use of corporate assets for personal use)
- Placing special emphasis on monitoring the personal and business activities of politicians and public officials

TECHNOLOGICAL
- Develop "fighting-fire-with-fire" strategies by using computer technology to fight white-collar computer crimes through the education of law enforcement on matters such as tracking illicit financial transactions, curbing credit card fraud and consumer scams, stopping fiduciary fraud, identifying child-pornography rings, and capturing identity thieves

EDUCATIONAL
- Increasing public awareness of the severe impact of white-collar crime
- Providing funding for additional ethics training in secondary schools and institutions of higher learning
- Providing education to the public by consumer protection groups, local government agencies, and law enforcement agencies regarding financial fraud, consumer scams, medical fraud, and other white-collar crimes

PROFESSIONAL ASSOCIATIONS
- Establish explicit ethical standards, prohibited practices, and guidelines that deal directly with fraud and client abuse
- Establish hearing panels or arbitration tribunals to deal with charges of unethical practices
- Impose public sanctions on members who violate the association's ethical standards and dismiss unethical practitioners from the association (including lifetime banishment)

Organizational Points of Attack

EXECUTIVE COMPENSATION
- Restricting the use of stock options in executive compensation
- Establishing stronger linkages between executive compensation and actual (not inflated) organizational performance

- Allowing shareholders to vote on the compensation of board members, CEOs, and top executives
- Increased monitoring of executive perquisite expenditures

ORGANIZATIONAL DESIGN AND HUMAN RESOURCE MANAGEMENT PRACTICES
- Allow corporate boards to monitor the daily activities of the corporation through a secure website
- Ensure that board members and CEOs are selected based on their professional expertise rather than on political or social factors
- Examine organizational structures and the design of jobs (autonomy, level of supervision, access to resources) to determine whether they create a criminogenic environment
- Perform thorough background checks on executive, managerial, and supervisory personnel as well as on personnel having access to money, valuable merchandise, computers, sensitive or proprietary information, or vulnerable clients

SECURITY AND ANTITHEFT MEASURES
- Implement specific antitheft policies that make it clear to employees that no form of theft will be tolerated; the policy should include misappropriation of company assets for personal use, expense accounts, and time management
- Establish procedures for protecting merchandise at points of receipt, storage, and sale; consider the cost-effective use of security personnel and technology to lower theft of merchandise
- Provide employees with antitheft training and confidential hotlines to report suspected acts of theft

ACCOUNTING SYSTEMS AND CONTROLS
- Carefully monitor cash flows and key accounting measures (e.g., inventory levels, receivables, payables, and expense categories) with special emphasis on observing the development of unusual trends (e.g., cash and receivables are decreasing while sales are increasing)
- Expand auditing activities to include fraud detection

ETHICS POLICIES
- Include ethics courses in professional degree programs
- Promulgate an ethics policy that provides as much detail as possible about proper and improper behaviors
- Provide periodic ethics training programs to employees and associates that reinforce the organization's ethics policy
- Executives and managers exhibit behavior that conforms to ethics policies and serve as models for employees and associates

The objective of these measures is to prevent or reduce the incidence of criminal and corrupt behavior by increasing the costs to criminals or prospective criminal of such behaviors. To a lesser extent, these points of attack may also reduce the benefits of white-collar crime.

Increasing the cost of crime may be achieved by increasing the effort required to commit a successful white-collar crime; increasing the risks of white-collar crime; and increasing the opportunity costs of white-collar crime compared with legitimate business activities.

Individuals often violate the law because the perceived costs are low and the benefits are high. They believe that they can earn more money through crime than by holding a regular job or by starting a legal business. Criminals prefer easy crimes to difficult ones. One approach to discouraging white-collar crime is to force the perpetrator or conspirator to expend more physical or mental energy during the commission of the crime. Surveillance devices, computer security software, and legislation aimed at executives who commit corporate and financial fraud all force the criminal to work harder and more intelligently.

Organizational crime and corruption have unique elements that require a concerted effort by the perpetrator.[2] Unlike many street crimes, white-collar crimes often depend on a disguise of purpose or intent. Documents such as falsified financial statements or verbal assurances such as a phony sales pitch are key ingredients to fraud. The use of disguise or deception necessitates increased efforts by the criminal. Many white-collar offenders rely on the ignorance or carelessness of victims as well as voluntary victim action to assist the offender, however, both of which make the criminal's work easier.

White-collar criminals often try to conceal their crimes. Concealment involves the criminal's ability to hide the fact that a crime has been committed and, failing that, to conceal their identity as the perpetrator. Ideally, a white-collar criminal would prefer that his or her crime remain undetected, but stealth often takes meticulous planning and patience. Concealment also allows the criminal to buy more time. The home-repair scam artist that journeys to a Gulf Coast community in the wake of a hurricane has only a few days to contact as many distraught homeowners as possible, collect cash deposits for the repair work, and leave town. Once the fraud is detected, the scam artist must be far from the scene of the crime. Measures taken to alert potential victims to the deceptive nature of white-collar criminals make their crimes more transparent and more difficult to carry out.

Vigilant local law enforcement, strict business-licensing requirements, and (most important) public awareness of scams all require that the criminal exert more effort to avoid detection and apprehension. Although some white-collar criminals are motivated to take on new challenges, most criminals are looking for a quick and easy score. If the task of committing a crime is too formidable, the criminal may give up and try something else.

Society and organizations may increase the level of risk for those who commit white-collar crimes. The Sarbanes-Oxley Act raised the risks of corporate fraud by holding executives personally liable if they sign off on fraudulent financial statements. Federal legislation enacted since 1998 has increased the severity of punishment (and risk) for identity thieves. Improved auditing and inventory practices and a zero-tolerance policy against theft discourage employees from pilfering merchandise. The prospect of being caught and punished serves as a deterrent to employees by raising the risk of theft.

Criminologists and others have long lamented the fact that white-collar criminals have traditionally avoided severe punishment. As prosecutors, judges, and juries have begun to take a hard-line stance toward crimes in the suites, white-collar criminals may perceive that the risks of crime are simply too great. The convictions and sentencing of Tyco's Dennis Koslowski, WorldCom's Bernard Ebbers, and Adelphia's John Rigas have undoubtedly sent a strong message to other executives whose actions border on the criminal. In the past, the prospect of damage to one's professional reputation was not always a sufficient deterrent. The additional prospect of a lengthy prison sentence, however, raises the risk of white-collar crime considerably.

Many white-collar crimes involve a great deal of planning and effort. The prospective criminal, especially one who already earns a large salary, must consider the alternative uses of his or her time. The opportunity costs of crime center on questions of: "Does crime pay?" "Is it better to work on illegal endeavors or on legal ones?" Time spent trying to cover one's tracks after evading taxes and bribing public officials is time that might be used more constructively in developing an effective marketing plan or performing due diligence on a corporate acquisition. Zealous prosecutors may force a corrupt executive to turn his entire attention to mounting an effective defense and enduring a trial that could last for weeks or even months. The trials of Kenneth Lay, Jeffrey Skilling, Bernard Ebbers, Richard Scrushy (who was acquitted), and John Rigas diverted hundreds of hours of executive talent away from more constructive activities. For white-collar criminals who are found guilty and sentenced to prison, the opportunity costs of crime are even greater.

Societal Responses to White-Collar Crime

Society's primary response to white-collar crime is through the enact-ment of new laws or the amendment and stricter enforcement of cur-rent laws. Legislation as a method of reducing white-collar crime raises several questions. First, are there unethical or corrupt acts that are not yet prohibited by law? If so, should a state or federal statute be enacted to proscribe such acts? How does a legislative body determine when the social problem reaches a specific threshold of severity and warrants leg-islative action? Should the law be criminal, civil, administrative, or some combination of these?

Second, if a new law is passed, should the law be administered through a board or regulatory agency, or directly through the courts?

Third, if a law already exists to prohibit a certain type of action, should regulatory mechanisms be strengthened to improve enforcement?

Not all acts of corruption are illegal. Nepotism in a private firm might be regarded as a mild form of corruption, but it is not illegal. Firing an employee who supports a college football team not favored by his or her boss appears grossly unfair, but it too is not illegal. Similarly, rejecting a well-qualified applicant because of his or her sexual orientation might be viewed as immoral, but it does not violate federal law (although dis-crimination based on sexual orientation does violate some state and local laws). More acts of corruption, however, have become illegal as the laws affecting white-collar crime have expanded.

Crime legislation is enacted because certain acts are perceived to be serious social problems. During the discussion of a proposed law, leg-islative bodies gather information from a variety of sources and experts. Legislative activity is often fueled by major events such as the Enron and WorldCom scandals. The swift passage of the Sarbanes-Oxley Act is a prime example. Regulatory overhaul began in mid-January 2002, and by the end of July of that year, the Act was signed into law. During this six-and-a-half-month period extensive debate, negotiations, and conces-sions were made; the law was a swift response to what Congress per-ceived to be a major economic and social problem.[3]

Some criminal statutes are enacted based, in part, on cost-benefit analyses. Using cost-benefit analyses to justify the passage of a law can be useful, but it can also be misleading. Cost-benefit studies are produced by government agencies or private groups that are concerned with crime. Legislators may not understand the intent of a particular study or its methodology. They may fail to delve into the research design, sampling methods, underlying assumptions, data-collection methods, or statistical tests of a cost-benefit study. Reducing the costs of a crime to a specific dollar value may invite misunderstandings with regard to its magnitude and impact. Cheating a wealthy investor out of $1,000, for example, may be of little consequence. But convenience-store owners in low-income neighborhoods who price gouge and cheat families out of an annual average of $1,000 per household create serious problems in their communities.

Politicians often take a harsh stance on a particular crime or category of crime based on a desire to appeal to constituents. The public's perception of the risk they face from such a crime may differ significantly from the real risk, a discrepancy that can be exacerbated by zealous politicians. Legislators and lobbyists may manipulate the data gathered during an economic analysis of crime to suit a particular purpose. Furthermore, cost-benefit analyses are often based on past assumptions or conditions that may not hold in the future. Changes in labor force demographics, for example, may affect the incidence of organizational crime and corruption.[4]

Estimating the impact of a new piece of crime legislation is full of pitfalls. Legislation usually has an uneven impact on different sectors of society. Medicare and Medicaid fraud legislation, for example, has a greater impact on the elderly and the indigent than it does on the younger and middle-class segments of society. In other instances, a law may actually work to the advantage of criminals as their attorneys discover loopholes and ambiguities in the statutory language. Studies that assess the impact of legislation may fall into the trap of *post hoc ergo propter hoc* (after this therefore because of this). If the number of financial fraud cases declines after the passage of the Sarbanes-Oxley Act, it will be tempting to credit the Act for this downturn. Yet, a greater awareness of financial fraud by investors, a rejuvenated ethical climate, or the harsh sentences received by high-profile corporate criminals may be the more significant factors in the decline in financial fraud.

Federal versus State Jurisdiction in White-Collar Crime Cases

Crimes such as murder, rape, robbery, assault, burglary, and larceny have traditionally been investigated and adjudicated at the state or local levels. Capital crimes such as first-degree murder, for example, are almost always prosecuted at the state level.[5] Most street crimes occur within a single jurisdiction and do not affect the movement of people or goods across state lines. White-collar crimes, however, usually involve multiple law enforcement jurisdictions and can be prosecuted at the state or federal level, or both. Mail and wire fraud, money laundering, computer crime, as well as medical, financial, and consumer fraud typically target victims in more than one state. Under the commerce clause of the U.S. Constitution, the federal government may prosecute white-collar crimes that impinge on federal interests or that affect the flow of commerce among the states.

Federal interests expanded greatly during the twentieth century. Laws on drug trafficking, driving stolen vehicles across state lines, racketeering, kidnapping, bank robbery, gambling, embezzlement from employee benefit plans, gun control, explosives, civil rights, identity theft and credit card fraud, occupational safety, contraband and counterfeit goods, and murder-for-hire illustrate the federal government's interest in expanding its jurisdiction over crime.[6]

During the later part of the twentieth century and the early part of the twenty-first century, the debate over federal jurisdiction intensified. It appears that white-collar crimes, especially high-profile white-collar crimes, will be prosecuted increasingly at the federal level. Crimes that have an impact on large corporations, financial markets, and the environment create a strong, substantive federal interest. Federal government prosecutors have the expertise and financial wherewithal to pursue wealthy defendants who can hire the best legal representation. Mississippi state prosecutors presumably had far fewer resources at their disposal than did federal prosecutors during the trial of WorldCom's Bernard Ebbers. Furthermore, wealthy white-collar criminals such as Ebbers are often philanthropists and local heroes. Prosecuting them at the federal level provides a buffer between the defendant and local politics.

State regulators may not be as strong as the federal government when it comes to fighting major corporations that commit fraud. The insurance industry, for example, is regulated largely by individual states, each with its own laws and insurance codes. State insurance commissions were established to set rates and to hear complaints from home and automobile owners. These commissions may be outgunned by large corporations that engage in elaborate reinsurance schemes and off-shore entities. "State regulators are doing the best they can, but they're not equipped to police multi-state or international scams," says Jay Aughtman, an Alabama attorney who represents insurance regulators.[7]

Allocating Resources to Fight White-Collar Crime

Passing laws and creating regulatory agencies to fight white-collar crime are important measures. Laws mean little, however, unless resources are allocated to enforce them. Cost-benefit analysis forms the foundation for allocating resources to fight crime. Assuming that federal, state, and local governments have fixed annual budgets available for crime control, they must decide what portion of the budget will be available for different categories of crime. More money spent on white-collar crimes means less money for fighting street crimes. Once the amount of money to be spent on fighting white-collar crime has been determined, it must be decided which crimes should receive enforcement priority. Should fighting multimillion-dollar financial-fraud cases, for example, take precedence over fighting environmental crimes?

When governments appropriate budgets for regulatory activity, police protection, and other security measures, they are making a statement as to how much crime they are willing to tolerate. In 2004, for example, the Florida Department of Corrections had a $1.8 billion budget, and the Chicago police department had a $1.1 billion budget. In essence, the budget amounts represent partial statements as to how crime is viewed and treated in those jurisdictions.

Residents of Florida and Chicago might debate whether these amounts are adequate. By spending less than $1.8 billion, some potentially dangerous felons in Florida might be free to roam the streets (perhaps under the supervision of overworked parole officers). By spending more than $1.8 billion, Floridians might waste money incarcerating criminals who pose little danger to society. Similarly, Chicago taxpayers are willing to allocate $1.1 billion to reduce the number of murders, sexual assaults, robberies, and other crimes in their city. By spending less, crime levels in Chicago might rise. Spending more than $1.1 billion might reduce crime in Chicago but at the expense of socially beneficial entities such as schools, parks, public hospitals, and important social programs.

The absolute dollar amount that a jurisdiction allocates to fighting crime provides little insight into its adequacy. Whether Florida's $1.8 billion corrections budget or Chicago's $1.1 billion police budget are adequate cannot be determined without additional analysis. According to some economists, society should increase crime-fighting expenditures to the point where the additional benefits of fighting crime equal the additional costs. These incremental benefits and costs are known as marginal benefits (MB) and marginal costs (MC). Additional benefits of fighting crime might include a reduction in financial frauds, fewer consumer scams, or a decline in deaths caused by occupational hazards. Additional costs include (respectively) the creation and enforcement of the Sarbanes-Oxley Act, more aggressive prosecution of mail and wire fraud cases, or additional OSHA inspectors in the workplace. Thus, the optimum amount spent on fighting crime occurs when marginal costs equal marginal benefits.

In the above examples, the $1.8 billion budget of the Florida Department of Corrections and the $1.1 billion budget of the Chicago police department represent total amounts. What we do not know is the impact of additional expenditures. If Florida increased its corrections budget to $2.5 billion, and the additional $700 million spent (MC) resulted in a reduction of $800 million in damage (the MB achieved by putting more criminals behind bars), then the additional expenditure would have been worthwhile. Once the marginal cost equals the marginal benefit, however, society should not be willing to spend additional funds on fighting crime.

A textbook description of marginal costs and marginal benefits is too basic. Assessing the costs and benefits of criminal activity can be a difficult task because of the multiple social, economic, and psychological impacts and repercussions that crime has on various segments of society. Marginal benefits and costs also vary from one crime to another. The marginal benefits and costs of environmental crimes might be higher than the marginal benefits and costs of employee theft from retail stores. As a general rule, society should allocate crime-fighting resources to those crimes whose marginal benefit to marginal cost ratio (MB/MC) is the highest. If the MB/MC for environmental crimes is 1.2 and the MB/MC for employee theft is 1.0, then society should give precedence to fighting environmental crimes. That is, society should allocate resources to crimes with MB/MC ratios greater than 1.0 and shift resources away from crimes with MB/MC ratios of 1.0 or less.[8]

Society can allocate resources to reduce crime, but it can not eliminate crime completely. Even if crime could be reduced to a minimum, citizens may not want to tolerate the oppressive measures needed to achieve this result. Two key points should be made with respect to white-collar crime and cost-benefit analyses. First, a significant amount of white-collar crime has traditionally been tolerated because the *perceived* MB/MC ratios for many of these crimes are less than 1.0. Instead, society has probably viewed the FBI index crimes (murder, robbery, rape, and so on) as having MB/MC ratios greater than 1.0. Second, assessing the benefits and costs associated with white-collar crimes is more difficult because of the morale ambiguity associated with these crimes. When moral ambiguity is high, cost-benefit analyses are suspect and subject to criticism.

Deciding Whether to Punish Organizations or Individuals

Legislators must decide whether white-collar corruption should be criminalized. The criminalization of an act means that the perpetrators are subject to incarceration or supervised probation. Yet, corporations cannot be tossed into a prison cell.[9] Organizations can be fined, banned from engaging in certain business endeavors, or lose their corporate charters or business licenses. Whether these sanctions deter future criminal acts is debatable. Civil litigation and fines are often viewed lightly by corporations, and shutting down a company does not necessarily prevent future white-collar crimes. Even when fines are assessed, they are often not paid. An Associated Press story reported that the amount of unpaid federal fines rose sharply between the mid-1990s and the first five years of this century. The federal government in 2006 was owed more than $35 billion in fines and other payments from criminal and civil cases, according to the U.S. Department of Justice. White-collar crimes accounted for the largest amount of uncollected debt with a restitution rate of only 7 percent.[10] Once civil penalties have been imposed on a corporation, the white-collar criminals are often free to start a new business or find employment elsewhere.[11]

Punishing a corporation often casts a wide net that ensnares innocent bystanders:

> In the case of a corporate conviction, a wide variety of individuals are punished, including the corporation's shareholders and its innocent employees. Such shareholders and innocent employees will have had no involvement in the wrongful conduct and may not have benefited from it. As a result, no just retribution is dispensed when they are punished along with the truly culpable parties. Moreover, because these individuals most likely lacked the ability to prevent the wrongful conduct, punishing such individuals does not provide any deterrent effect on other, similarly situated shareholders and innocent employees who may likewise, be unable to stop wrongful conduct in their own organization.[12]

Culpable executives, in addition, may be able to use the corporate structure to cover their tracks and avoid responsibility for their actions. Mid-level and low-level managers may commit illegal acts at the behest of top executives. This strategy enables those in the upper echelons to feign ignorance when confronted with acts such as accounting fraud, the manufacturing of unsafe products, or violations of occupational health and safety laws.

To date, deciding whether to prosecute corporations or their individual officers remains uncertain. As the *Economist* reported,

> a common element in both the Tyco and the Adelphia cases was the decision by local and federal prosecutors to go after individuals rather than the companies that employed them, a strategy that sharply diverged from the approach taken by New York state's attorney general Eliot Spitzer, in his pursuit of errant big financial firms. Mr. Spitzer preferred to extract large financial settlements from the firms, leave most of the executives in place, and prosecute almost none. With the key executives, alone, facing the music, shareholders and employees of Adelphia and Tyco were not only spared from having to suffer the continued management of crooks, but also from paying for the privilege. Tyco post-Koslowski, has

made a brilliant recovery, saving thousands of jobs and providing a huge financial bounce for investors. Adelphia's assets were auctioned off: bids have exceeded expectations and investors have enjoyed at least some bounce.

These contrasting prosecutorial strategies raise difficult questions about the correct way to address corporate malfeasance. Even in the Tyco and Adelphia cases, where the targeting only of individuals did much to spare the firms, there is controversy about whether investors would have been better off had the culprits been pursued with civil rather than criminal charges. Then, the emphasis would have been on recovering still more money from the firm, rather than on punishment. But what about retribution? And what about deterring future crimes?[13]

Federal Prosecution of White-Collar Crime

Prosecutors appear more poised than ever to pursue white-collar cases. Between 2002 and 2005, the U.S. Department of Justice prosecuted more than nine hundred individuals in more than four hundred corporate frauds. Once in the federal government's sights, white-collar criminals face formidable odds. Of the nine hundred individuals charged, five hundred were convicted. The more federal authorities deal with white-collar criminal cases, the more competent they become in prosecuting them.[14] Federal prosecutors favor two strategies in white-collar crime cases: deferred prosecution and bottom-to-top prosecution. The first strategy attempts to resolve the case without a criminal trial, and the second strategy is directed at undermining the denial-of-knowledge excuse that is often offered by board members, CEOs, and top managers who are accused of wrongdoing.

Federal government attorneys are making increased use of a strategy known as deferred-prosecution agreements to encourage corporations not to contest allegations of fraud. Under this arrangement, the company agrees to take certain actions such as terminating a CEO or a management team. Computer Associates International was accused of accounting and securities fraud. The company accepted a deferred-prosecution agreement to replace its top managers. The agreement led to the resignation of chairman and CEO Sanjay Kumar. Computer Associates also agreed to place $225 million into a fund for investors. According to one senior Justice department lawyer, Computer Associates "is a good example of a case in which a deferred-prosecution agreement, combined with the indictment of individual wrongdoers, was used to send a strong deterrent message, recover significant compensation for victims, and ensure the company's continued cooperation, all while giving the organization a chance to reform."[15]

Prosecutors may use a bottom-to-top or building-block strategy in large, complex criminal cases. This tactic starts with less-complicated cases and, "building to a crescendo," takes aim at key targets. As convictions or plea bargains are obtained in the less-complex cases, more pressure to cooperate with the government is placed on figures at higher levels.[16]

It was no coincidence that federal prosecutors set their sites on underlings at WorldCom and Enron before working their way up the corporate ladder to Bernard Ebbers and Kenneth Lay. Shortly before he was to go on trial in January 2006, Richard Causey, Enron's chief accountant, agreed to cooperate with federal prosecutors in the trial against Kenneth Lay and Jeffrey Skilling. By doing so, Causey stood to serve as little as five years in prison rather than a possible twenty years had he gone to trial and been convicted as a major player in Enron's massive financial fraud.

Many white-collar crimes are committed by middle-level managers who are taking direct orders from superiors. Once these managers are ensnared by prosecutors, they plea bargain to lesser charges (or bargain for amnesty) in return for revealing information that will implicate those higher up. Once those at the next level are indicted, they turn on their superiors. The process is repeated until prosecutors reach the CEO and, possibly, the board members.

This bottom-to-top strategy does not always work. When evidence of direct orders to commit a crime from higher level managers is not available, prosecutors may find it difficult to pin responsibility on those at the pinnacle of the organization. A CEO or board may quietly condone the corruption at lower levels because doing so benefits the corporation and its top management. In the absence of corroborating evidence, the mere suspicion that top management was aware of the malfeasance is not adequate proof of guilt.[17]

Another concern with this prosecutorial strategy is the credibility of turncoat witnesses in the eyes of jurors. Witnesses in white-collar crimi-

nal cases who agree to cooperate with prosecutors usually do so to mitigate the severity of their punishment. Since these individuals have admitted to engaging in fraud, and fraud involves deception and lies, the
veracity of their testimony becomes questionable. Defense attorneys
often emphasize the unreliability of these witnesses during cross-
examination as they attempt to convince the jury that the witness's motives are not based on a guilty conscience or on a desire to see justice
served but rather on the self-serving motive of staying out of prison.

Finally, the bottom-to-top strategy may be contributing to a sentencing backlash against high-profile white-collar criminals. Some judges appear to be compensating for the light sentences meted out to lower-
ranking informants by throwing the book at the executives whose
criminal activities the informants have exposed. The law professors Al-
bert Alschuler (University of Chicago) and Frank Bowman (University
of Missouri-Columbia) stated during a 2005 Chicago Public Radio interview that the twenty-year-plus sentences imposed on well-known white-
collar criminals may be unduly harsh. They noted that murderers, by
contrast, receive an average prison sentence of only fifteen years while
those adjudged guilty of kidnapping are sentenced to an average of ten
years.[18]Much has been said about the light sentences and lack of prison
time for less-notorious white-collar criminals. Reasons such as the fact
that white-collar criminals come from higher social classes than street
criminals or that white-collar criminals do not pose a physical danger to
the public have enabled them to have their jail time suspended or reduced to probation or house arrest.

In addition to incarceration, white-collar offenders may be required
to forfeit their ill-gotten gains under federal forfeiture laws. They may
also be ordered to pay fines and provide restitution to their victims. In
theory, these make-whole remedies attempt to restore the perpetrator
and victim to the same financial position they were in before the crime
occurred. Fines and jail sentences, conversely, are punitive in nature.
Such remedies go beyond restoring the economic equity that existed before the white-collar crime was committed, and they impose (or have
the potential to impose) severe economic and social sanctions on white-
collar criminals.

In 1987, the Federal Sentencing Guidelines were established to ensure consistent sentences for similar crimes. For white-collar crimes,
the guidelines allowed federal judges to consider factors such as the im-

pact of the crime, the degree to which the defendant cooperated with prosecutors and expressed remorse, and the defendant's prior brushes with the law. It was the use of this last factor that led the U.S. Supreme Court in January 2005 to rule that the Federal Sentencing Guidelines were unconstitutional under the Sixth Amendment, which guarantees the right to trial by jury.[19]

In sentencing convicted criminals, judges were allowed to use the criminal's previous crimes, including charges that the individual neither confessed to nor was convicted of by a jury. Thus, the guidelines created dilemmas for defendants similar to the following:

> Lawrence Braun learned the hard way that being acquitted of a crime doesn't always stop you from being punished for it. . . . Mr. Braun, a former co-owner of a New York company that defrauded the U.S. Postal Service, was convicted by a New York federal jury in 2002 of racketeering and conspiracy. Had he been punished just for those crimes, he probably would have gotten around 2½ years in prison. . . . But the federal judge who sentenced Mr. Braun also decided he should serve time for many of the 23 counts of which he was *acquitted*, calling it "relevant conduct." This last-minute add-on—called an enhancement—doubled Mr. Braun's prison sentence to five years.[20]

The Supreme Court held that judges could still regard the guidelines as advisory. If so, federal judges now have more discretion in weighing aggravating and mitigating factors when imposing sentences on those convicted of federal crimes. But in white-collar crime cases, aggravating factors tend to outweigh mitigating factors. This imbalance has created an ominous situation for professionals and managers accused of serious white-collar offenses. Although the Court's ruling may allow criminal defendants greater leverage for plea bargaining, it also creates more uncertainty when sentences are determined.

Congress will likely be pressured by consumer and victims' rights groups to rewrite the federal sentencing guidelines.[21] The new guidelines could be harsher than the previous ones if Congress recalibrates the point system and sentence structure. In the meantime, the Court's decision could open a floodgate of litigation as criminals sentenced under the now-unconstitutional guidelines file appeals.[22]

A crucial question surrounding the fate of white-collar criminals is the issue of whether judges should impose prison time. The judicial trend appears to be toward lengthier prison sentences as the public has become more aware of the tremendous damage inflicted by white-collar criminals.[23] The U.S. Sentencing Commission in 2003 increased the odds of an errant executive receiving a lengthy prison sentence. An officer of a publicly traded company who defrauds more than 250 individuals of more than $1 million, for example, may receive more than ten years in prison.[24]

In 2002 U.S. Attorney (Southern District of New York) James B. Comey Jr. gave the following testimony regarding penalties for white-collar offenses before the U.S. Senate Judiciary Committee, Subcommittee on Crime, Corrections, and Victims' Rights:

Chairman Biden, Senator Grassley, Members of the Subcommittee—I thank you for the invitation and very much welcome the opportunity to appear before this Subcommittee today to discuss the important issue of penalties for white collar crime.

Mr. Chairman, as you know, the swift and certain punishment of financial crimes helps protect our country's economy. The prosperity of the United States is, in part, made possible by the federal, state, and local laws that bring a degree of order and predictability to commerce and protect citizens from the predation of criminals who use a pen or a computer, rather than a knife or a gun. But as you know, the real and immediate prospect of significant periods of incarceration is necessary to give force to law. Nothing erodes the deterrent power of our laws—and breeds contempt for obeying the law—more quickly than if certain criminals appear to receive punishment not according to the gravity of the offense, but according to their social or economic stature. We think it absolutely critical—not only to maintain trust and confidence in our economy and in our criminal justice system, but also for the sale of justice itself—that there be appropriate and stiff penalties for what we commonly call "white collar" criminals. We thank you for your leadership in convening this hearing and for raising the important issues being discussed today.

The Department of Justice is committed to the vigorous enforcement of the laws against all forms of financial crime. Our position on this issue is straightforward, and we hope, inarguable: White collar criminals have broken serious laws, done grave harm to real people—like the people who just testified—[and] should be subject to the same serious treatment that we accord all serious crimes: substantial periods of incarceration. While we have made significant progress on some issues in recent years, especially in improving the applicable sentencing guidelines, we believe that current federal penalties for white collar offenses should be toughened. We are pleased that last year the United States Sentencing Commission amended the sentencing guidelines for these offenses to raise penalties on white collar offenders who are responsible for significant financial loss, although penalties were decreased to some extent for criminals who are responsible for less. Both the Department and the Commission will be closely examining the effects of those recent amendments on cases that are just now being prosecuted, and we at the Department will pay particular attention to what happens with lower-level cases, which constitute a significant number of prosecutions.[25]

Prison sentences serve several functions. Time behind bars serves as a deterrent to crime. The prospect of going to prison is daunting, and it provides a strong incentive for professionals and managers to steer clear of felonious behaviors. Much has been said about the amenities found in minimum-security federal prisons. But for executives who have had the power and resources to travel the world, deal with others strictly on their own terms, and enjoy the luxuries of life, even a minimum-security "Club Fed" is a rude awakening. State prisons and local jails, in contrast, are especially harsh environments for convicted white-collar criminals who are prosecuted at the state level. For defendants such as Bernard Ebbers (early sixties when sentenced), Dennis Koslowski (late fifties when sentenced), John Rigas (eighty years old and in poor health when sentenced), and former Louisiana governor Edwin Edwards (in his seventies while incarcerated in a federal prison), the idea of spending the rest of one's natural life in confinement is bleak.

Prison sentences serve as retribution. This form of punishment extracts revenge on the perpetrator. Victims of white-collar crime probably receive a dark sense of satisfaction from knowing that the executives who cheated them are now behind bars. The public is reassured that the prison cells stand ready to house both the wealthy and powerful as well as the common street criminal. Some citizens may get further satisfaction from knowing that white-collar criminals and their rough-and-tumble street counterparts will be rubbing elbows and, perhaps, sharing a prison cell.

Time behind bars serves as a form of incapacitation. Incarcerated white-collar criminals are removed from the economic mainstream and may find it difficult or impossible to conduct business activities from inside a prison compound. Cellular telephones are regarded as contraband in prison, and communication with the outside world is restricted. Business associates may sever ties and create as much distance as possible between themselves and a fallen executive. Assets not seized by federal authorities are often consumed by legal expenses, and a high-profile prisoner's ability to make money through book publishing contracts is limited by department of corrections or institutional policy. Without financial resources or outside contacts, the white-collar criminal's business dealings are put on hold unless, as was the case with Martha Stewart, they anticipate serving an extremely short sentence.

Incarceration can be used to rehabilitate the white-collar criminal. Given the general inadequacy of prison rehabilitation programs and the difficulties associated with changing the way that criminals view the world, however, the goal of rehabilitation is probably not realistic. Rehabilitation should not be confused with a lack of recidivism. White-collar criminals are less likely than street criminals to reoffend and return to prison. But their manipulative view of the world often remains unchanged.[26]

Federal White-Collar Crime Legislation

The web of federal legislation affecting organizational crime is extensive. The appendix at the end of the book summarizes federal legislation that affects cases of organizational crime and corruption. Some of these laws such as the mail and wire fraud statutes are related directly to white-collar crime and are staples in the repertoire of federal prosecutors. Other laws apply only rarely to white-collar crimes or are used only incidentally in white-collar crime prosecutions.

The federal laws highlighted in the appendix illustrate the complex legal network that regulates a variety of potential white-collar crimes. Some of these laws, such as the mail fraud statutes and the Sherman Antitrust Act, have been on the books for over a century. Other laws, such as the identity-theft laws, computer-fraud laws, and the Sarbanes-Oxley Act, were enacted in the late 1990s and early years of the twenty-first century.

The international nature of many white-collar crimes poses problems for prosecutors. With the growth of multinational enterprises and computer technology along with the increased mobility of the population, crimes are more likely to cross international borders. This problem is especially true for identity theft, credit card fraud, counterfeiting, and piracy. Countries may establish treaties and pacts to foster the investigation of white-collar crimes and the apprehension and extradition of white-collar criminals. In China, for example, authorities are cracking down on counterfeit goods and piracy. But in places such as Russia, criminals may be able to elude authorities, especially if they have cultivated friendships with politicians. Despite governmental pledges to clean up music piracy, few cases in Russia have resulted in convictions. For those that have, suspended sentences are the norm.[27]

Regulatory agencies may be granted the authority to investigate and charge parties with a violation, or an agency may refer the case to a branch of the U.S. Government for prosecution. Once established by legislative authority, these agencies make rules covering their specialized areas of regulation, administer programs, and adjudicate disputes and rule violations. Regulatory agencies affecting businesses have traditionally emphasized cooperation and compliance rather than punishment.[28]

Federal laws are enforced through independent regulatory agencies and nonindependent regulatory agencies. Independent regulatory agencies such as the SEC and the EPA have the power to investigate and enforce their regulations through administrative proceedings, civil action, or criminal referral. Nonindependent agencies such as the IRS and FBI refer criminal and civil cases to the U.S. Department of Treasury and the U.S. Department of Justice respectively.[29] Similar regulatory agencies exist at the state level.

Business regulation has been the subject of considerable debate by politicians, business people, and academicians. Regulations govern economic issues such as antitrust or interstate commerce, social issues such as worker health and safety and consumer protection, and environmental issues such as air and water standards. Proponents of governmental regulations affecting organizational crime and corruption claim that some businesses act strictly in their own economic interests. If executives and their corporations are left unregulated, regulatory proponents claim, they will engage in anticompetitive practices, commit financial fraud, design and manufacture unsafe products, force employees to work under dangerous conditions, and pollute the environment. Regulation has also been cited as being helpful to businesses by leveling the playing field among competitors who might otherwise use their size and resources to unfair advantage. A development on the federal regulatory front is the increased attention that Congress is giving commodities and futures industries. This development occurred coincidentally as futures and commodities broker Refco Inc. filed for bankruptcy amid allegations of fraud.[30]

Opponents of governmental regulation argue that these measures impose unnecessary costs on businesses and that these costs and accompanying inefficiencies are borne ultimately by the consumer. Increased regulation creates new federal bureaucracies and forces corporations to employ additional corporate staff to wade through the quagmire of rules and handle the ubiquitous government paperwork. The time spent satisfying a state or federal bureaucracy is time that could be spent on more constructive business activities. A prime example is the Sarbanes-Oxley Act. Although estimates vary, corporations may eventually spend as much $1.4 trillion dollars in compliance costs.[31] Opponents of governmental control also claim that regulations stifle innovation, exacerbate inflation and unemployment, and place U.S. corporations at a competitive disadvantage in international markets. There is also concern among antiregulators that regulatory agencies are staffed with political appointees and civil servants who lack the technical expertise and managerial skill to create and administer rules. Finally, regulatory agencies have been accused of being subject to control and manipulation by the very industries they are supposed to regulate (agency capture).

Other Societal Responses

The distinction is sometimes unclear between a societal response and an organizational response to white-collar crime.[32] One alternative is for regulatory agencies to beef up the enforcement of existing laws that affect white-collar crime. An examination of the myriad laws in the appendix of this book suggests that stronger enforcement rather than additional legislation might be the most effective measure for reducing white-collar crime. The attorney general of one southern state, for example, decided in 2005 to step up its enforcement of insurance scams (beneficiary fraud, staged automobile accidents, and illicit insurers that collect premiums but fail to pay legitimate claims) by allocating additional staff and resources to this type of fraud.[33] Congress has also given agencies such as the SEC more money and personnel positions. Between 2002 and 2004, the SEC's budget increased from $483 million to $842 million with 850 new positions and merit pay raises for SEC employees.[34]

Establishing a national database that improves the measurement and analysis of white-collar crime will help place this social problem into perspective. A national database will provide a foundation for assessing the costs and benefits of white-collar crime, making the public aware of its seriousness. Legislators and members of the executive branch can use the national database as a foundation for enacting new legislation and allocating resources to fight white-collar crime. Furthermore, a national database may allow better comparisons between the impact of white-collar crime and the impact of the FBI's index of violent crimes.

Fines and restitution combined with lengthier prison terms are shown to be a deterrent to crime in general.[35] Corporations should be required to pay restitution to defrauded or injured customers, short-changed investors, and victims of environmental crimes. The most likely way of significantly reducing white-collar crime is to force executives to forfeit a significant amount of their personal assets and to endure lengthy prison terms with less opportunity for plea bargaining. The IRS should also have greater latitude to punish corporations and executives who use off-shore entities to evade tax obligations.

Several measures regarding executive compensation are relevant to the reduction of white-collar crime. First, corporations will now have to expense stock options under FAS 123(R) of the Financial Accounting Standards Board (FASB).[36] This requirement should reduce the attractiveness of stock options as a method of executive compensation, and it should reduce the incidence of accounting, financial, and corporate fraud. Although many corporations have expensed stock options voluntarily, some financial officers have claimed that expensing stock options is not practical (although they have no trouble doing so when filing corporate income-tax returns). The real objection to expensing stock options, it seems, is that it reduces corporate net profits on the income statement. Smaller net profits (or perhaps a net loss) make publicly held corporations less attractive to investors. For this reason, stock options may lose their appeal for CEOs and executives.[37]

Second, consideration should be given to allowing shareholders to vote on the compensation packages (base pay, incentives, stock options, and perquisites) of top executives. Beginning with 2006 annual reports, the SEC requires publicly held companies to disclose the total compensation of their CEO, chief financial officers, and the next three highest-paid executives. The SEC policy also requires disclosure on the dating of stock options and the pay of nonexecutive employees who make decisions about corporate strategy and policy. Allowing shareholders to know exactly what executives are being paid may force executives to rethink their role as financial stewards. Furthermore, executives may become more cognizant of and accountable for the relationship between what they earn and the financial performance of their corporations.

Third, greater shareholder knowledge of executive spending on perquisites such as corporate aircraft, business retreats that double as lavish family vacations, and exorbitant spending on entertainment may give executives pause to think before indulging at shareholder expense. As noted, Dennis Koslowski of Tyco and John Rigas of Adelphia are prime examples of executives whose extravagant spending led to their demise.

Finally, shareholders and corporate boards may discover that competent and ethical executives who place company stakeholder interests above their personal financial interests can be hired for much less than the multimillion-dollar sums currently paid to many CEOs. Perhaps the columnist Robert J. Samuelson said it best:

> CEOs justify their compensation by saying they get what "the market" dictates, just like everyone else. Rubbish. Their market is highly artificial. CEOs match their pay with that of other CEOs, as revealed by surveys. But this comparison isn't especially relevant because other CEO jobs aren't open. A CEO dismissed today can't easily get a comparable job tomorrow. Compensation levels are what economists call "administered prices," set by corporate direc-

tors who are usually top executives or retired executives. The result is an artificial welfare system designed to ensure that even mediocre executives do well—and everyone else receives repeated chances to make a fortune.[38]

Organizational Responses to White-Collar Crime

White-collar crime imposes costs on organizations. These costs are of two types: the costs of being victimized by white-collar crime and the costs of preventing future white-collar crimes. Organizations victimized by white-collar crimes incur costs that include embezzled money, pilfered merchandise, the purchase of inferior goods, loss of customer confidence, damaged employee morale, and investigation and litigation expenses. To reduce the incidence of white-collar crime, organizations tighten inventory and accounting controls, reconstitute corporate board membership and responsibilities, alter compensation practices, hire more security personnel, install surveillance devices, dig deeper into the background of job applicants, redesign organizational structures and job functions, and institute ethics-training programs. All of these measures cost money and divert managerial time and resources from the organization's mission.

Corporate boards have the responsibility for overseeing the operation of the organization, and CEOs typically report to the board of directors. The role and effectiveness of corporate boards in corporate strategy formulation has received a great deal of attention from journalists and academicians. Less attention, however, has been paid with respect to how corporate boards affect the incidence of white-collar crime.[39] Ten outside directors at WorldCom reached a class-action settlement, agreeing to pay $18 million from their own pockets. A contributing factor to the scandal and ensuing demise of WorldCom was the board's "near complete deference" to CEO Bernard Ebbers and other senior executives.[40]

Several steps can be taken that might improve the effectiveness of corporate boards in fighting white-collar crime:

1. Corporate board members should be selected carefully based on their expertise to make decisions that will be in the best interests of the stakeholders and on their reputation for integrity.

2. Corporate board members need to receive information on the daily operations of a company. Since most boards meet only several times a year, members should be given access to secure online sources to monitor key measures such as productivity, labor costs, stock prices, top-management decisions, financial performance and cash flows, human resource levels, and any other factors that the board deems appropriate. Management could, of course, feed the board false information, but instant access to key factors would provide the board with better controls for managing the company.

3. Corporate boards should institute policies that clarify appropriate and inappropriate behaviors. These policies should address compliance with federal and state laws, the relationship with and treatment of stakeholders (customers, employees, investors, suppliers, auditors, government inspectors, labor organizations, lobbyists, and industry interest groups), the design and manufacture of products or the provision of services, adherence to relevant professional codes of conduct, and other behaviors that the board deems appropriate.

4. Policies and codes of conduct should be communicated clearly and forcefully to all employees. Communications media should include training and development programs and internal memos that are distributed at least once a year.

5. Corporate board members should be compensated well for their services but should be held personally responsible for any acts of malfeasance that they either commit or condone.

6. Corporate board performance should be subject to an annual self-evaluation.[41]

Serving on corporate boards has become increasingly risky and less appealing. As noted, WorldCom board members were personally liable in a class-action settlement. Enron board members also paid $13 million in settlements. Furthermore, as board members are held to a higher standard of accountability, they will have to spend additional time performing their duties. This increased accountability will make it more difficult for prospective board members to serve on multiple boards and receive the generous compensation that comes with being a corporate board member. Simply stated, the risk-reward ratio for board members is becoming increasingly unsatisfactory.[42]

Accounting systems are designed to measure income and revenue streams, value assets, provide information for the preparation of financial statements and tax returns, and establish controls to protect corporate resources. Most corporate accounting is conducted by the company's in-house accounting staff. Experts from outside the corporation are frequently consulted on new accounting rules, information systems, and changes in tax laws.

Outside auditors are employed periodically to ensure compliance with corporate accounting procedures. Auditor and client interests are supposed to remain independent to ensure an objective assessment of the client firm's accounting procedures and financial statements. Over time, however, client companies and auditors can develop consulting relationships that go beyond traditional auditing practices. As client-consulting activities by auditing firms increase, so do the conflicts of interest that eventually compromise the integrity of the accounting and financial auditing process. This conflict of interest was at the heart of the Enron–Arthur Andersen scandal. Once Arthur Andersen auditors lost control at Enron, it enabled Enron executives to manipulate cash flows, distort financial results, and fool investors. The Sarbanes-Oxley Act now restricts accounting firms from engaging in both auditing and consulting activities with a client. It also mandates that the CEO personally guarantee that corporate financial statements are accurate and in compliance with generally accepted accounting principles.

Auditors have traditionally been more concerned with accounting system irregularities than with fraud detection. FAS 99 and the Sarbanes-Oxley Act require publicly traded companies to place more emphasis on fraud detection. In the area of compensation and benefits, companies must validate retirement expense accruals and liabilities, screen workers' compensation claims, ensure that stock options are calculated accurately and disclosed properly, maintain tighter control of payroll functions, and protect confidential information on employees.[43] These measures all represent viable points of attack against white-collar crime.

Background checks are one of the most underutilized tools for reducing white-collar crime. First, background checks enable a firm to verify the employment and educational history of a job applicant. Applicants have been known to falsify their employment history, educational credentials, and even their identities. Second, background checks can enable a prospective employer to discover information that an applicant might try to conceal such as a criminal conviction, history of substance abuse, termination from a job for just cause, or acts of corruption. Finally, a background check is based on the premise that past behavior is predictive of future behavior. If a job applicant has a history of criminal or corrupt activities, reckless driving, or a poor credit history, then it is reasonable to assume that this individual is likely to engage in future counterproductive behaviors.

Background checks are especially critical because many white-collar job applicants are older and have lengthy employment histories. When a fraud is detected and a perpetrator is identified by corporate management or security, the easiest and least controversial solution is to terminate the offending employee and avoid the publicity of a criminal prosecution. The white-collar criminal then looks elsewhere for employment, and banks on the fact that his or her past offenses will not be revealed. But white-collar crimes cannot be kept completely under wraps. Former supervisors, co-workers, and business associates are likely to be aware of an applicant's corrupt actions, and a shady employment history can be discovered if a background check is thorough.

A major obstacle facing firms that try to check the backgrounds of job applicants is a former associate's fear of a defamation-of-character lawsuit. When the hiring firm contacts a job applicant's previous employer, they may be given little information other than the person's job title and employment dates. A lack of critical information on the employee's job performance, attendance, reliability, interpersonal skills, and integrity makes intelligent hiring decisions difficult. Furthermore, the applicant's former employer may be reluctant to reveal why the employee left his or her job or whether the firm would rehire that person.

Concern by former employers or business associates about defamation-of-character suits is often overblown. A qualified business interest privilege usually protects organizations and individuals who exchange truthful information about a job applicant in furtherance of a legitimate business purpose. As long as information about former employees and job applicants is exchanged in good faith through normal business channels to individuals who have a legitimate need for the information, the likelihood of being held liable for defamation is low.

An inadequate background check could lead to the hiring of a criminally inclined, dangerously incompetent, or violent individual. If an employee has a history of fraud and property crimes, and the employer fails to discover this history during a pre-employment background check, then the employer may be liable for fraudulent acts that cause damage to clients, vendors, or business associates. Similarly, if a hospital hires a physician and it is later discovered that the physician possesses false credentials, the hospital would be liable for any deaths or injuries caused by the physician's incompetence. This problem is known as negligent hiring.

Negligent hiring has several important elements. First, an employer has a duty to investigate an applicant's background before making the final decision to hire. This duty varies, depending on the nature of the job. Negligent hiring has most often been an issue for employees with a history of violence, sexual predation, or larceny. The duty to investigate an applicant for a white-collar job may actually be less than the duty associated with hiring a maintenance worker in an apartment complex. The latter possesses a passkey and has twenty-four-hour-a-day access to tenant living quarters, while the former is less able to commit violent acts (directly) against clients or co-workers.

Second, negligent hiring must be linked to bad conduct that was foreseeable. There may be little excuse for a bank that hires a clerk with an extensive history of embezzlement or a day care center that hires a sexually predatory pedophile. Their subsequent misconduct on the job would have been easy to foresee. Background checks, however, are less likely to snare white-collar applicants with a history of unscrupulous office politics, unethical business dealings, or hushed terminations at a previous job. Even so, individuals with a potential to cross the line into criminal or corrupt acts may send out danger signals such as a poor driving record, a low credit score, excessive civil litigation, and other evidence that suggests irresponsible and impulsive behavior.

The previously mentioned research analyst who fell from grace and was banned from the financial securities industry, had a reputation as a prevaricator. He told people that he grew up in the rough section of a major city when, in fact, he came from a middle-class background. Furthermore, he falsely claimed on his resume that he held a degree from one of the most prestigious institutions of higher learning in the United

States. Even the stories he told about his athletic prowess appear to have been contrived.

His proclivity to lie eventually had a devastating impact on investors who relied on the veracity of his corporate analyses. In retrospect, this research analyst's dishonest boasting should have been a danger signal to those who did business with him.

The final element of negligent hiring is proximate cause. A relationship must be demonstrated between a person's past and present behaviors. A proximate cause probably exists if a jewelry store hires an individual with a recent history of retail theft who subsequently steals from customers. The element of time, however, may reduce or eliminate proximate cause. The issue of proximate cause may not be relevant, for example, if the former jewelry thief had maintained a crime-free record for the past twenty years.

For a white-collar criminal to create a negligent hiring liability, the organization must have had a duty to investigate, the criminal or corrupt act must have been foreseeable, and there must be a link (proximate cause) between the perpetrator's previous activities and the crime. Suppose a mail-order retailer hires a customer service representative who commits credit card fraud and identity theft by stealing proprietary customer information. It is discovered subsequently that the employee has a history of computer crimes and spent time in a federal prison for attempting to hack into a Social Security Administration information system. The company's duty to investigate the background of someone whose job provides them access to confidential information is fairly high in light of current concerns over credit card fraud and identity theft. Given the employee's criminal background, the ability to anticipate these crimes was also high. Establishing proximate cause is also straightforward because of the short time between the previous and current crimes.

Persons with felony and misdemeanor convictions are finding it increasingly difficult to find employment. Companies such as Wal-Mart, General Motors, Ford Motor Company, General Electric, Citigroup, IBM, and American International Group have stepped up efforts to uncover the criminal backgrounds of job applicants. The Internet has made criminal background checks easier, faster, and cheaper than ever before. These developments enable firms to check the backgrounds of all applicants from entry-level jobs to top management positions for as little as \$10 to \$20 per applicant.

The downside of the easy access to criminal background checks are the obstacles encountered by exconvicts who need work but suffer one rejection after another:

> "Forty-six million people in this country have been convicted of something sometime in their lives and our economy would collapse if none of them could get jobs." says Lewis Maltby, president of the National WorkRights Institute, a non-profit human-rights organization founded by former staff of the American Civil Liberties Union. That figure includes everybody in the FBI criminal records database, which includes people convicted of a relatively minor misdemeanor.[44]

One line of thought is: Exconvicts are supposed to have been rehabilitated. If they cannot find employment, they will eventually return to crime. The validity of this argument is questionable, and it reinforces the view of the recidivist exconvict as a victim rather than as a perpetrator. There is also long-held concern that rejecting applicants because of their criminal records will have a disparate impact on minorities.

Organizations should also consider periodic background checks on current employees. Long-term employees may experience behavioral changes that make them unsuitable for continued employment. Background checks on current employees should include criminal, driving, and credit checks. An employee who has never embezzled funds may be tempted if he or she has recently encountered severe financial pressures. A driving-record check may reveal that an employee has begun to abuse alcohol or controlled substances. Illegal activities away from work may be predictive of illegal activities at work. Checks should also be made on employees whose jobs require periodic relicensure to ensure that they remain legal to perform their job duties (and to avoid a negligent retention lawsuit).

Another method for detecting dishonest attitudes among applicants for professional and managerial positions is through integrity testing. The popularity of paper-and-pencil integrity tests stems directly from the elimination of polygraph examinations in hiring decisions (Employee Polygraph Protection Act of 1988). Dozens of commercially available integrity tests have been developed. Overt integrity tests such as the Stanton Survey and the Reid Report ask questions that are linked directly to honesty (e.g., attitudes toward theft and previous dishonest acts). Personality-based tests are used to predict a variety of counterproductive behaviors such as theft, physical aggression, and litigious behavior.

The validity of integrity tests has been questioned by industrial psychologists and others. These tests often have high false positive rates (i.e., honest applicants are labeled as being dishonest), and they may also discriminate against religious persons who want to forgive rather than punish dishonesty. Integrity tests may not be valid predictors of white-collar crime because of the aforementioned low detection and reporting rates of these crimes. Since honesty and integrity are correlated with conscientiousness and emotional stability, it might be more prudent to focus on examining these personality traits rather than on using integrity tests.

Security and Antitheft Measures

Thefts, breaches of computer security systems, threats of industrial sabotage, and concerns over terrorist activities have led to the creation of a multibillion-dollar security industry. Organizations realize that local, state, and federal law enforcement agencies cannot begin to provide adequate protection. Instead, organizations create their own private police forces through the use of security guards, electronic surveillance devices, global positioning technology, inventory control systems, and other state-of-the-art security technology.

Security and antitheft measures are not foolproof, but they do increase the effort required and the risks associated with committing crimes such as computer fraud, theft of cash and merchandise, and identity theft. For many white-collar crimes, however, the use of sophisticated security measures makes little difference. An army of security guards and an abundance of surveillance technology and computer firewalls could not have prevented the acts of malfeasance that occurred at Enron, WorldCom, Adelphia, and Tyco. But since the major damage associated with organizational crimes occurs at mid and lower levels of an organization, these controls can help. Policies and technology that restrict employee access to certain areas within a facility, control the disbursement of funds, safeguard merchandise, or limit the autonomy that employees have when performing their jobs all serve to reduce white-collar crime.[45]

Organizations that use expensive security personnel and technology must be aware of previously discussed cost-benefit analysis. On the surface it makes little sense to spend $1 million for additional security to avoid $500,000 in losses. Although tracking expenditures on security is easy, estimating the economic benefits of security technology is difficult. The problem lies in estimating the dollar value of crimes that were prevented. If a company spends $1 million on security and notes a $500,000 drop in thefts, it is hard to know whether the added expenditures on security prevented these losses or whether other factors contributed to the decline. The reduction in thefts could have been attributed to the termination of several employees who were caught using and selling illegal drugs. What management never realized was that once the drug problem was eliminated so too was much of the employee theft; the addition of the security technology was simply a coincidence. Thus, a problem that continues to frustrate criminologists is tracking and isolating the relationships among criminal activities and crime-prevention measures.

Educational and Whistle-Blowing Programs

Professionals, managers, and other employees understand that white-collar crimes are wrong. What they may not comprehend fully, however, is the devastating cumulative impact of these crimes. Education and awareness programs can accomplish several objectives. They can teach employees to recognize the wide range of white-collar crimes and perpetrators. In addition, they can learn more about the economic, psychological, and social impacts of these crimes. Armed with this knowledge, organizational stakeholders are in a better position to appreciate how these crimes can lead to poor financial performance, the alienation of customers, bad publicity, and the loss of jobs. Finally, employees can help to reduce white-collar crime.

Whistle-blowing programs encourage employees to report criminal and corrupt practices in the workplace. Employee reporting can be done through ombudsmen, telephone hotlines, and e-mail accounts that ensure anonymity. The use of both confidential reporting channels and monetary rewards appear to be the most effective approach for encouraging employees to report illegal or corrupt acts. Some organizations use vendors to handle reports from whistleblowers.

Many employees silently witness crime and corruption and fail to take action to stop it. For this reason, whistle-blowing programs may require changes in an organization's culture. Educating employees on the deleterious effects of white-collar crime should be the first consideration followed by the implementation of a confidential whistle-blowing program. This approach must be supplemented with other measures such as the equitable treatment of employees (fair pay, a good benefits package, and respect for employee dignity), the rotation of employees through work groups to prevent the development of close personal ties that can lead to conspiracies, and periodic retraining on ethical issues and workplace crime prevention.

Conclusion

This chapter describes the major societal and organizational responses to white-collar crime. White-collar crime and white-collar criminals are dynamic, not static. Criminals respond to societal and organizational measures in several ways. Some may decide that society and organizations have created too many obstacles and imposed too much risk on their criminal activities. Working their way through an elaborate security system or covering up evidence of a financial fraud is simply too burdensome. They may decide that the opportunity costs of white-collar crime are too high and that they would be better off directing their time and energies to legitimate endeavors. Other white-collar criminals view newly erected societal and organizational barriers as a challenge, much in the same way that law-abiding business people view new customers and markets as a challenge. Career criminals (opportunity seekers) may adjust their modus operandi and either continue committing the same crimes or experiment with new ones.

Conclusion and Future Directions

Twenty Points to Take from This Book

This book presents a dynamic model of organizational crime and corruption. Many points have been covered. Here are the top twenty:

1. White-collar crime is a major social problem. It inflicts billions of dollars in economic damage, and it extracts a major psychological and social toll. A wide range of individuals, organizations, and segments of society bear the costs of white-collar crime.

2. White-collar crime has not been defined with clarity. There is not complete agreement among criminologists or law enforcement agencies as to how white-collar crime should be defined. Furthermore, there is no coherent database to track the incidence and trends of white-collar crime. We cannot be certain whether white-collar crime is increasing, decreasing, or remaining constant. This problem is compounded by the fact that many white-collar crimes go undetected and unreported.

3. White-collar crimes consist of a variety of specialized-access crimes. These crimes overlap and share several common elements: they are usually committed within an organization; they almost always contain an element of fraud or endanger-

ment to others; and their primary purpose is to acquire wealth (although that is not the only goal).

4. White-collar crime has become international in scope because of the growth of multinational enterprises, computer technology, and the ease with which people can travel from one part of the world to another. The international nature of white-collar crime has made it harder for governments to identify, capture, and punish white-collar criminals.

5. White-collar criminals and street criminals have different personal characteristics and operating modes, but they possess similar thought processes.

6. White-collar crimes are more complex than street crimes (murder, robbery, burglary, assaults). Street crimes, however, are viewed by the public as being more serious than white-collar crimes.

7. White-collar crimes are caused by a confluence of individual traits, organizational arrangements, and societal forces. Complex issues have complex causes, and a multitude of theories have been developed to explain crime. There is probably an element of truth in all of these theories, but we do not have a definitive understanding of what triggers criminal behavior. It is easier to explain criminal behavior after the fact than before the fact.

8. The typical white-collar crime usually consists of a primary crime (e.g., consumer fraud) and one or more facilitating crimes (e.g., mail fraud and conspiracy).

9. White-collar criminals have different motives and preferences for crime. Some criminals operate alone while others operate as part of a conspiracy.

10. White-collar criminals are not usually impulsive or careless. They assess the risks and rewards of crime in a rational fashion and act accordingly. White-collar criminals, however, do not have complete or perfect information as they plan and execute their crimes. Incomplete information and superoptimism on the part of the criminal may lead to their apprehension and prosecution.

11. White-collar criminals use a variety of psychological coping mechanisms before, during, and after they commit a crime.

These mechanisms enable them to justify their acts, save face, and set themselves apart from other criminals.

12. White-collar crimes may be more costly than street crimes to individuals, organizations, and society. The economic, psychological, and social destruction wrought by white-collar criminals is huge but difficult to estimate accurately.

13. The degree of moral ambiguity of white-collar crimes is high, whereas the moral ambiguity of street crimes is low. The morally ambiguous nature of white-collar crime makes it difficult for the public to know how this social problem should be addressed.

14. The concept of moral intensity provides an alternate, but subjective, mechanism for individuals to assess the impact of a white-collar crime (or other social problems).

15. White-collar crime can be reduced but not eliminated. Reducing it involves imposing additional costs on the criminal by increasing the effort needed to commit a white-collar crime, increasing the risks of white-collar crime, and increasing the opportunity costs of white-collar crime, making legal options more attractive than illegal options.

16. Society responds to white-collar crime by enacting laws (and supporting regulations) to proscribe corrupt behaviors. The federal government has expanded its jurisdiction over white-collar crime, and Congress has enacted dozens of laws that impinge, to varying degrees, on the activities of white-collar criminals.

17. The passage of laws and the promulgation of regulations require that resources be allocated to fight white-collar crime. The optimal amount of resources allocated to fight white-collar crime is attained when the marginal costs of fighting crime equal the marginal benefits of additional anticrime expenditures.

18. Society is becoming less tolerant of white-collar crime. White-collar criminals are facing harsher sentences that include longer stretches in prison, forfeiture of assets, and financial restitution. Although prison time serves as deterrence, retribution, incapacitation, and rehabilitation, controversy contin-

ues as to whether prison is an appropriate punishment for white-collar criminals.

19. To reduce major white-collar crimes, organizations must take measures to control the behaviors of board members, CEOs, and other top executives. Most high-profile white-collar crimes are precipitated by the misuse of stock options, bonuses, commissions, and perquisites. Controlling executive compensation practices will represent a significant step toward reducing white-collar crime.

20. To reduce white-collar crime among other employees, organizations should fortify financial controls, perform thorough background checks on job applicants, use state-of-the-art security systems, and establish educational and whistle-blowing programs.

Future Directions

The future of white-collar crime encompasses three questions: Will white-collar crime increase, decrease, or remain the same? What shape will white-collar crime take in the future? Will society's perception of white-collar crime change? In closing, I offer observations on these important questions. Table 6.1 summarizes my projections.

Will White-Collar Crime Go Up, Down, or Stay the Same?

For those who have followed the events and personalities of corporate scandals such as Enron, WorldCom, Adelphia, and Tyco, it appears that white-collar crime is a growing social problem. As noted, however, we cannot be sure of the direction that white-collar crime is moving without a more comprehensive database or a better idea of how many crimes go undetected or unreported. I predict that the incidence of white-collar crime will not change significantly. Furthermore, as the U.S. labor force continues to age as post–World War II baby boomers reach the twilight of their careers, we might experience a decline in white-collar crime. Baby boomers approaching retirement will become increasingly concerned about their job security and retirement nest eggs and may decide that committing a white-collar crime is too risky to their personal and financial futures. As white-collar baby boomers age out of crime, however, it is possible that Generation Xers and others may commit more white-collar offenses.

What Shape Will White-Collar Crime Take in the Future?

In the future, the mix of white-collar crime is likely to change. There are two major crimes that may increase: health care fraud and crimes that use computer technology. The health care field will continue to grow in terms of its economic impact and complexity. Its vast size will provide white-collar criminals with many points of attack, and it will be impossible to defend it against criminals who are intent on embezzlement and fraud. The complex integration of private enterprises into the Medicare drug plan, for example, will provide additional opportunities for white-collar crime and corruption.

Computer technology and the Internet will continue to provide a springboard for white-collar crime. The proliferation of laptop computers and wireless Internet access provides white-collar criminals with an unprecedented degree of mobility and access to financial and personal information. Crimes against financial institutions and consumer scams may be driven by the ubiquity of computers. The displacement theory of crime posits that a decrease in one type of crime may lead to an increase in another type of crime. Telemarketing fraud may decrease as consumers become increasingly wary of cold calls from strangers, but Internet-based consumer fraud may increase. Similarly, the passage of federal identity theft legislation coupled with a growing public awareness of safeguards and preventive measures may reduce identity theft.

The corruption of domestic and foreign public officials will also continue to be a problem. As capitalism expands and markets become more competitive and international in scope, public officials in the U.S. and other countries will be confronted by business people who are eager to pay bribes and kickbacks in exchange for favorable treatment. Furthermore, successful political campaigns require huge sums of cash and create temptations to violate campaign finance laws. As noted, Representative Randy "Duke" Cunningham, the former congressman from California, pleaded guilty to taking bribes from defense contractors. Cunningham's plea came amid a series of Republican scandals that in-

Table 6.1. Projected White-Collar Crime Trends

Crimes That May Increase	Reasons
health care fraud	huge sums of money, complex system, inadequate fraud controls
computer crimes	proliferation of laptop computers and wireless Internet enables thieves to hack into bank and brokerage accounts and steal personal information
corruption by public officials	people willing to pay bribes, money to be made at every turn
bribes, gratuities, and extortion	highly competitive markets, international expansion
consumer scams	growing number of elderly, real-estate and get-rich-quick schemes
fiduciary fraud	accumulation of pension funds, inadequate insurance regulation
employee theft	less worker loyalty, small thefts that are difficult to detect

Crimes That May Decrease	
antitrust violations	federal government is watching mergers, acquisitions, and competitive practices closely
financial fraud and insider trading	Sarbanes-Oxley provisions and increased SEC scrutiny
telemarketing fraud	consumers may be more skeptical of telemarketers
identity theft	federal legislation and heightened public awareness of the dangers of disclosing private information
counterfeit and unsafe products	increased cooperation between U.S., Chinese, and other governments in cracking down on the manufacture and distribution of counterfeit goods

Crimes That May Either Increase of Decrease	
environmental crimes	depends on EPA enforcement and movement of manufacturing jobs out of United States
worker injuries and deaths	if manufacturing jobs leave the United States, occupational safety and health violations may decrease; increased OSHA enforcement may contribute to a decline

clude Representative Tom DeLay's indictment on campaign finance irregularities, majority leader Bill Frist's investigation on irregular stock
sales, and the indictment of vice president Dick Cheney's chief of staff
on CIA leaks.[1] Democrats are quick to point to the corruptive tendencies of Republicans, but the main problem is that politicians encounter
enticements for corruption at nearly every turn.

Major white-collar crimes of the magnitude of Enron, WorldCom,
Global Crossing, Adelphia, and Waste Management may decrease. The
passage of the Sarbanes-Oxley Act should reduce accounting, financial,
and corporate fraud because board members, CEOs, and members of
top management know that the SEC is keeping a closer eye on corporate behaviors that involve financial fraud and insider trading. Also,
there is a growing fear that board members and CEOs are more likely to
be held criminally and civilly liable for acts of fraud. The personal threat
of financial ruin is a strong incentive to avoid criminal behavior. The federal government appears to be especially vigilant in policing antitrust vi-
olators and insider traders.

The number of less-consequential white-collar crimes may increase.
U.S. workers have shorter job tenures and feel less loyalty toward employers. According to the U.S. Department of Labor, the average U.S.
worker has held an average of nine jobs by the age of 32. Employers are
more likely to view employees as dispensable, employing them only as
long as they are productive and can add value. The lack of a long-term
commitment in the employment relationship breeds a degree of disloy-
alty that encourages counterproductive workplace behaviors such as
petty white-collar crimes. Furthermore, employers tend to underestimate the importance of pay to middle- and lower-level employees. Employers who fail to understand what is important to workers are probably more susceptible to being victimized by white-collar crime. Thus, I
predict a decrease in major white-collar crimes and an increase in
minor white-collar crimes. Organizations may witness an increase in
crimes such as embezzlement, employee theft, shortchanging customers or vendors, padding expense accounts, falsification of time
sheets or sales reports, misappropriation of company assets, and defrauding workers' compensation programs. These "crimes on the mar-
gin" are easy for management to ignore, but as noted, their cumulative
effect can be significant.

Will Society's Perception of White-Collar Crime Change?

The public's view of white-collar crime will be determined by the media's portrayal of white-collar crime and the extent to which the public believes they are the victim of white-collar crimes. As the major headline-grabbing white-collar crimes decrease, the public's memory of Enron, WorldCom, and major political scandals will eventually fade. The media is not likely to provide substantial coverage of less-prominent white-collar crimes.

Barring a catastrophic white-collar crime that (1) has a devastating impact on the economic security of tens of thousands of individuals (such as Enron or WorldCom) or (2) is an occupational and safety violation that leads to a high number of injuries and deaths (such as the fire in the poultry processing plant in Hamlet, North Carolina) or (3) is a major environmental crisis (such as the Exxon *Valdes* oil spill), I speculate that the public will continue to view street crimes with more concern than white-collar crimes.

Parting Comments

To a certain extent, white-collar crime is a product of a free and capitalistic society. Eliminating it—or any other type of crime for that matter—is an unrealistic goal. A key question concerning white-collar criminals is: How do we explain such aberrant behavior of otherwise law-abiding adults? Most white-collar crimes involve fraud, but there may be two elements of this social problem that are especially prominent. First, white-collar crime and corruption exist because many professionals place their personal and financial needs above those of their customers, clients, and other stakeholders. Unless organizations and society can find a way to convince more individuals to subordinate their personal goals to the goals of others, white-collar crime will continue to flourish. Second, white-collar crime is often a quick, easy, and clandestine route to wealth, sometimes extreme wealth. Unless organizations and society can discourage individuals from taking the white-collar crime shortcut to riches and convince them to build businesses and business relationships through hard work, intelligent management, and trust, white-collar crime will continue to proliferate.

Rather than asking why certain people commit white-collar crimes and what can be done to prevent or reduce these crimes, we might ask why most people *do not* engage in the nefarious activities described in this book. The fact that most professionals and managers resist the temptation to commit crimes and engage in unethical or corrupt behaviors is worthy of consideration, and it raises questions as to why most people continue to do the right thing even in the face of seductive routes to quick and easy wealth or the avoidance of hardship.

In closing, I offer two simple quotations. Mark Twain, an irreverent humorist who possessed great insight into human nature, parlayed his writing and speaking skills into enduring worldwide fame. He was inept, however, as a business person. For much of the 1890s, he teetered on the edge of personal bankruptcy. Rather than shirking his obligations to creditors, he fought valiantly to pay back his debt. One of his aphorisms seems especially appropriate for marking the end of this book: "Honor is a harder master than the law. It cannot compromise for less than one hundred cents on the dollar."

Another piece of wisdom of more recent vintage comes from Alto "Bud" Adams, a successful Florida cattle rancher:

"I tell my boys, 'Tell the truth. It makes doing business a lot easier.'"

Professionals, managers, and employees alike would do well to heed the simple advice of Messrs Twain and Adams.

Appendixes

A Model of Organizational Crime and Corruption

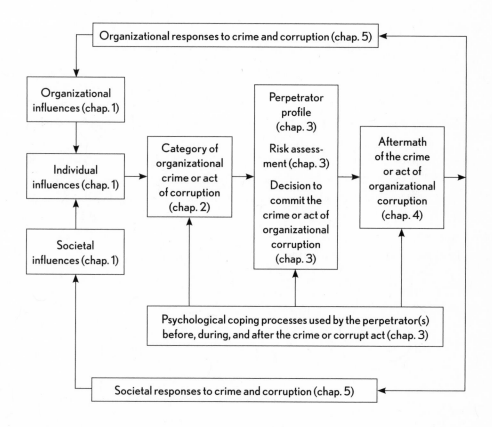

Organizational responses to crime and corruption (chap. 5)

Organizational influences (chap. 1)

Individual influences (chap. 1)

Societal influences (chap. 1)

Category of organizational crime or act of corruption (chap. 2)

Perpetrator profile (chap. 3)

Risk assessment (chap. 3)

Decision to commit the crime or act of organizational corruption (chap. 3)

Aftermath of the crime or act of organizational corruption (chap. 4)

Psychological coping processes used by the perpetrator(s) before, during, and after the crime or corrupt act (chap. 3)

Societal responses to crime and corruption (chap. 5)

Selected Theories on the Causes of Criminal Behavior

There is an abundance of theories in criminology. Theories have two primary functions: to explain a phenomenon such as crime or to predict outcomes. Some theories of crime examine differences in individual criminal behavior: Who is most likely to commit a crime? Why do younger people commit more street crimes than older people? Other theories examine geographic differences in crime rates: Why do crime rates differ between Los Angeles and Minneapolis? Why is drug trafficking a major problem in Mexico? Why do low income neighborhoods have higher rates of petty crime than affluent neighborhoods?

Theories on crime and criminals can be categorized as follows (this categorization is based on Tittle 2000, 51–101; Howard, Newman, and Pridemore 2000; and Frederichs 2004, 191–217):

1. individual-level theories;
2. lifecycle change theories;
3. theories that explain societal variations in crime rates; and
4. theories that explain differences in criminal behavior among situations.

Individual-Level Theories

Control and integration: Criminals fail to integrate or become connected to others. They share little or no concern, moral beliefs, or involvement with others. The criminal's social and psychological detachment makes it easier to commit crimes.

Identity: Criminal behavior is explained through labeling or stigmas attached to a specific individual. It might be best summarized by: "If I have the name (criminal), then I will play the game (commit crimes)." Identity is linked to labeling theory and secondary deviance.

Learning: Criminal behavior is learned through observing or being taught by other criminals, usually through a process of continuous reinforcement. Learning is also known as differential association.

Neutralization: Criminals attempt to rationalize or excuse their behaviors. By using these defense mechanisms, the psychological discomfort (e.g., guilt or remorse) associated with committing a crime is reduced.

Personal defects: Criminal behavior is attributable to personal defects such as genetic inheritance, birth defects, exposure to toxic substances, or traumatic life experiences.

Rational choice: Criminals weigh the potential benefits and costs before committing a crime. The criminal's goal is to maximize pleasure and to minimize pain.

Social control theory: People with strong bonds to family, school, church, and community are less likely to commit crimes because of the social control imposed by these institutions. Criminals have less exposure to these positive influences resulting in less social control.

Status deprivation theory: Criminals commit crimes because they have been deprived of respect or status.

Strain: Criminal behavior is the result of economic deprivation, stressful events, loss of valued possessions, abuse, or frustrated goals.

Lifecycle Change Theories

Age-graded theory: Changes toward or away from criminal behavior depend on the criminal's life circumstances (employment, marriage, major life changes).

Two-path theory: Criminals exhibit one of two patterns of behavior: (1) offending behavior that ceases after their teen years, or (2) offending behavior that is fairly constant throughout life.

Societal Variations in Crime Rates (exclusive macro-level themes)

Civilization theory: As governments and their citizens become more civilized, crime rates decrease.

Conflict theory: Rates of crime among societies vary with the degree to which their economic systems are capitalistic and internally competitive. Capitalism promotes selfishness and greed, undermines moral feelings, and leads to higher levels of crime. One version of conflict theory is Marxist or neo-Marxist theory.

Modernization theory: Rapid social change within a nation causes traditional values to break down, resulting in (among other things) higher rates of crime.

Routine activities theory: Crimes require motivated offenders, suitable targets, and the absence of guardians (security personnel, bystanders, alert co-workers, or police). For crime to occur, these three elements must be present at the same time and place.

Social disorganization theory: Large heterogeneous populations, rapid population movement, economic deterioration, and a lack of close relationships and interests among citizens create unstable communities and higher levels of crime.

World system theory: As market economies expand around the globe, the national autonomy of countries is diminished and weaker countries are exploited by stronger ones. Shifts in political, economic, and social conditions together with poverty, inequality, and poor living conditions produce an array of criminogenic conditions.

Societal Variations in Crime Rates (mixed macro-level themes)

Anomie: Crime is caused by a lack of norms (anomie). Social goals and the means for achieving those goals are not consistent with the realities of life. Anomie creates higher rates of deviance, including criminal behavior.

Defiance: Societies impose or threaten criminal sanctions. The success of deterrence measures depends on an offender's motivation for rehabilitation and bonds to the community. Sanctions must be imposed with dignity and respect.

Deprivation of law: Crime rates vary inversely with the availability of legal mechanisms for resolving disputes.

General strain theory: The presence of large numbers of strained individuals in a community leads to higher levels of crime.

Shaming: Society may ignore criminal behavior, punish it, or shame it. The more a society attempts to shame criminals, the lower the rates of crime. Shaming is effective in socially cohesive societies, and it is preferable to ignoring or punishing crime.

Social learning: Rates of crime increase in a society as crime-favorable messages exceed messages unfavorable to crime.

Variations in Criminal Behavior among Situations

Opportunity: Crime is explained by the presence of opportunities that attract motivated offenders. The presence of police patrols, lighting, valuable merchandise, and potential victims all represent opportunities for crime.

Symbolic interactionism: Criminal behavior can be explained in terms of the individuals' reaction to the behavior of others. The theory focuses on sequences of behavior and other individuals' reaction to that behavior. Barroom fights that are escalated by drunken boasting and insults as well as gang violence are explained by this theory.

Federal Laws Affecting White-Collar Crime

Anti-Drug Abuse Act: Maintaining a drug-free workplace.

Antitrust Laws: Price-fixing, monopolies, mergers, and other practices that limit competition (Sherman Act, Clayton Act, Celler-Kefauver Act, Federal Trade Commission Act, Hart-Scott-Rodino Act, Robinson-Patman Act).

Archaeological Resources Protection Act: Excavations on public land.

Civil False Claims Act: Fraudulent activities against the government.

Civil Rights: Equal employment opportunity (Title VII of 1964 Civil Rights Act, Age Discrimination in Employment Act, Americans with Disabilities Act, Civil Rights Act of 1991), fair housing, public accommodation, educational opportunities.

Comprehensive Crime Control Act: Forfeitures of assets obtained during the commission of a crime.

Comprehensive Drug Abuse Prevention Act: The manufacture and distribution of illegal drugs; a foundational law in the government's fight against drug trafficking.

Comprehensive Thrift Act: Banking fraud and misconduct, asset concealment, obstruction of bank examiners.

Computer Fraud and Abuse Act: Unauthorized access to protected computers, illicit trafficking of passwords and other protected information. (Also National Information and Infrastructure Protection Act, Homeland Security Act, Digital Millennium Copyright Act, Economic Espionage Act, Patriot Act, Cyber Security Enhancement Act, No Electronic Theft Act, Electronic Communications Privacy).

Conspiracy: Crimes or precursor actions to crimes involving multiple perpetrators.

Consumer Product Safety Act: Unsafe products, product defects, and related crimes.

Copyright Act: Misappropriation of copyrighted material.

Dyer Act: Interstate transportation of stolen vehicles.

Economic Espionage Act: Misappropriation of proprietary information.

Employee Retirement Income Security Act: Retirement programs and related fiduciary obligations.

Environmental Laws: Regulate substances and practices that cause damage to the ecosystem (Clean Air Act, Clean Water Act, Resource Conservation and Recovery Act, Toxic Substances Control Act, Comprehensive Environmental Response, Compensation, and Liability Act, Insecticide, Fungicide and Rodentcide Act, Water Pollution Control Act, Pollution Prevention Act, Migratory Bird Treaty Act, Refuse Act, Ports and Waterways Act).

Ethics Reform Act: Restrictions on the ability of federal employees to earn money from outside employment.

Fair Housing Act: Discrimination in the real estate market based on race, sex, familial status, or disabilities.

False Statements Statute: False declarations before a federal grand jury or court.

Federal Election Campaign Act: Political campaign contributions and spending.

Federal Food, Drug, and Cosmetics Act: Safety of food, drugs, and cosmetics.

Federal Trade Commission Act: Antitrust activities, false advertising.

Financial Crime Kingpin Statute: Continuing financial crime enterprises, freezing assets prior to court judgments, victim restitution.

Financial Institutions and Reform, Recovery, and Enforcement Act: Real estate appraisals and transactions.

Financial Privacy Act: Access to personal financial information.

Foreign Corrupt Practices Act: Bribery of foreign officials.

Freedom of Information Act: Access to public information.

Health Care Fraud: Medicare and Medicaid fraud, false billing, unnecessary health care services, collusion. (Medicare and Medicaid Anti-

Fraud and Abuse Amendments, Health Insurance Portability and Accountability Act).

Hobbs Act: Racketeering, extortion, robbery, physical violence.

Identity Theft: Identity Theft and Assumption Deterrence Act, Fair Credit Reporting Act, Fair and Accurate credit Transactions Act, Fair Credit Billing Act, Fair Debt Collections Practices Act, Electronic Fund Transfer Act

Insider Trading: Stock trading based on nonpublic information for personal enrichment; leaking information to outside parties who profit unfairly (Security Exchange Act, Insider Trading Sanctions Act, Sarbanes-Oxley Act).

Inspector General Act: Auditing of federal programs.

Internal Revenue Restructuring and Reform Act: Taxpayer rights and IRS reorganization.

Lacey Act: Game and wildlife preservation.

Landrum Griffin Act: Regulation of labor union elections and activities.

Mail Fraud: Engaging in fraudulent activities using the U.S. mails.

Major Fraud Act: Frauds against the U.S. Government used to receive property or services valued at $1 million or more.

McDade Act: Ethical acts of federal prosecutors and law enforcement officials.

Meat Inspection Act: Practices within the meatpacking industry (sanitation, processed foods).

Money Laundering: Concealing the source of money generated by illegal activities or for the purpose of evading income taxes. (Annunzio-Wylie Anti-Money Laundering Act, Bank Secrecy Act, Tax Reform Act, Money Laundering Control Act, Criminal Forfeiture Act, RICO, International Money Laundering Abatement and Anti-Terrorist Act).

National Labor Relations Act: Regulation of concerted labor activity and collective bargaining.

National Stolen Property Act: Interstate or international transport of stolen money or goods.

Occupational Safety and Health Act: Workplace health and safety standards.

Organized Crime and Control Act: Gambling and witness protection.

Pesticides: Manufacture, distribution, and use of pesticides (Food,

Drug, and Cosmetic Act, National Environmental Policy Act, Food Quality Protection Act).

Pure Food, Drug, and Cosmetics Act: Regulation of food, drugs, medical devices, and cosmetics to protect consumers from tainted, misbranded, or dangerous merchandise.

Racketeer Influenced Corrupt Organizations Act (RICO): Ongoing illegal enterprises that exhibit a pattern of racketeering, bribery, counterfeiting, embezzlement, loan sharking, mail and wire fraud, prostitution, bankruptcy fraud, and more.

Sarbanes-Oxley Act: Accounting and financial fraud, consulting and auditing practices, liability of corporate officers.

Securities Act of 1933: Investor information on securities offered for public sale.

Sentencing Reform Act: Sentencing for federal crimes.

Truth in Lending and Credit Protection Laws: Protects credit rights of individuals (Fair Credit Billing Act, Fair Credit Reporting Act, Equal Credit Opportunity Act, Consumer Leasing Act, Fair Debt Collection Practices Act).

Uniform Trade Secrets Act: Patents and trade secrets.

Violent Crime Control and Law Enforcement Act: Comprehensive law affecting law enforcement funding, firearms, federal death penalty, fraud, gang crimes, and other offenses.

Williams Act: Disclosure of certain business relationships.

Wire fraud: Fraudulent activities by telephone, computer, or other mechanisms that utilize the wires for transmission.

Notes

Introduction: The Big Picture

1. Leung 2004.
2. Associated Press 2006b.
3. Darr 2006.
4. Napoleon III appointed Georges-Eugène Haussmann as Prefect of the Seine and charged Haussmann with the Herculean task of coordinating the rebuilding of Paris. Napoleon and Haussmann were concerned with the potential for corruption that was likely to accompany such a massive and ambitious project. See Pinkney 1958, 48.
5. The term "crime" refers to any act committed by a person that violates a criminal statute or common law principle, regardless of whether that act is detected or reported. A "criminal" is any person who commits a criminal act, even though that person may escape detection or prosecution. The government (federal, state, or local) is the initial plaintiff in a criminal charge, and it must prove beyond a reasonable doubt that the accused has committed the crime for which he or she is charged. I use the term "convicted" to describe individuals who have been found guilty of a criminal act. The focus in this book is on criminals whose actions normally constitute a felony. Civil suits are brought by private individuals, and the burden of proof—"the preponderance of evidence"—is a less rigorous standard than that required in a criminal case. Criminals may also face civil suits filed by individuals who have suffered harm by their actions. Thus, a person who has been accused of securities fraud may face both criminal and civil prosecution. It is also possible for an individual to be acquitted of criminal charges yet held liable in a civil suit. The O.J. Simpson case is an example.
6. Samenow 2004, 12.
7. See Geis, Meier, and Salinger 1995, 25.
8. Criminologists and academicians are concerned about the definition of social terms such as *white-collar crime* because of the need to carefully define and measure variables used in their research. Law enforcement is interested in precise definitions of various categories of crime because of the need to gather crime statistics and monitor trends.
9. Some white-collar criminals also engage in robbery, assault, and other violent crimes. The widest range of crimes by a criminal of which this author is aware was com-

mitted by John Robinson, who lived in the Kansas City area. For many years, Robinson engaged in a variety of white-collar crimes and serial murders of women. See Douglas 2003.

10. Felson 2002, 94–95.

11. Embezzlement is the misappropriation of assets that have been entrusted to the care of the person committing the misappropriation. Thus, embezzlement differs from other types of theft where the assets are not in the care, custody, or control of the perpetrator.

12. U.S. Department of Justice n.d.

13. This assumption is based on that used by the U.S. judicial system, which assumes that a criminal defendant is sane unless he or she is ruled innocent on the grounds of insanity, a rarity in white-collar crime cases. A major point of contention among persons who deal with white-collar crimes is the issue of culpability. Under what circumstances are corporations punished, and under what circumstances should their executives be held individually liable? This question is critical because it has a profound effect on the motivations behind organizational crime and corruption. Corporations can be fined, ordered to cease committing certain actions, or even disbanded. But only employees, not corporations, can receive jail time. Since executives, managers, and other employees act as agents for a company, it is hard to know when they cross the line between organizational liability and individual liability.

14. Friedrichs 2004, 200.

15. Weisburd, Waring, and Chayet 2001, 51–90.

16. Felson 2002, 100–101

17. My views of criminal thinking and behavior are based primarily on the work of the psychologists Stanton E. Samenow and his mentor, the late Samuel Yochelson, both of whom spent the bulk of their careers working with criminals and writing extensively about their experiences and insights on criminal behavior. See Samenow 2004.

18. Felson discusses several fallacies associated with crime in general. It is probably common for law-abiding persons to entertain momentary thoughts of crime only to be repulsed at the thought of doing something that would be illegal or harmful to others. The "not-me fallacy" posits that the difference between criminals and law-abiding citizens is not as large as we might assume. Many adults have violated the law to some extent, whether it be driving too fast, failing to report earnings paid in cash on an income tax return, inflating a travel expense voucher, pilfering office supplies, or misappropriating items for personal use.

19. The seminal work for the use of neutralization (rationalization) techniques by criminals is Sykes and Matza 1957.

20. See, in general, Denenberg and Braverman 1999, 141–153, and Warchol 1998.

21. The probability of being the victim of workplace violence has been compared to the probability of being struck by lightning. According to the National Institute for Occupational Safety and Health (NIOSH), approximately twenty workers are murdered and 18,000 are assaulted per week. See NIOSH, "Violence in the Workplace," http://www.cdc.gov/niosh/violfwd.html.

22. Mass murders occur when an individual kills three or more people in a single episode. Mass murderers, such as Timothy McVeigh, are often themselves killed during the commission of a crime, captured at the crime scene, or captured shortly after the crime has been committed. Spree killers, rapists, or arsonists commit their crimes within a short period of time and remain in an agitated state without a cooling-off period

during their crime spree. The two snipers who terrorized the Washington, D.C., area in 2001 are examples of spree offenders. Serial murders, rapes, and acts of arson typically occur over a period of months or years, and the perpetrator does experience a cooling-off period in which he resumes living a normal, law-abiding life. Weeks or months later, the serial offender commits another murder, rape, or act of arson. White-collar crimes may also be committed on a mass basis (e.g., stealing several million dollars from a bank vault and disappearing to a Caribbean retreat), spree basis (tapping into secure government databases during a four-week period and selling the information to agents of a country whose interests are hostile to the United States), or serial basis (periodically embezzling cash from customer receipts over a span of months or years).

23. Predicting that an individual or class of individuals will commit a particular type of crime is highly speculative. Given that only a very small percentage of the population will commit a serious white-collar crime (low base rate), such predictions are difficult to make and lack scientific credibility. Thus it is safer to say: "The person who violently assaulted the pedestrian and stole his wallet was probably a male under the age of thirty with only a high school education" (an accurate profile after the fact), than it is to say, "If you are a male under the age of thirty with only a high school education, you will likely commit a violent assault or robbery" (an inaccurate prediction before the fact). Although most violent crimes are committed by males under the age of thirty with only a high school education, the vast majority of people fitting this profile do not commit such crimes. If they did, college campuses as well as many cultural and sporting events where young people gather would be extremely dangerous places. White-collar crimes, however, are probably less amenable to profiling than street crimes.

24. For a discussion of how incarcerated criminals manipulate corrections personnel, see Allen and Bosta 1981.

25. Weiss 2003.

26. Carter 1994.

27. National White Collar Crime Center 2002.

28. Lyman and Potter 2000, 35–37.

29. President's Commission on Organized Crime 1986.

30. Bryan-Low 2005a.

31. Lyman and Potter 2000, 2–13.

32. Calavita and Pontell 2002.

33. Not all harmful acts of deception or misrepresentation are fraud. An elderly person of sound mind who signed a land sales contract without reading it and later realized that the contract contained unfavorable provisions normally has no legal recourse.

34. Associated Press 2005c.

35. Shafer 2003.

36. Cooke 1980.

37. Broder 2003.

38. May 2005.

39. See Douglas, Burgess, and Ressler 1992, which focuses on serious violent crimes rather than white-collar crimes.

40. Braithwaite and Geis 2001, 365.

41. Douglas 2003, 241–243.

42. Young, Latour, and Pulliam 2005.

43. Nossen 2002, 8.

1. What Influences Organizational Crime and Corruption?

1. Samenow 2004, 5.

2. For an excellent discussion of the demise of WorldCom, the largest bankruptcy in U.S. history, see the PBS video, "The Wall Street Fix."

3. Over a period of thirty years, the Harvard psychologist Gordon Allport investigated over 18,000 separate personality traits and developed a personality classification scheme.

4. Ones and Viswesvaran 2003, 230.

5. The *Diagnostic and Statistical Manual of Mental Disorders*, 4th ed. (DSM-IV-TR) provides a classification scheme for sixteen major diagnostic classes of mental disorders. See American Psychiatric Association 2000.

6. Comer 2001, 510.

7. There is also a phenomenon known as adult antisocial behavior, which can be found among some career criminals. Professional thieves, racketeers, or drug dealers who are loyal and responsible toward family and friends, who show remorse, and who engage in constructive activities outside of their criminal activities may not meet the diagnostic criteria for antisocial personality disorder. Don Corleone, the fictional crime family boss in Mario Puzo's novel *The Godfather*, is probably an example of this disorder. See American Psychiatric Association 2000, 740.

8. Deutschman 2005.

9. Hare 1993, 113–114.

10. This term was coined originally by Hervey Cleckley (1941).

11. Persons with antisocial personality disorder rarely seek professional help, and when they do receive counseling (usually at the behest of the legal system) they are manipulative and evasive with mental health professionals. Since few white-collar criminals are sentenced to prison, they often avoid mandatory counseling. Absent a formal diagnosis, however, if one reads about the lives of some major white-collar criminals, it appears that antisocial personality disorder may have played a prominent role in their crimes.

It would be both difficult and unethical for a mental health professional to label a person with a personality disorder based solely on news accounts of that person's behavior. Mental health diagnoses require extensive interviewing and testing of patients before a reliable assessment can be made. Historical figures such as Joseph Stalin, Adolf Hitler, and Saddam Hussein, however, would probably have been diagnosed with antisocial personality disorder. These individuals illustrate the rare possibility of rising to prominent positions while suffering from a serious mental problem. For additional insights into this disorder, see Black 1999.

12. American Psychiatric Association 2000, 714–717. White-collar criminals who are narcissists are of the cerebral variety in that they derive their narcissism from their intellect and academic and professional achievements. Somatic narcissists derive their gratification from their physical and sexual prowess. See "Narcissistic Personality Disorder, Fact Sheet and Tips," http://Healthyplace.com.

13. Raghaven 2002.

14. American Psychiatric Association 2000, 665–666.

15. See, for example, Mason 2003.

16. Bryan-Low 2005.

17. Although many criminals have little formal education, they can be extremely resourceful when planning and committing crimes.

18. See Abagnale 2001, 26–87.

19. Junger, West, and Timman 2001, 439.

20. Bruno 1993, 186.

21. Grover 2005, 148.

22. See, for example, Skorupski 2003, 202–230.

23. Adams 1965, 267–299.

24. Johnson 2003, 3.

25. Needleman and Needleman 1979.

26. See, in general, Purpura 2002.

27. Baucus and Near 1991, 14; and Daboub, Rasheed, Priem, and Gray 1995, 143–146.

28. Organizations may have three distinct subcultures that affect the incidence of white-collar crime: the organizational subculture, the industry subculture, and the occupational subculture. See Coleman 2001, 352.

29. Mills 2003, 94–95.

30. Lagace 2003.

31. Huffington 2003, 194–201.

32. Forelle and Bandler 2006.

33. Janis 1982.

34. Forelle 2005.

35. Stanford Graduate School of Business, news release, "Dueling for Dollars," http://www.gsb.stanford.edu/research/faculty/news_releases/edward.lazear/lazear.htm   (no date).

36. Huffington 2003, 62–65.

37. Farberman 1975, 438–457; and Denzin 1977, 905–920.

38. Zahra, Priem, and Rasheed 2005, 808–812.

39. There is evidence that a low rate of sales or employment growth, for example, appears to be a good predictor of environmental crime and that environmental crime tends to occur in industries that have had relatively high rates of sales and employment growth. Alexander and Cohen 1996, 421–435.

40. The acronym CRAVED (concealable, removable, available, valuable, enjoyable, and disposable) has been used to describe the characteristics of merchandise that is especially susceptible to theft. Felson 2002.

41. States have criminal and civil laws that are similar to federal laws. The focus here, however, is on federal laws.

42. See Strader 2002; and Abrams and Beale 2000.

43. Albanese 1995, 118–119.

44. Douglas 2003, 121–123.

45. Abagnale 2001, 26–81, 138–166.

46. Grow 2005, 36.

47. Lipman 1989, 288.

48. Mitchell et al. 1996, 442.

2. The Many Facets of White-Collar Crime

1. Uniform Crime Reports are tabulated by the FBI based on arrest information from over 17,000 police jurisdictions throughout the United States. The National Crime Victimization Survey is based on information obtained from a sample of households. The NCVS conducts interviews with persons over the age of twelve in these households and

obtains information from them about their experiences with crime (excluding homicides). Even though the UCR and NCVS focus on the same crimes (with the NCVS exclusion of murder), the survey results are often dramatically different. Criminologists believe that the UCR exaggerates crime rates because of double counting (e.g., two drunken patrons assault a bartender at a nightclub, and the UCR records this crime twice, once for each assailant) and because law enforcement agencies may be tempted to skew crime statistics to attract more funding from federal and state sources. The UCR does, however, provide an accurate count of homicides. For these reasons, criminologists regard NCVS statistics as more accurate, and they prefer to use them when measuring and tracking crime trends. Because it is based on surveys of households, NCVS does not account for thefts from commercial or business establishments. See Donzinger 1996, 2–5; and Steffensmeier and Harer 1999, 236–237.

2. Group A offenses are fraud offenses (false pretenses/swindle/confidence game, credit card/ATM fraud, impersonation, welfare fraud, and wire fraud), bribery, counterfeiting/forgery, embezzlement, and arson plus fraud. The lone Group B offense is bad checks.

3. Barnett n.d.

4. In addition, the increased sophistication of security technology and the increased use of security personnel in residences and commercial establishments has increased the risk for burglars.

5. Robberies usually provide quick cash that can be used by the perpetrator for purchasing illegal drugs, whereas burglaries usually require the time-consuming activity of fencing the stolen property to obtain cash. The displacement theory of crime holds that a reduction of crime in one area will result in an increase in crime in another area. Evidence indicates that the displacement theory of crime often lacks validity.

6. The fifth and sixth points are based on Steffensmeier and Harer 1999, 235–274.

7. France 2005, 32–35.

8. Most mail and wire fraud cases are under federal jurisdiction because the mails are under federal control and the transmission of information through the wires typically travels across state lines and is subject to the Commerce Clause.

9. Strader 2002, 59–60.

10. *United States v. Schmuck*, 489 U.S. 705 (1989).

11. Simpson 2004.

12. Criminals such as drug traffickers accumulate huge sums of cash in small denominations. The problem is the sheer bulk and weight of the cash. For example, $1 million in $20 bills weighs approximately 113 pounds. Converting small bills to large bills reduces this problem.

13. U.S. Department of Treasury 2005. This report presents a comprehensive analysis of money laundering techniques, and it illustrates how money launderers have become adept at using intricate financial networks to move money within the United States as well as across international borders.

14. Wingfield 2004.

15. The Bank Secrecy Act (1970) also requires a report if more than $10,000 cash (including foreign currency) is shipped into or out of the United States or when more than $10,000 is kept in a foreign bank account. The Tax Reform Act of 1984 requires that a report must be filed with the IRS by persons engaged in a trade or business who receive more than $10,000 cash in one or more related transactions (e.g., purchasing an automobile for cash).

16. The filing of a CTR, by itself, is not indicative of criminal activity. Many individuals deposit or withdraw cash for legal activities such as the sale of an automobile, obtaining traveler's checks for vacations, or the purchase of expensive items such as furniture. It is only when patterns of unusual behavior emerge that a SAR is filed or law enforcement officials become involved.

17. See Liddick 2004, 59–69, 93–102; Block and Weaver 2004; and Powis 1992.

18. See Strader 2002, 237–264.

19. Income tax evasion is different from income tax avoidance. In the latter case, an individual is attempting to minimize tax liability while complying with applicable federal and state tax laws. In the former, tax liabilities are reduced by failing to comply with tax laws.

20. CNN.com 2002.

21. Forensic accountants may use one of two methods to determine the illegal income of white-collar criminals for criminal prosecution or tax evasion purposes. The net worth method examines the manner in which a suspect criminal's assets and liabilities have changed over time, whereas the expenditure method examines cash expenditures over a specific period of time. Both methods attempt to distinguish between income from legal sources and income from illegal sources.

22. Federal conspiracy cases have relaxed standards with regard to the hearsay rule. In federal law, hearsay is "a statement (either a verbal assertion or nonverbal assertive conduct), other than one made by the declarant while testifying at the trial or hearing, offered in evidence to prove the truth of the matter asserted." Garner 2000, 578–579. *Federal Rules of Evidence*, Rule 801, Definitions (d)(2)(e) classfies "a statement by a co-conspirator of a party during the course and in furtherance of a conspiracy" as a statement that does not constitute hearsay. According to the State (Michigan) Appellate Defender Office, "the co-conspirator hearsay exception represents a formidable prosecutorial weapon." Lippman 1997.

23. *Pinkerton v. United States*, 328 U.S. 640 (1946).

24. Horizontal price fixing occurs among competitors in the same industry. Vertical price fixing occurs in the same chain of distribution as manufacturers and retailers attempt to control the price of a product.

25. Langley and Francis 2004; and Langley and McDonald 2004.

26. U.S. Department of Justice, Antitrust Division 2005.

27. Companies that mislead investors do not necessarily have to resort to accounting and financial fraud. Generally accepted accounting principles provide adequate leeway for chief financial officers and accountants to construct financial statements that are legal, yet misleading. "Indeed, today's financial reports are more difficult to understand than ever. They're riddled with jargon that's hard to fathom and numbers that don't track. They're muddled with inconsistent categories, vague entries, and hidden adjustments that disguise how much various estimates change a company's earnings from quarter to quarter," says Donn Vickers, a former accounting professor and cofounder of Camel-Back Research Alliance, Inc., an Arizona firm used by investors to detect inflated earnings. Henry 2004, 80.

28. Brady and Vickers 2005.

29. McDonald and Francis 2005.

30. Powell 2006.

31. Young, Solomon, and Berman 2004.

32. Swartz 2003; Mclean and Elkind 2003; and Smith and Emshwiller 2003.

33. Partnoy 2003, 370.
34. Foust and Grow 2005.
35. McDonald and Dugan 2005.
36. Greene 2005.
37. Solomon 2005.
38. Insurance companies frequently transfer insurance obligations to a reinsurer. If you purchase automobile insurance from Company A, Company A may transfer your policy to Company B (the reinsurer). Reinsurance is used to enable insurance companies to write insurance coverage and comply with state financial laws that limit the amount of coverage an insurance company can have on its books at a particular time.
39. The laws dealing with insider trading are the Security Exchange Act of 1934, the Insider Trading Sanctions Act of 1984, the Insider Trading and Securities Act of 1988, and the Sarbanes-Oxley Act of 2002.
40. Lucchetti and Scannell 2005.
41. Young 2005.
42. The term *public official* includes not only elected officials of the legislative, executive, and judicial branches but also political appointees, civil servants, and officers of the law.
43. Soto 2006, and Henry and Preston 2005.
44. Pasztor and Karp 2004.
45. Gray 2005.
46. Percy 2002.
47. Rhoads 2004.
48. Fritsch and Mapes 2005.
49. Gold and Fleming 2004.
50. Liederbach 2001.
51. Armstrong 2005.
52. Physicians are protected against prosecution because of their high professional status, altruistic and trustworthy image, the self-regulating history of the medical profession, and the lax enforcement standards of many state medical boards. Liederbach 2001, 146–147.
53. Levy 2004, 12–33.
54. Anderson 2004, ES-1-ES-8, 1–24.
55. Hollinger and Langton 2005.
56. Anderson 2005.
57. Lublin 2005.
58. For example, employees may condone certain thefts but not others by co-workers. Restaurant employees may tolerate the theft of food but not money from the cash register. Office workers may look the other way when co-workers pilfer small amounts of supplies, but they may not tolerate the unauthorized use of long-distance telephone services.
59. Bryan-Low 2004.
60. See Bryan-Low 2005b.
61. *BusinessWeek* 2005, 13.
62. Borrus 2005, 38.
63. Borrus 2005, 40.
64. Perez and Brooks 2005.
65. Perez and Brooks 2005, A1.

66. Sidel 2005.
67. Levy and Stone 2005, 40.
68. Guth 2005.
69. McQueen 2006.
70. Conkey 2005.
71. The public relations director of an aircraft manufacturing company told me that his firm made a multi-million-dollar settlement with the estate of a pilot who perished while attempting to fly a single-engine aircraft into a thunderstorm. The individual killed was an experienced airline pilot who, presumably, knew full well the dangers of flying any aircraft into a thunderstorm. This case presents a prime example of how products liability cases have become a major concern in the aviation industry. Cases such as these have inflated the cost of aircraft ownership tremendously.
72. A family member of mine witnessed her neighbor's unsupervised preteen children jumping onto the trampoline from a second-story window.
73. Schmidt 2004.
74. Schmidt 2004.
75. Felson 2002, 100–101
76. There are several classifications of theft. They include cyber theft (theft using computer access), theft by deception, theft by extortion, theft by false pretext, theft of property lost, mislaid, or delivered by mistake, and theft of services. See Garner 2000, 1200.
77. Maremont 2005.
78. Grant and Nuzum 2004.
79. Balfour et al. 2005.
80. Wonacott and McBride 2005.
81. An Illinois couple was burned after an appliance with a fake UL label caught fire. See "Buyer Beware: Counterfeit Goods," A&E Investigative Reports video (New York: New Video, 2000).

3. White-Collar Criminals: Risks and Rationalizations

1. Weisburd, Waring, and Chayet 2001, 51–90.
2. Krause 2002, 3.
3. Gamiz 2005.
4. Anand, Ashforth, and Joshi 2004, 46.
5. Moore, Tetlock, Tanlu, and Bazerman 2006, 17.
6. Anand, Ashforth, and Joshi 2004, 46.
7. For an interesting and bizarre illustration of the use of economic theory applied to the decision to commit crime, see Marché 1998.
8. Hellman and Alper 2000, 1.
9. If given the choice between $100,000 in cash and $50,000 in cash, the rational person with a positive utility for money would select the $100,000 option. Similarly, if the rational individual is offered the opportunity to receive $1 every time a coin flip comes up heads and nothing if it comes up tails, then he should be willing to pay $50 for 100 tosses of the coin (the 0.5 probability of heads x $1 x 100 tosses). Even with a "fair" coin, it is unlikely that 100 tosses will yield exactly 50 heads and 50 tails. A risk-prone person might pay more than $50 for this bet with the hope that the number of heads will exceed 50 when the coin tosses are made. Conversely, a risk-averse person would not be willing

to pay $50 for this bet owing to the possibility that the number of tails will exceed the number of heads.

10. Yochelson and Samenow 1976, 424.

11. CBSNews.com 2003.

12. Regaldo and Fairclough 2005; and Fairclough and Regaldo 2005.

13. Hammond, Keeney, and Raiffa 1989, 163.

14. CBSNews.com 2003.

15. Lemert 1951.

16. Comer 2001, 54.

17. To reiterate a point made earlier, guilt or innocence has two levels of meaning. From a legal standpoint, a person accused of a crime must be proven guilty beyond a reasonable doubt—a high standard of proof that forces the judicial system to err on the side of allowing a guilty person to be acquitted. At a second level, persons accused, tried, and acquitted of a crime may have been guilty of a criminal act but not punished because the "beyond a reasonable doubt" standard was not met.

18. The "ignorance of the facts" defense is not applicable in strict liability situations such as products liability cases.

19. Emshwiller and Smith 2005.

20. Shmukler 2005. Scrushy was later found guilty, however, of state fraud charges.

21. *Wall Street Journal* 2005.

22. Buell 2006. http://blogs.chron.com/legalcommentary/archives/2006/02/big_picture.html.

23. Employees who appear to be overly conscientious, arriving for work early, leaving late, and never taking time off for vacations might be involved in an embezzlement scheme such as lapping. For this reason, banks and other organizations insist that employees take periodic vacations. It is usually during the time that the dishonest employee is away from work that the crime is detected.

24. This incident was relayed to me by a manager in a large firm who wishes to remain anonymous.

25. Katz 1988, 318.

26. Delattre 2002, 77–78.

27. Fausto Tonna, a key figure in the accounting fraud that crippled Parmalat SpA, stated, "There are people more responsible than I am." Galloni 2004.

28. "Stolen Identities," A&E "Investigative Reports" video (New York: New Video, 1999).

29. Calavita and Pontell 2002, 118–122.

30. Black-hat hackers, in contrast, infiltrate systems for the purposes of sabotage and theft. What white-hat hackers frequently have ignored is that the very act of hacking into a computer system can cause significant damage.

31. Morse 2005.

32. Dreazen 2005.

33. Krause 2002, 13.

34. Psychologists have labeled this defense mechanism *reaction formation*. People who voice strong feelings against homosexuals and gay rights, for example, might be doing so to suppress their own sexual attraction toward the same sex.

35. Bancroft 2002, 296.

36. Wolpe 1998, lecture one.

37. See Durkheim 1966.

4. The Elusive Impact of White-Collar Crime

1. Horn 2005.

2. Cohen 2000. Cost adjustments for 2005 were made using the U.S. Department of Labor, Bureau of Labor Statistics, and CPI indexes.

3. For an excellent discussion of moral ambiguity see Green 2004. Green discusses ten factors associated with moral ambiguity and white-collar crimes: (1) the ambiguity between criminality and "merely aggressive" behavior, (2) the overcriminalization of some crimes and the problem of "sticky norms," (3) the complexity of white-collar crimes and the difficulties of defining harms and identifying victims, (4) the diffusion of responsibility associated with the fact that white-collar crimes often have multiple participants with varying degrees of culpability, (5) the inchoate nature of many white-collar crimes, (6) the difficulties of demonstrating mens rea (a guilty mind) for some white-collar crimes, (7) the fact that illegal activities may be surrounded by legitimate conduct, (8) the fact that legislatures treat white-collar crime differently from other crimes, (9) the fact that prosecutors and judges view white-collar criminals differently from other criminals, and (10) the differences in the way defense attorneys, publicists, the media, and academicians view white-collar and other crimes. In my opinion, Green's first seven factors focus on the causes of moral ambiguity, whereas his final three factors focus on the effects of this phenomenon.

4. Green 2004, 506–508.

5. Compare the conviction of WorldCom's Bernard Ebbers with the acquittal of HealthSouth's Richard Scrushy. Ebbers's trial was held at a neutral site (New York, New York) away from the influence of his Jackson, Mississippi, family and friends. Scrushy's trial was held in Birmingham, Alabama, a community where he is deeply revered. There is speculation that Scrushy's "home court advantage" led to his acquittal. See Terhune, Morse, and Latour 2005.

6. *Economist* 2005e.

7. Armour 2006.

8. Anders 2004.

9. Foust, Grow, and France 2005, 34.

10. Emshwiller 2005.

11. Bravin 2005.

12. Ted Allen, "Citigroup, J.P. Morgan Agree to Pay $4.2 Billion to Enron Investors," Institutional Shareholder Services (ISS Global), 2006, http://www.issproxy.com/governance/publications/2005archived/112.jsp.

13. Weil and Sidel 2005.

14. Associated Press 2006a.

15. Baucus and Baucus 1997.

16. Leung 2004.

17. The Ford Pinto case is probably the best example of the public outrage that may occur when dollar amounts are assigned callously to a human life. Parties in wrongful death suits frequently hire expert witnesses to place a dollar value to a deceased person's life as part of the calculation of damages to be imposed on a negligent defendant who caused the death. The net present value of a twenty-six-year-old Harvard Law School graduate's lifetime income stream, for example, might be several million dollars, whereas that of an unskilled 64-year-old laborer might be only $100,000 or so. The dif-

ference between a case of this type and the Ford Pinto case is that Ford calculated the loss of life *before* Pinto passengers had perished in fiery crashes and decided that a certain number of lost lives was tolerable from a cost-benefit standpoint.

18. National Victim Assistance Academy 2002.

19. I was a resident of Louisiana from 1978 to 1983. Before moving there, I was aware of the reputation for corruption among the state's elected officials. I was not prepared, however, for the corruption that seemed to permeate the day-to-day activities of businesses and governmental and other institutions.

20. Gasparino 2005, 87, 96, 161, 308.

21. The Sarbanes-Oxley Act has required accounting firms to avoid providing both auditing and consulting services to the same client, but the net effect is that the act has increased compliance costs and has boosted the business of accounting firms. See Bulkeley and Forelle 2005.

22. Jones 1991.

23. Jones 1991, 376.

24. Singhapakdi, Vitell, and Franke 1999.

25. Leap and Crino 1998.

26. Cohen 2000, 283.

5. Responses to White-Collar Crime

1. I use the term "rehabilitation" with some reservation. Rehabilitation, by definition, implies that the criminal was once a law-abiding, functional citizen. Some criminals might be converted into law-abiding citizens even though they have always preferred to operate on the wrong side of the law. Thus, we should consider taking the "re" out of rehabilitation for many criminals.

2. Adapted from Nossen 1977, 22–26.

3. Zhang 2005, 5.

4. Cohen 2000, 303–305.

5. Violent crimes that occur on government property such as the Oklahoma City bombing that destroyed a U.S. government building and killed 168 people fall under federal jurisdiction. White-collar crimes affecting federal funds or personnel might also be prosecuted at the federal level.

6. Abrams and Beale 2000, 62–63.

7. McNamee 2005.

8. Suppose the MB/MC ratio of environmental crimes was $100 million/$80 million (1.25). This ratio means that every $1.00 spent on fighting environmental crime yields a benefit of $1.25. Thus, it would behoove policymakers to continue allocating funds to fight environmental crime. If the MB/MC ratio for employee theft was $250/$250 (1.0), then spending an additional dollar to reduce employee theft would quickly yield a benefit of slightly less than $1.00. There is an additional twist. When society fails to provide adequate protection against crime, organizations and individuals may take up the slack. Large organizations hire security personnel and purchase security technology. Individuals also make expenditures on security against both street crime and white-collar crime. Private anticrime strategies fall outside public cost-benefit analyses.

9. As Donald Cressey adds, "even though the language of ordinary citizens endows corporations with human attributes, this language also suggests that everyone knows the

difference between a 'person' and a 'thing.' Thus, the gas company is never referred to as a 'she' or a 'he.' It, like other companies, is always called 'it.' This usage characterizes legal language too, suggesting that the regulation of corporations might be more effective if corporation codes of ethics as well as regulatory laws pertained to the real persons in charge of inanimate objects, not to the objects themselves." Cressey 1988, 177.

10. Mendoza and Sullivan 2006.

11. One variation of this dilemma is the college athletic coach who commits serious violations of NCAA rules. The institution, its student-athletes, and fans are penalized through scholarship reductions, bans from post-season play, and loss of television revenues. It is possible, however, for the coaches who committed the violations to take positions at other institutions and incur no further penalties. To add insult to injury, a coach who is fired in the wake of an NCAA enforcement action may receive a lucrative severance package.

12. Whitley, Garber, McCarty, and Henry 2002, 14–15.

13. *Economist* 2005b.

14. Solomon and Squeo 2005.

15. Solomon and Squeo 2005, A10. See also Hamm 2005.

16. Emshwiller and Scannell 2005.

17. The bottom-up prosecutorial strategy bears a striking resemblance to game theory's well-known Prisoner's Dilemma in which one person accused of a crime tends to implicate another to avoid possibly more severe punishment.

18. "White Collar Crime," on *Odyssey*, Chicago Public Radio (July 18, 2005), www.chicagopublicradio.org.

19. *U.S. v. Booker* 543 U.S. 220 (2205)(and *U.S. v. Fanfan*), Nos. 04-104 and 04-105.

20. Cohen and Fields 2004.

21. Woellert and France 2005.

22. Savage 2005.

23. Young and Grant 2005.

24. Solomon and Squeo 2005.

25. Testimony, United States Senate Committee on the Judiciary, "Penalties for White Collar Offenses: Are We Really Getting Tough on Crime?" by the Honorable James B. Comey Jr., United States Attorney, Southern District of New York (June 19, 2002). http://judiciary.senate.gov/print_testimony.cfm?id=280&wit_id=650.

26. See Shover and Hochstetler 2006, 136–149.

27. Chazan 2005.

28. McGregor 2005. After years of complaints that the government is not doing enough to catch and punish white-collar criminals, the SEC and the Justice Department are being accused of engaging in unfair double teaming against white-collar criminals accused of financial crimes. See Lattman and Scannell 2006.

29. Albanese 1995, 118–119.

30. Economist 2005c, 77; and Thorton 2005.

31. Zhang 2002, preface. See also Shuit 2005; Gullapalli 2005; and *Economist* 2005a, 72.

32. See Mills 2003.

33. Associated Press 2005a.

34. Solomon and Squeo 2005.

35. Polinsky and Shavell 1984.

36. "Beginning in 2005, companies will have to show the fair value of their stock option

awards on their income statements. That value will be determined using an option-pricing model. In the past, under FAS 123, companies have shown the Black-Scholes value of their stock options in the footnotes to their income statements, but not reflected them as a line item. Most other kinds of equity compensation already show up as an expense on companies' income statements." The National Center for Employee Ownership. http://www.nceo.org/library/fasb-final-accounting-rules.html.

37. Economist 2005d, 69.
38. Samuelson 2003.
39. Schnatterly 2003.
40. Weil and Young 2005.
41. Stybel and Peabody 2005.
42. Raghaven 2005.
43. Grossman 2005.
44. Zimmerman and Stringer 2004.
45. Reducing the theft and pilferage, for example, entails controlling merchandise receiving-and-storage areas as well as safeguarding merchandise that is being shipped or placed in retail areas. Sources of theft in receiving areas include collusion between drivers and warehouse employees, theft from delivery vehicles, leaving merchandise unprotected in staging areas, covering up thefts by pilfering merchandise from the center of shipping pallets, frequently shorting a shipment by one or two items, recording undamaged merchandise as damaged, allowing goods to be stolen in transit between staging and storage areas, and allowing unloaded vehicles to remain in a loading area. Thefts from storage areas occurs when unauthorized persons are allowed access to stored merchandise (e.g., to use a lounge or restroom), merchandise is in close proximity to personal vehicles or dumpsters, a storage area has several unguarded doorways, high-risk merchandise is easily accessed by personnel (instead of being stored in a restricted area or in an area that is not easily accessible). Shipping areas are conducive to theft when drivers and order personnel are not screened carefully when hired, when control seals on vehicles are handled improperly, or when discarded packing material accumulates (perhaps as a sign that someone has removed the packaging and has stolen the merchandise). Employees in retail sales areas may conceal theft by hiding merchandise in their clothing, newspapers, umbrellas, trash, or dumpsters. Employees with pass keys or other access devices may return after hours and steal merchandise. See http://crime prevention.rutgers.edu/crime/emp_theft/warehouses.

Conclusion and Future Directions

1. Associated Press 2005b.

References

Abagnale, Frank W. 2001. *The Art of the Steal*. New York: Broadway Books.

Abrams, Norman, and Sara Sun Beale. 2000. *Federal Criminal Law and Its Enforcement*. 3rd ed. St. Paul, Minn.: West Group.

Adams, J. Stacy. 1965. "Inequity in Social Exchange." In *Advances in Experimental Social Psychology*, edited by L. Berkowitz, 2:267–299. New York: Academic Press.

Albanese, Jay. 1995. *White Collar Crime in America*. Englewood Cliffs, N.J.: Prentice-Hall.

Alexander, Cindy R., and Mark A. Cohen. 1996. "New Evidence on the Origins of Corporate Crime." *Managerial and Decision Economics* (17): 421–435.

Allen, Bud, and Diana Bosta. 1981. *Games Criminals Play*. Sacramento, Calif.: Rae John.

American Psychiatric Association. 2000. *Diagnostic and Statistical Manual of Mental Disorders (DSM-IV-TR)*. 4th ed. Washington, D.C.: American Psychiatric Association.

Anand, Vikas, Blake E. Ashforth, and Mahendra Joshi. 2004. "Business as Usual: The Acceptance and Perpetuation of Corruption in Organizations." *Academy of Management Executive* (18): 39–55.

Anders, George. 2004. "Moving after Enron Means Being Humble and Minimizing Role." *Wall Street Journal*, July 27: B1.

Anderson, Claire. 2005. "Ex-BMW Worker Charged in Theft." *Greenville News*, September 29: B1.

Anderson, Keith B. 2004. *Consumer Fraud in the United States: An FTC Survey*. Washington, D.C.: Federal Trade Commission.

Armour, Stephanie. 2006. "Enron Woes Reverberate through Lives." *USA Today*, January 26, http://news.yahoo.com/s/usatoday/20060126/bs_usatoday/enronwoesreverberatethroughlives.

Armstrong, David. 2005. "How Doctors Turn a $90 Profit from a $17 Test." *Wall Street Journal*, September 30: A1.

Associated Press. 2005a. "Attorney General Hiring More Fraud Prosecutors." *Greenville News*, October 9: 5B.

Associated Press. 2005b. "Lawmaker Pleads Guilty to Taking Bribes, Resigns." *Greenville News*, November 29: 8A.

Associated Press. 2005c. "Three More Indicted in Junior College Fraud Case." *Hannibal Courier Post*, December 16, http://www.hannibal.net/cgi-bin/printme.pl.

Associated Press. 2006a. "Alma Mater Wrestles with Lay Donation after Enron Conviction." *Hannibal Courier Post*, May 27, http://www.hannibal.net/stories/052706/happenings_20060527004.shtml.

Associated Press. 2006b. "Coastal Transit Agency Wants Ex-CEO's Pay Back." *Greenville News*, February 20: 2B.

Balfour, Frederick, et al. 2005. "Fakes." *BusinessWeek Online*, February 7, http://www.businessweek.com/magazine/content/05_06/b3919001_mz001.htm.

Bancroft, Lundy. 2002. *Why Does He Do That? Inside the Minds of Angry and Controlling Men*. New York: Putnam's Sons.

Barnett, Cynthia. n.d. "The Measurement of White-Collar Crime Using Uniform Reporting (UCR) Data." U.S. Department of Justice, Federal Bureau of Investigation, http://www.fbi.gov/ucr/whitecollarforweb.pdf.

Baucus, Melissa S., and Janet P. Near. 1991. "Can Illegal Corporate Behavior Be Predicted? An Event History Analysis." *Academy of Management Journal* (34): 14.

Baucus, Melissa S., and David A. Baucus. 1997. "Paying the Piper: An Empirical Examination of Long-Term Financial Consequences of Illegal Corporate Behavior." *Academy of Management Journal* 40 (February): 129–151.

Black, D., with C. Larsen. 1999. *Bad Boys, Bad Men: Confronting Antisocial Personality Disorder*. New York: Oxford University Press.

Block, Alan A., and Constance A. Weaver. 2004. *All Is Clouded by Desire: Global Banking, Money Laundering, and International Organized Crime*. Westport, Conn.: Praeger.

Borrus, Amy. 2005. "Cybercrime: Invasion of the Stock Hackers." *BusinessWeek*, November 14: 38.

Brady, Diane, and Marcia Vickers. 2005. "AIG: What Went Wrong." *BusinessWeek*, April 11: 32–35.

Braithwaite, John, and Gilbert Geis. 2001. "On Theory and Action for Corporate Crime Control." In *Crimes of Privilege: Readings in White-Collar Crime*, edited by Neal Shover and John Paul Wright. New York: Oxford University Press.

Bravin, Jess. 2005. "Justices Overturn Criminal Verdict in Andersen Case." *Wall Street Journal*, June 1: A1, A6.

Broder, David S. 2003. "The Perils of Arrogance." *Washington Post*, June 11: A35.

Bruno, Frank J. 1993. *Psychological Symptoms*. New York: John Wiley & Sons.

Bryan-Low, Cassell. 2004. "Seeking New Payoff: Hackers Now Strike Web Sites for Cash." *Wall Street Journal*, November 30: A1, A8.

——. 2005a. "Identity Thieves Organize." *Wall Street Journal*, April 7: B1, B2.

——. 2005b. "Tech-Savvy Blackmailers Have a New Form of Extortion." *Wall Street Journal*, May 5: B1, B3.

——. 2005c. "As Identity Theft Moves Online, Crime Rings Mimic Big Business." *Wall Street Journal*, July 13: A1, A6.

Buell, Samuel. 2006. "Big Picture." February 6, http://blogs.chron.com/legalcommentary/archives/2006/02/big_picture.html.

Bulkeley, William M., and Charles Forelle. 2005. "How Corporate Scandals Gave Tech Firms a New Business Line." *Wall Street Journal*, December 9.

Calavita, Kitty, and Henry N. Pontell. 2002. "'Heads I Win, Tails You Lose': Deregulation, Crime, and Crisis in the Savings and Loan Industry." In *Readings in White-*

Collar Crime, edited by David Shichor, Larry Gaines, and Richard Ball, 111–142. Mt. Prospect, Ill.: Waveland Press.

Callahan, David. 2004. *The Cheating Culture*. Orlando, Fla.: Harcourt.

Carter, David L. 1994. "International Organized Crime." East Lansing, Mich.: School of Criminal Justice, Michigan State University, http://www.cj.msu.edu/~outreach/security/orgcrime.html.

CBSNews.com. 2003. "Stephen Glass: I Lied for Esteem." August 15, http://www.cbsnews.com/stories/2003/05/0760minutes/main552819.shtml.

Chazan, Guy. 2005. "In Russia, Politicians Protect Movie, Music Pirates." *Wall Street Journal*, May 12: B1, B8.

Cleckley, Hervey. 1941. *The Mask of Sanity*. St. Louis, Mo.: Mosby.

CNN.com. 2002. "Koslowski Wants Charges Dropped." August 29, http://money.cnn.com/2002/08/29/news/companies/koslowski/.

Cohen, Laura P., and Gary Fields. 2004. "How Unproven Allegations Can Lengthen Time in Prison." *Wall Street Journal*, September 20: A1.

Cohen, Mark A. 2000. "Measuring the Costs and Benefits of Crime and Justice." *Criminal Justice 2000* (4): 263–315.

Coleman, James William. 2001. "Competition and Motivation to White-Collar Crime." In *Crimes of Privilege: Readings in White-Collar Crime*, edited by Neal Shover and John Paul Wright, 341–358. New York: Oxford University Press.

Comer, Ronald J. 2001. *Abnormal Psychology*. New York: Worth.

Conkey, Christopher. 2005. "A Radical Tool to Fight ID Theft." *Wall Street Journal*, July 8: D1, D2.

Cooke, Janet. 1980. "Jimmy's World." *Washington Post*, September 28: A1.

Cressey, Donald R. 1988. "The Poverty of Theory in Corporate Crime Research." In *Advances in Criminological Theory*, vol. 1, edited by W. S. Laufer and F. Adler. New Brunswick, N.J.: Transaction Publishers.

Daboub, Anthony J., Abdul M. A. Rasheed, Richard L. Priem, and David A. Gray. 1995. "Top Management Team Characteristics and Corporate Illegal Activity." *Academy of Management Review* (20): 143–146.

Darr, Bev. 2006. "Owner Says Manager Admitted Stealing." *Hannibal Courier Post*, February 10, http://hannibal.net/stories/021006/happenings_20060210008.

Delattre, Edwin J. 2002. *Character and Cops: Ethics in Policing*. 4th ed. Washington, D.C.: AEI Press.

Denenberg, Richard V., and Mark Braverman. 1999. *The Violence-Prone Workplace*. Ithaca, N.Y.: Cornell University Press.

Denzin, N. K. 1977. "Notes on the Criminogenic Hypothesis: A Case Study of the American Liquor Industry." *American Sociological Review* (42): 905–920.

Deutschman, Alan. 2005. "Is Your Boss a Psychopath?" New York: Fast Company, http://www.fastcompany.com/subscr/96/open_boss.html.

Donzinger, Steven, ed. 1996. *The Real War on Crime: The Report of the National Criminal Justice Commission*. New York: Harper Perennial.

Douglas, John E., Ann W. Burgess, and Robert K. Ressler. 1992. *Crime Classification Manual: A Standard System for Investigating and Classifying Violent Crimes*. San Francisco: Jossey-Bass.

Douglas, John, with Stephen Singular. 2003. *Anyone You Want Me to Be*. New York: Pocket Star Books.

Dreazen, Yochi J. 2005. "Some Firms Hired in Katrina's Wake Have Checkered Pasts." *Wall Street Journal*, September 20: B1.

Durkeim, Emil. 1966. *Suicide*. New York: Free Press.

Economist. 2005a. "Teething Troubles: One Company's Experience of Sarbanes-Oxley." May 21.

Economist. 2005b. "Corporate Crime: Off to Jail." July 23. http://www.economist.com/printedition/displayStory.cfm?Story_ID=4113198.

Economist. 2005c. "Refco, Rotten yet Robust." October 22.

Economist. 2005d. "No Compensation without Cost." October 29.

Economist. 2005e. "A Crackdown Too Far." November 5.

Eichenwald, Kurt. 2005. *Conspiracy of Fools*. New York: Broadway Books.

Emshwiller, John R. 2005. "A Felon's Wife Picks Up the Pieces of Her Luxury Life." *Wall Street Journal*, November 29: A1, A12.

Emshwiller, John R., and Kava Scannell. 2004. "Enron Trial Results in Five Guilty Verdicts." *Wall Street Journal*, November 4: C1, C6.

Emshwiller, John R., and Rebecca Smith. 2005. "For Enron's Ex-Chief, Spotlight Shines on His Public Statements." *Wall Street Journal*, January 5: A1, A6. Fairclough, Gordon, and Antonio Regaldo. 2005. "Fraud Allegations Deal New Setback to Cloning Effort." *Wall Street Journal*, December 24–25: A1, A6.

Farberman, H. A. 1975. "A Criminogenic Market Structure: The Automobile Industry." *Sociological Quarterly* (16): 438–457.

Felson, Marcus. 2002. *Crime and Everyday Life*. Thousand Oaks, Calif.: Sage.

Forelle, Charles. 2005. "Seeking Restitution, Government Targets Tyco Duo's Fortunes." *Wall Street Journal*, June 30: A1, A6.

Forelle, Charles, and James Bandler. 2006. "Five More Companies Show Questionable Options Pattern." *Wall Street Journal*, May 22: A1 and A10.

Foust, Dean, and Brian Grow. 2005. "Sharks in the Housing Pool." *BusinessWeek*, September 5: 32–35.

Foust, Dean, Brian Grow, and Mike France. 2005. "Scrushy Has a Score to Settle." *BusinessWeek*, July 11: 34.

France, Mike. 2005. "Court Room Strategies on Trial." *BusinessWeek*, July 4: 32–35.

Friedrichs, David O. 2004. *Trusted Criminals*. 2nd ed. Belmont, Calif.: Wadsworth.

Fritsch, Peter, and Timothy Mapes. 2005. "In Indonesia a Tangle of Bribes Creates Trouble for Monsanto." *Wall Street Journal*, April 5: A1, A6.

Galloni, Alessandra. 2004. "Parmalat Executive Tries Out New Role: Mr. Nice Guy." *Wall Street Journal*, December 27: A1, A7.

Gamiz, Manuel, Jr. 2005. "Police: Woman Stole $618,000 from Employer." *Morning Call*, January 27: 1.

Garner, Bryan A., ed. 2000. *Black's Law Dictionary*. 7th ed. St. Paul, Minn.: West Group.

Gasparino, Charles. 2005. *Blood on the Street*. New York: Free Press.

Geis, Gilbert, Robert F. Meier, and Lawrence Salinger. 1995. *White-Collar Crime: Classic and Contemporary Views*. New York: Free Press.

Gold, Russell, and Charles Fleming. 2004. "In Halliburton Nigeria Probe, a Search for Bribes to a Dictator." *Wall Street Journal*, September 24: A1, A6.

Grant, Peter, and Christine Nuzum. 2004. "Adelphia Founder and One Son Are Found Guilty." *Wall Street Journal*, July 9: A1, A6.

Gray, Steven. 2005. "How an Analyst Got Nabbed for Extortion." *Wall Street Journal*, April 18: C1, C4.

Green, Stuart P. 2004. "Moral Ambiguity in White-Collar Criminal Law." *Notre Dame Journal of Law, Ethics, & Public Policy* (18): 501–519..

Greene, Kelly. 2005. "Theft from 401(k)s Is on the Rise." *Wall Street Journal*, March 2: D1, D2.

Grossman, Robert J. 2005. "Demystifying Section 404." *HR Magazine* (October): 48.

Grover, Steven. 2005. "The Truth, the Whole Truth, and Nothing but the Truth: The Causes and Management of Workplace Lying." *Academy of Management Executive* (10): 148.

Grow, Brian. 2005. "A Painful Lesson: E-Mail Is Forever." *BusinessWeek*, March 21: 36.

Gullapalli, Diya. 2005. "Take This Job and File It." *Wall Street Journal*, April 4: C1.

Guth, Robert A. 2005. "Microsoft Tests Software to Fight Identity Theft on the Web." *Wall Street Journal*, March 28: B1, B6.

Hamm, Steve. 2005. "Computer Associates: Clearing a Cloud." *BusinessWeek*, November 21: 70–72.

Hammond, John S., Ralph L. Keeney, and Howard Raiffa. 1989. *Smart Choices: A Practical Guide to Making Better Decisions*. Boston: Harvard Business School Press.

Hare, Robert D. 1993. *Without Conscience: The Disturbing World of the Psychopaths among Us*. New York: Guilford Press.

Hellman, Daryl A., and Neil O. Alper. 2000. *Economics of Crime*. 5th ed. Boston: Pearson Custom Publishing.

Henry, David. 2004. "Fuzzy Numbers." *BusinessWeek*, October 4: 80.

Henry, Ed, and Mark Preston. 2005. "Congressman Resigns after Bribery Plea." CNN.com, November 28.

Hollinger, Richard C., and Lynn Langton. 2005. "2004 National Retail Security Survey: Final Report." Gainesville, Fla.: University of Florida Department of Criminology, Law, and Society, www.crim.ufl.edu/research/srp/srp.htm.

Horn, Stacy. 2005. "Counting Corporate Crooks." *New York Times*, July 16, http://web .lexis-nexis.com/universe/document?_m=31a285f7958579d81fc8d5d25350ae36& _docnum=2.

Howard, Gregory J., Graeme Newman, and William Alex Pridemore. 2000. "Theory, Method, and Data in Comparative Criminology." *Criminal Justice 2000* 4: 139–211.

Huffington, Arianna. 2003. *Pigs at the Trough: How Corporate Greed and Political Corruption Are Undermining America*. New York: Crown.

Israel, Jerold H., Ellen S. Podgor, Paul D. Borman, and Peter J. Henning. 2003. *White Collar Crime Law and Practice*. 2nd ed. St. Paul, Minn.: West Publishing Company.

Janis, Irving. 1982. *Groupthink*. Boston: Houghton-Mifflin.

Johnson, Craig. 2003. "Enron's Ethical Collapse: Lessons for Leadership Educators." *Journal of Leadership Education* 2 (Summer): 3.

Jones, Thomas M. 1991. "Ethical Decision Making by Individuals in Organizations: An Issue Contingent Model." *Academy of Management Review* 16 (April): 366–395.

Junger, Marianne, Robert West, and Reinier Timman. 2001. "Crime and Risky Behavior in Traffic: An Example of Cross-Situational Consistency." *Journal of Research in Crime and Delinquency* 38 (November): 439.

Katz, Jack. 1988. *Seductions of Crime*. New York: Basic Books.

Krause, M. S. 2002. "Contemporary White Collar Crime Research: A Survey of Findings Relevant to Personnel Security Research and Practice." Working paper, the Personnel Security Manager's Research Program: (August): 3.

Lagace, Martha, ed. 2003. "How to Build a Better Board." Based on an Interview with Jay Lorsch. December 22, Boston: Harvard Business School Working Knowledge, http://hbswk.hbs.edu/item.jhtml?id=3834&t=corporate_governance.

Langley, Monica, and Ian McDonald. 2004. "Marsh Averts Criminal Case with New CEO." *Wall Street Journal*, October 26: A1, A10.

Langley, Monica, and Theo Francis. 2004. "Insurers Reel from Bust of a 'Cartel.'" *Wall Street Journal*, October 18: A1, A14.

Lattman Peter, and Kara Scannell. 2006. "Slapping Down a Dynamic Duo." *Wall Street Journal*, January 25: C1, C3.

Leap, Terry L., and Michael D. Crino. 1998. "How Serious Is Serious?" *HR Magazine*, May.

Lemert, E. 1951. *Social Pathology*. New York: McGraw-Hill.

Leung, Shirley. 2004. "Despite Best Efforts, Doughnut Makers Must Fry, Fry Again." *Wall Street Journal*, January 5: A1, A12.

Levy, Joel. 2004. *The Scam Handbook: The Secrets of a Con Artist*. New York: Barnes & Noble Books.

Levy, Steven, and Brad Stone. 2005. "Grand Theft Identity." *Newsweek*, July 4: 40.

Liddick, Donald R. 2004. *The Global Underworld: Transnational Crime and the United States*. Westport, Conn.: Praeger.

Liederbach, John. 2001. "Opportunity and Crime in Medical Professions." In *Crimes of Privilege: Readings in White-Collar Crime*, edited by Neal Shover and John Paul Wright, 144–156. New York: Oxford University Press.

Lipman, Ira A. 1989. How to Protect Yourself from Crime. 4th ed. New York: Reader's Digest Association.

Lippman, Mark. 1997. "Co-Conspirator Hearsay Exception." *Criminal Defense Newsletter* 20, no. 12 (September), http://www.sado.org/21cdn1.htm#21cdu1a.

Lublin, Joann S. 2005. "Travel Expenses Prompt Yale to Force Institute Chief Out." *Wall Street Journal*, January 10: B1, B5.

Lucchetti, Aaron, and Kara Scannell. 2005. "How Day Traders Turned Squawk-Box Chatter into Profits." *Wall Street Journal*, August 23: A1, A8.

Lyman, Michael D., and Gary W. Potter. 2000. *Organized Crime*. 2nd ed. Upper Saddle River, N.J.: Prentice-Hall.

Marché, Gary. 1998. *Murder as a Business Decision: An Economic Analysis of a Criminal Phenomena*. San Francisco: Austin & Winfield.

Maremont, Mark. 2005. "Amid Crackdown, the Jet Perk Suddenly Looks a Lot Pricier." *Wall Street Journal*, May 25: A1, A8.

Mason, Bill, with Lee Gruenfeld. 2003. *Confessions of a Master Jewel Thief*. New York: Villiard Books.

May, Allan. 2005. "The Lufthansa Heist," http://www.crimelibrary.com/gangster_out laws/gang/heist/8.html.

McDonald, Ian, and Ianthe Jean Dugan. 2005. "Investigators Probe Locations of Bayou Funds." *Wall Street Journal*, August 25: C1, C2.

McDonald, Ian, and Theo Francis. 2005. "AIG Probe Brings First Charges." *Wall Street Journal*, May 27: C1, C3.

McGregor, Michael. 2005. "Reform and Regulation," and "Regulatory Enforcement."

In *Encyclopedia of White-Collar and Corporate Crime*, edited by Lawrence M. Salinger, 670–679. Thousand Oaks, Calif.: Sage.

McLean, Bethany, and Peter Elkind. 2003. *The Smartest Guys in the Room: The Amazing Rise and Scandalous Fall of Enron*. New York: Portfolio.

McNamee, Mike. 2005. "Watchdogs with Eyes Wide Shut." *BusinessWeek*, April 25: 34.

McQueen, M. P. 2006. "Employers Offer Help Fighting ID Theft." *Wall Street Journal*, May 24: D1, D3.

Mendoza, Martha and Christopher Sullivan. 2006. "Billions in Fines Never Get Collected." Associated Press, *Greenville News* March 19: 2A.

Mills, D. Quinn. 2003. *Wheel, Deal, and Steal: Deceptive Accounting, Deceitful CEOs, and Ineffective Reforms*. Upper Saddle River, N.J.: FT/Prentice-Hall.

Mitchell, Terence R., et al. 1996. "Perceived Correlates of Illegal Behavior in Organizations." *Journal of Business Ethics* (15): 442.

Moore, Don A., Philip E. Tetlock, Lloyd Tanlu, and Max H. Bazerman. 2006. "Conficts of Interest and the Case of Auditor Independence: Moral Seduction and Strategic Issue Cycling." *Academy of Management Review* 31, no. 1 (January): 10–29.

Morse, Dan. 2005. "For Former HealthSouth Chief, an Appeal to Higher Authority." *Wall Street Journal*, May 13: A1, A10.

Murphy, Kevin. 1993. *Honesty in the Workplace*. Pacific Grove, Calif.: Brooks-Cole.

National Victim Assistance Academy. 2002. "Financial Crimes." In *Foundations in Victimology and Victims' Rights and Services*, chap. 16, http://www.ojp.usdoj.gov/ovc/assist/nvaa2002/.

National White-Collar Crime Center. 2002. "WCC Issue: Organized Crime." Fairmont, W. Va.: National White Collar Crime Center, http://www.nw3c.org.

Needleman, Martin L., and Carolyn Needleman. 1979. "Organizational Crime: Two Models of Criminogenesis." *Sociological Quarterly* 20 (Autumn): 517–528.

New York Times. 2003. "Correcting the Record: Times Reporter Who Resigned Leaves Long Trail of Deception." May 11: 1:1.

Nossen, Richard A. 2002. *The Investigation of White-Collar Crime: A Manual for Law Enforcement Agencies*. New York: Hong Kong Books for Business.

Ones, Deniz S., and Chockalingam Viswesvaran. 2003. "The Big-5 Personality and Counterproductive Behaviors." In *Misbehaviour and Dysfunctional Attitudes in Organizations*, edited by Abraham Sagie, Shmuel Stashevsky, and Meni Koslowsky, 211–249. New York: Palgrave Macmillan.

Partnoy, Frank. 2003. *Infectious Greed*. New York: Times Books.

Pasztor, Andy, and Jonathan Karp. 2004. "How an Air Force Official's Help for a Daughter Led to Disgrace." *Wall Street Journal*, December 9: A1, A10.

Percy, Kumar. 2002. "Fighting Corporate and Government Wrongdoing: A Research Guide to U.S. and Federal Laws on White-Collar Crime and Corruption." August 15, http://www.llrx.com/features/whitecollarcrime.htm.

Perez, Evan, and Rick Brooks. 2005. "For Big Vendor of Personal Data, A Theft Lays Bare the Downside." *Wall Street Journal*, May 3: A1, A6.

Perry, Tony. 2005. "Rep. Cunningham Pleads Guilty to Bribery, Resigns." *Los Angeles Times*, November 29, latimes.com.

Pinkney, David H. 1958. *Napoleon III and the Rebuilding of Paris*. Princeton, N.J.: Princeton University Press.

Polinsky, A. Mitchell, and Steven Shavell. 1984. "The Optimal Use of Fines and Imprisonment." *Journal of Public Economics* (24): 89–99.

Powell, Eileen Alt. 2006. "AIG Agrees to Pay Out $1.64 Billion in Settlement." *Greenville News,* February 10: 9A.

Powis, Robert E. 1992. *The Money Launderers.* Chicago: Probus.

President's Commission on Organized Crime. 1986. *The Edge: Organized Crime, Business, and Labor Unions.* Washington, D.C.: U.S. Government Printing Office.

Purpura, Philip P. 2002. *Security and Loss Prevention: An Introduction.* 4th ed. Boston: Butterworth-Heinemann.

Raghavan, Anita. 2002. "Accountable: How a Bright Star at Andersen Fell along with Enron." In *Best Business Crime Writing of the Year,* edited by James Surowiecki, 190–196. New York: Anchor Books.

———. 2005. "More CEOs Say 'No Thanks' to Board Seats." *Wall Street Journal,* January 28: B1.

Regaldo, Antonio, and Gordon Fairclough. 2005. "Cloning Scientist Falsified Data, Colleague Says." *Wall Street Journal,* December 16: B1, B2.

Rhoads, Christopher. 2004. "Lucent Faces Bribery Allegations in Giant Saudi Telecom Project." *Wall Street Journal,* November 16: A1, A18.

Samenow, Stanton E. 2004. *Inside the Criminal Mind.* Rev. and updated ed. New York: Crown Publishers.

Samuelson, Robert. 2003. "Welfare for Capitalists." *Newsweek,* May 5: 54.

Savage, Charlie. 2005. "High Court Overturns Sentencing Guidelines." *Boston.Com,* January 13, http://www.boston.com/news/nation/washington/articles/2005/01/13/.

Schmidt, Charles W. 2004. "Environmental Crimes: Profiting at the Earth's Expense." *Environmental Health Perspectives* 12, no. 2 (February), http://www.ehponline.org/members/2004/112-2/focus.html.

Schnatterly, Karen. 2003. "Increasing Firm Value through Detection and Prevention of White-Collar Crime." *Strategic Management Journal* (24): 587–588.

Shafer, Jack. 2003. "The Jayson Blair Project: How Did He Bamboozle the *New York Times*?" May 8, http://slate.msn.com/id/2082741.

Shmukler, Evelina. 2005. "Witness Says Scrushy Skipped 'Family' Meetings." *Wall Street Journal,* February 2: C4.

Shover, Neal, and Andy Hochstetler. 2006. *Choosing White-Collar Crime.* New York: Cambridge University Press.

Shuit, Douglas P. 2005. "Ebbers' Costly Legacy." *Workforce Management* (April): 15–16.

Sidel, Robin. 2005. "Identity Theft—Unplugged." *Wall Street Journal,* October 8: B1, B4.

Simpson, Glenn R. 2004. "As Investigations Proliferate, Big Banks Feel under the Gun." *Wall Street Journal,* December 30: A1, A4.

Singhapakdi, Anusorn, Scott J. Vitell, and George R. Franke. 1999. "Antecedents, Consequences, and Mediating Effects of Perceived Moral Intensity and Personal Moral Philosophies." *Academy of Marketing Science Journal* 27 (Winter): 19–36.

Skorupski, John. 2003. "Ethics." In *The Blackwell Companion to Philosophy,* edited by Nicholas Bunnin and E.P. Tsui-James, 202–230. Malden, Mass.: Blackwell Publishing.

Smith, Rebecca, and John R. Emshwiller. 2003. *24 Days.* New York: Harper Business.

Solomon, Deborah. 2005. "After Pension-Fund Debacle, San Diego Is Mired in Probes." *Wall Street Journal,* October 10: A1, A8.

Solomon, Deborah, and Anne Marie Squeo. 2005. "Crackdown Puts Corporations, Executives in New Legal Peril." *Wall Street Journal*, June 20: A1, A10.

Soto, Ornell R. March 4, 2006. "8 Years, 4 Months." *The San Diego Union-Tribune*, SignOnSanDiego.com.

Stanford Graduate School of Business. n.d. News release, "Dueling for Dollars," http://www.gsb.stanford.edu/research/faculty/news_releases/edward.lazear/lazear.htm.

Steffensmeirer, Darrell, and Miles D. Harer. 1999. "Making Sense of Recent U.S. Crime Trends, 1980 to 1996/1998: Age Composition Effects and Other Explanations." *Journal of Research in Crime and Delinquency* 36 (August): 235–274.

Strader, J. Kelly. 2002. *Understanding White Collar Crime*. Newark, N.J.: LexisNexis.

Stybel, Lawrence J., and Maryanne Peabody. 2005. "How Should Board of Directors Evaluate Themselves?" *MIT Sloan Management Review* 47 (Fall): 67–72.

Sutherland, Edwin H. 1940. "White Collar Criminality." *American Sociological Review* 10: 132–139.

Swartz, Mimi, with Sherron Watkins. 2003. *Power Failure: The Inside Story of the Collapse of Enron*. New York: Doubleday.

Sykes, Gresham M., and David Matza. 1957. "Techniques of Neutralization: A Theory of Delinquency." *American Sociological Review* 22: 664–670.

Terhune, Chad, Dan Morse, and Almar Latour. 2005. "Why Scrushy Won, Ebbers Lost." *Wall Street Journal*, June 30: C1, C3.

Thornton, Emily. 2005. "Refco: The Reckoning." *BusinessWeek*, November 7: 114–116.

Tittle, Charles R. 2000. "Theoretical Developments in Criminology." *Criminal Justice 2000* 1: 51–101.

U.S. Department of Justice, Antitrust Division. 2005. "An Antitrust Primer for Federal Law Enforcement Personnel." Rev. ed. Report, April, Washington, D.C.: U.S. Department of Justice.

U.S. Department of Justice, Federal Bureau of Investigation. n.d. "The Measurement of White-Collar Crime Using Uniform Crime Reporting (UCR) Data." Report, http://www.fbi.gov/ucr/whitecollarforweb.pdf.

U.S. Department of Treasury. 2005. "U.S. Money Laundering Threat Assessment." Report, December .

Wall Street Journal. 2005. "Sullivan Calls Ebbers 'Hands-On.'" February 8: C1, C4.

Warchol, Greg. 1998. "Special Report: Workplace Violence, 1992–1996." Washington, D.C.: U.S. Department of Justice, http://www.ojp.usdoj.gov/bjs/pub/pdf/wv96.pdf.

Weil, Jonathan, and Robin Sidel. 2005. "J.P. Morgan's WorldCom Risk." *Wall Street Journal*, March 11: C1, C4.

Weil, Jonathan, and Shawn Young. 2005. "WorldCom's Steep Price." *Wall Street Journal*, January 7: C1, C3.

Weisburd, David, Elin Waring, and Ellen F. Chayet. 2001. *White-Collar Crime and Criminal Careers*. New York: Cambridge University Press.

Weiss, Gary. 2003. *Born to Steal: When the Mafia Hit Wall Street*. New York: Warner Books.

Whitley, Joe D., Marc N. Garber, Mark A. McCarty, and Steven D. Henry. 2002. "The Case for Reevaluating DOJ Policies on Prosecuting White-Collar Crime." Working Paper Series no. 108, Washington Legal Foundation.

Wingfield, Nick. 2004. "Problems for Cops on eBay Beat: Crooks Keep Getting Smarter." *Wall Street Journal*, August 3: A1, A8.

Woellert, Lorraine, and Mike France. 2005. "Corporate Cases: Time to Cut a Deal." *BusinessWeek*, January 24: 43.

Wolpe, Paul Root. 1998. "Explaining Social Deviance." audiotape. Chantilly, Va.: The Teaching Company.

Wonacott, Peter, and Sarah McBride. 2005. "To Catch Film Pirate, U.S. China Follow Spy Flick to Shanghai." *Wall Street Journal*, March 7: A1, A10.

Woyke, Elizabeth. 2005. "Another Spammer Flames Out." *BusinessWeek*, July 18: 13.

Yochelson, Samuel, and Stanton E. Samenow. 1976. *The Criminal Personality*, vol. 1, *A Profile for Change*. New York: Jason Aronson.

Young, Shawn. 2005. "Qwest's Ex-CEO to Base Defense on Federal Pacts." *Wall Street Journal*, November 21: C1, C9.

Young, Shawn, Almar Latour, and Susan Pulliam. 2005. "Linking Ebbers to the Fraud at WorldCom Proves Difficult." *Wall Street Journal*, February 18: A1, A8.

Young, Shawn, Deborah Solomon, and Dennis K. Berman. 2004. "Qwest Engaged in Fraud, SEC Says." *Wall Street Journal*, October 22: A3.

Young, Shawn, and Peter Grant. 2005. "More Penstripes Get Prison Stripes." *Wall Street Journal*, June 20: C1, C2.

Zahra, Shakar A., Richard L. Priem, and Abdul A. Rasheed. 2005. "The Antecedents and Consequences of Top Management Fraud." *Journal of Management* (December): 808–812.

Zhang, Ivy Xiying. 2005. "Economic Consequences of the Sarbanes-Oxley Act of 2002." Working paper, Rochester, N.Y.: University of Rochester.

Zimmerman, Ann, and Kortney Stringer. 2004. "Background Checks Proliferate, Ex-Cons Face Jobs Lock." *Wall Street Journal*, August 26: B1, B3.

Index